PERMANENT
WAR

Books by Sidney Lens

Left, Right and Center (1949)

The Counterfeit Revolution (1952)

A World in Revolution (1956)

The Crisis of American Labor (1959)

Working Men (1960)

Africa, Awakening Giant (1962)

The Futile Crusade (1964)

A Country Is Born (1964)

Radicalism in America (1966)

What Unions Do (1968)

Poverty: America's Enduring Paradox (1969)

The Military Industrial Complex (1970)

The Forging of the American Empire (1972)

The Labor Wars (1973)

Poverty, Yesterday and Today (1973)

The Promise and Pitfalls of Revolution (1974)

The Day before Doomsday (1977)

Unrepentant Radical (1980)

The Bomb (1982)

The Maginot Line Syndrome: America's Hopeless Policy (1983)

Strikemakers and Strikebreakers (1985)

PERMANENT *WAR*

The Militarization of America

SIDNEY LENS

Foreword by Stanley Aronowitz

SCHOCKEN BOOKS · NEW YORK

First published by Schocken Books 1987
10 9 8 7 6 5 4 3 2 1 87 88 89 90

Library of Congress Cataloging-in-Publication Data
Lens, Sidney.
Permanent war.
Bibliography: p.
Includes index.
1. Militarism—United States—History—20th century. 2. United States—Politics and government—1945–. 3. United States—Armed Forces—Political activity—History—20th century.
I. Title.
E840.4.L46 1987 322'.5'0973 86–22005

Design by Cassandra Pappas
Manufactured in the United States of America
ISBN 0–8052–4025–X

Research for this book was made possible in part by grants from the A. J. Muste Memorial Institute and the World Policy Institute

Contents

Foreword

This book is as hot as today's headlines. Completed in 1986, *Permanent War* documents the long history of CIA, FBI and the U.S. government agency efforts to undermine the democratic process in our country. There was, of course, no way that Lens could have known about the Iran/Contra affair. His death occurred before November when the sordid details began to trickle out of this secret effort at the highest levels of the national administration to free American hostages by selling arms to our ostensible arch enemy, Iran, and sidestep the decision of the U.S. Congress to prohibit military shipments to the counter-revolutionary forces in Nicaragua. Nevertheless, what we have in this book is a description of the mechanisms by which government agencies charged with protecting our national security are, instead, responsible for creating mayhem at home and abroad.

The actions of these agencies directly belie the repeated declarations, both by the Reagan and previous national administrations, that America stands for the "rule of law" against terrorists and others who would violate international compacts and standards of human decency. Lens shows how powerful political and economic forces in American society are working against these precepts because they believe—with political scientist, Samuel Huntington and other conservative ideologues—that national and international policy is thwarted by "too much democracy." Faced with the growing unpopularity of U.S. foreign policy, especially in Central America, officials in high places simply take actions that contravene the lawful processes of democratic decision making. What they do at home and abroad often amounts to state terrorism.

Lens's book is not clairvoyant. That is, his indictment does not just happen to describe practices that are now in full public view.

Rather, his profound understanding of the fact that there have been two governments ruling this country for at least forty years leads to an understanding of current events as more than the work of a few willful and zealous individuals who, however misguided, believed they were serving the best interests of their country. Lens shows that there exists massive institutional and financial support for secret government, that many in both major political parties and in corporate board rooms have never trusted the American people or, indeed, any people who seek to control their own destiny. *Permanent War* reveals a pattern of lawlessness and pervasive contempt among people in high places for the democracy in whose behalf they regularly issue public statements. Beyond merely indicting, Lens reveals how fragile our democracy really is, and how dissent is routinely met by government agents with a wholesale denial of civil rights and, upon occasion, murder.

In contrast to the majority of the media who view these events as discrete, Lens is able to establish the connections between them: his moral outrage is not directed at individuals but at whole areas of public policy. As a result, *Permanent War* offers a coherent picture. It reveals a history that is routinely erased from public memory by the fragmented images of violence and subterfuge often embodied in the idiosyncratic behavior of individuals. Oliver North, in Lens's account, would not appear to be a highly motivated ideologue who misdirects his passion to nefarious ends, but a "normal" operative in a long chain of similar people whose work is sanctioned as patriotism by the leaders of the secret government.

Such coherency does violate the picture of the American presidency and the federal government over which it presides as essentially honest. If Lens is to be believed, Watergate is merely the first open revelation of the work of the secret government and its antidemocratic policies. The level of detail contained in this book shows that "dirty tricks" have been a routine practice of the warfare state across presidents and that few, if any of them, are able to halt or even circumvent its imperatives.

Sidney Lens was one of the rarest of Americans: a labor intellectual. Having attained maturity during the most exciting period of U.S. labor history—the years in which millions joined unions as a protest against the poverty and work hardships imposed on American workers during the Great Depression—he shared both the glory and the struggle of workers who emerged from its depths to improve their living standards and, even more importantly, he became part of the history of that time. Lens was a worker and a union organizer and, until the 1970s, a leader of a local union of retail employees in Chicago. If these activities had fully encompassed his contribution to the causes of freedom and equality, they would have been acknowledged as both honorable and complete. For Sidney Lens was a devoted and tireless labor militant who turned his back on the perquisites of trade union office to which too many of his fellow officers aspired and, having achieved, held onto for dear life.

But Lens was made of different material. For he was not only a veteran of the labor wars, he was a committed radical and thinker. These qualities made for an extraordinary person. A catalyst and leader of social and political movements organized not only in the name of the emancipation of workers but for general emancipation, he simply refused to take reversals as more than temporary. My last contact with him was a telephone call in 1985. Lens asked if I would help organize a conference on "socialism and activism" which he thought could be held in New York later in the year. I was skeptical. After all this was a period when the right wing seemed to be gaining ground at an exponential rate, when Congress showed little inclination to oppose the conservative policies of the Reagan administration and, equally depressing, the radicals were in disarray. Lens wanted to pick the left up from the ground and make it ready, yet another time, to oppose U.S. intervention in Central America and other developments that have become known as the permanent war machine. In other words, he was proposing to sidestep the question of whether a left was possible in America and simply start afresh.

Although I joined his effort with some reluctance, in the fall of 1985 Lens, nevertheless, succeeded in holding a conference that was attended by nearly a thousand activists. His main hope was that the participants would work together beyond the conference. As part of the labor panel, I was glad to see that his wishes were partially fufilled in some areas. While preparations were being made for a second annual conference, Lens died suddenly, leaving a legacy of writing and leadership that will outlive the limitations of a single life.

This was not my first encounter with Sidney Lens. In the early 1960s when I had formed a committee to defend a group of miners in Southeastern Kentucky who had defied both the owners and their own union in order to hold on to the dignity that their union had once helped them gain, Lens was among the first to support this effort. Shortly thereafter, we joined with a fairly small group of trade unionists to oppose U.S. policy in Vietnam and Southeast Asia. During these years, it wasn't popular in the labor movement to be against the war. AFL-CIO policy was not only strongly proadministration, but its president, George Meany, did not suffer lightly opposition to official labor's foreign policy. After all, anti-Communism had long been a political litmus test within organized labor and witch-hunts against those who refused to support its program were not infrequent. Nevertheless some labor leaders—notably Frank Rosenblum of the Clothing Workers, Pat Gorman of the then Meatcutters Union, Ralph Helstein of the Packinghouse Workers, and independents such as the Electrical and Longshore Unions—joined with dozens of local union officials in forming a Labor for Peace movement. Later, the powerful president of the Autoworkers union Walter Reuther joined the effort. At the heart of this movement was Sidney Lens whose relationships with many of these people in Chicago and throughout the Midwest had been close.

During the postwar period Lens distinguished himself by producing two of the most influential books on American labor ever written. The first, *Left Right and Center* (1949), was a veritable manifesto for independent radicals in the labor movement, those who would follow neither the Cold War policies of CIO and AFL leaders who were all too anxious to get on the bandwagon, nor the pro-Soviet politics of the Communists and their supporters. Lens did not advocate a "middle-ground" but stood forthrightly for a "third" way that accomplished several goals. First, it viewed the interests of the workers and their unions as primary; it stood fast against railroading American labor into an anti-Communist crusade at the expense of the democratic and militant traditions of the new industrial and service unions that had been born in the heat of the thirties battles; and, finally, it pointed to independent political action—free of subordination of labor to the two main political parties—as a road for labor.

A decade later, Lens published his *Crisis of American Labor* (1959), which was an eloquent plea for a new strategy for a labor movement already showing signs of considerable wear and tear. In this book, Lens advanced a remarkable analysis, which is as fresh in 1987 as it was nearly thirty years ago: unions had been transformed into business organizations dispensing benefits like insurance companies. And, like organizations dominated by managers, many had lost the strong participation of their membership, even as they retained considerable strength and grass roots loyalty. Further, Lens theorized that in the coming decades unfavorable economic conditions and conservative governments might make the strategy of collaboration between business and labor disastrous for workers. Against this trend, he proposed the idea of social unionism that grew with the industrial unions during the depression. These unions believe that the labor movement is constituted on grounds broader than bread and butter. For Lens, these unions must be the basis for a major renovation and revival of the labor movement. Large national unions, after all, are constituted by collective bargaining with equally large national and sometimes international corporations. They are ill-suited to deal with the everyday needs of workers both on the shop floor and in their communities where as parents, homeowners, tenants, or consumers, workers face multiple problems which their unions seem unable, or unwilling to face—except through fattening the wage packet.

Lens proposed strengthening the local central labor councils as the focus of labor's organizing political action and community service. It is a radical idea only to those who see unions as a kind of bank. For others, like the independent radicals and trade union activists for whom he characteristically spoke, Lens's arguments had the ring of truth and his analysis the unmistakable quality of authenticity. I was working in a plant when I read his book, *Crisis*, and it shaped my own understanding of the labor movement, its problems and possibilities for years thereafter.

But Lens was restless. From a base in working-class interests, he soon became not only a fearless organizer of the peace movement, but one of its most distinguished theorists as well. His work on nuclear destruction, the permanent war economy, the relationship between foreign policy and issues such as poverty and his questions of social and historical change enlivened the pages of magazines such as the *Progressive* and *The Nation*. For the past quarter of a century his voice has been raised against the narrow parochialism of radical and progressive political movements, insisting that the question of war and peace is the leading edge of social change.

Lens never saw the "labor question" in isolation from the larger landscape of politics and, in the last decades of his life, he articulated the position of the centrality of the Cold War to all aspects of social, economic, and labor policy. Today, this perspective seems self-evident and, to some, even commonplace. If it has entered the vernacular of political talk, credit must be given, to a large extent, to Sidney Lens. For in my own thirty-five years of labor and political activism, I can recall many groups, movements, and individuals, who, at various times, insisted that to go beyond the "single" issue of civil rights, peace, trade union militancy, or environmentalism, would dilute the force of protest, divert the necessary single-mindedness of the effort. This tendency, widespread among activists and leaders of key elements of the left since the end of the Second World War, was always a particular target of Lens's pen. He understood that issues sometimes require sharp focus; that was not in contention. What was under scrutiny is whether those fighting for peace and justice against an increasingly aggressive corporate-dominated war machine could ignore the interconnections at the bottom, even as they recognized them at the top of the social hierarchy.

The polemics and controversies with which Lens was embroiled did not always make him a popular figure among those who were content to ignore warnings that they were taking the line of least resistance, a stance that could only work in the short run. For Lens was not hesitant to take on issues, even when discretion might have been the better part of valor. Yet, he always looked for a basis of agreement; he was always trying to free the left and the labor movement from divisive ideologies and acrimony. If he fought for his own position, it was never in a spirit of venality; on the contrary, he was personally engaging and always compromising without surrendering principle.

Permanent War was his last effort to call attention to the perils of the war machine (Lens died before he could complete his work on the Notes). Written in his usual lively and engaging style—the result of a mind eager to engage his audience as well as persuade them—the book provides an astute analysis of the many-sided effort by official government agencies to undermine the struggle for peace and democracy around the world. The section on the Philippines will be illuminating to many who have followed recent developments there, especially with respect to U.S. policy, which alternated between resolute support for the Marcos dictatorship and endorsement for his liberal opponents after their coming to power. Lens spares few details of the intricate course of U.S. policy, one that was informed, in his analysis, by the interest of "global imperialism." This is his perspective on such phenomena as "dirty tricks," secret wars conducted by the CIA and the FBI against real and imagined external and internal opponents of what Lens calls the "National Security State." He shows that global dirty tricks were not confined to Third World countries or Europe. For example, acting under the banner of internal security, the FBI made massive interventions into black civil rights and radicals' organizations, intending to crush them and the resistance to racism that they represented.

This sharply written analysis of the inevitable confrontation between the National Security State of U.S. imperialism and the American and world peoples will be read as extreme by those who want to believe that the accumulations of violence and subversion of popular movements by official and semiofficial agents of the U.S. government is somehow the product of a few conservative zealots operating without authority from the top. Yet, Lens's documentation is ultimately persuasive because of its historical perspective. *Permanent War* is a fine legacy to us by one of the leading American radicals of the past half century.

STANLEY ARONOWITZ

1
The Permanent War

Since 1945 the United States has been engaged in a permanent war. It is not permanent in the sense that it will never end, for all things must eventually end but, rather, permanent in the sense that it is fought every day on every continent and there is no single day when either side can claim definitive victory. This permanent war is unique because it takes two forms: one is the kind of war we have known throughout history, with armies, navies, and air forces confronting each other in open battle; the other is a new type of war fought by subversion, dirty tricks, secret manipulation, coups d'état, even assassinations. Korea and Vietnam are examples of the first form, with the United States directly engaged against two Soviet proxies. The 1973 overthrow of the Allende government in Chile by an American-supported group is an example of the second. That there has been no decision in the permanent war does not mean that it has been effete. Millions have been killed as a result of this new type of war (which is mistakenly called the "cold" war) and many millions more either have been injured or had their lives disrupted.

Like all wars the permanent war has restructured the institutional life of the nations involved, in particular the United States. War, after all, is the worst emergency a nation-state ever confronts, and special measures and institutions are required to meet the emergency. In World War II, for instance, the government exacted a no-strike pledge from the labor movement so that war production might proceed with little interruption. To deny war material to the men at the front while workers and employers in the rear resolve their differences in work stoppages would be intolerable—a major battle could be lost, even the war itself, because of supply shortages. As a corollary to the no-strike pledge, the Roosevelt administration had to create a number of institutions to avoid economic hazards such as uncontrolled inflation. If workers could not strike they at least needed some mechanism to adjudicate contractual disputes and grievances; hence a War Labor Board was established with powers to resolve such differences. A lid also had to be placed on prices; hence an Office of Price Administration was created to pass on price increases. There was also a rationing board to see to it that scarce items—gasoline, meat, cigarettes—were distributed equitably and a Selective Service system and draft board were needed to see to it that men were enrolled in the military on an orderly basis. A host of new bodies were fashioned: the Office of Production Management, the War Production Board, the Office of Strategic Supply, the Supply, Priorities, and Allocation Board, the Office of Technical Development, and the Office of Emergency Management.[1] A censorship office was created to guard against publication of "sensitive" material, and the Office of Strategic Services was charged with espionage and subversion behind enemy lines. Not only were new agencies added, but the structure and size of government changed decisively. Richard Barnet tells us that "in 1939 the federal government had about eight hundred thousand civilian employees, about 10 percent of whom worked for national security agencies. At the end of the war the figure approached four million, of which more than 75 percent were in national security activities."[2]

Changes of this magnitude were made in order to deal with a relatively short war—four years. The permanent war under way since 1945–47 has already lasted ten times as long. Inevitably, it was bound not only to rearrange the old institutional patterns, but to modify attitudes toward law and order, alter traditional beliefs, refashion the economy and above all, sire a new form of government—a twin government. Hanson Baldwin, military writer for the *New York Times*, foresaw the problems ahead when he expressed concern in 1947 over "the militarization of our government and of the American state of mind."[3]

We still have one president and one Congress in the United States but, in effect, we now have two governments. One government remains open, formally democratic; the other operates in the shadows, secretive and authoritarian. The open government is not untainted, but at least in the formal sense it tolerates the freedoms we have become accustomed to: free speech, free press, and the rest. The average American, then, believes we are still a "free people," living in a true democracy.

The government that counts, nevertheless, is the second one constructed around the National Security Council (NSC) and an imperial presidency, which makes secret, far-reaching decisions about war, foreign policy, and, indirectly, the economy, without consulting either the Congress or the American people. This National Security State is an authoritarian state which has removed itself from most popular controls to avoid punishment for violations of American and international law and the central principle of the American way of life, "government by consent of the governed." It doesn't act this way as a lark or to enjoy the perquisites of power, but because there is no other way to carry out the day-to-day activities dictated by the existence of the permanent war. To function as a democracy would make it impossible to continue the war.

The best known transgressions of legality by the National Security State are those which have been directed against foreigners and foreign governments. The attempts (sometimes with the aid of the Mafia) to assassinate Fidel Castro, the financing of counterrevolutionary forces against the governments of Jacobo Arbenz Guzmán in Guatemala, Mohammed Mossadegh in Iran, the Sandinistas in Nicaragua are a few examples of covert foreign activity. But the true measure of the National Security State includes what it has done to shred democratic rights and values at home. If none of this seems immediately apparent it is because the subversion has taken place over a period of four decades, step by step, and we have slowly imbibed the values of the authoritarian way of life, to the point where few of us question it.

For example, in 1956 the Federal Bureau of Investigation (FBI) established the Counterintelligence Program (COINTELPRO) to ferret out alleged radicals, disrupt their organizations, and discredit them personally.[4] This was the same kind of tactic that the Soviet KGB had been criticized for carrying out in its sphere of influence. The FBI committed 239 actual break-ins and burglaries against fifteen organizations—more than 90 against the Socialist Workers

Party alone. None of these activities was conducted with legal search warrants; all were patent violations of American law. Yet, apart from a small number of leftist and liberal publications there was no public outcry for an investigation. Then FBI chief, J. Edgar Hoover was never indicted for having ordered these criminal acts, even though he had taken an oath to uphold the law without fear or bias when he was installed in office. None of the attorneys general or the presidents whom they served while these illegal acts were taking place was impeached or even reprimanded, even though they too had taken an oath to uphold the law.

Americans generally have a decent respect for the law, but the permanent war has eroded their values. Their attitude is not unlike that of the late Dr. Martin Niemöller, the German Protestant minister who ultimately spent many years in Hitler's prisons. When the Nazis began arresting communists, Niemöller recalled, he was indifferent—"after all I was not a communist." When the arrests began to include Jews, socialists, and other critics of the Nazis he began to feel concern, but not enough to spark involvement. By the time he decided to do something about it the secret police were knocking at his own door.

There are many examples of how Americans have become indifferent to law-breaking by their government. For instance, in April 1959 Fidel Castro came to New York to speak to a group of journalists. President Eisenhower refused to see him but Vice President Richard Nixon met with him privately, and, based on that talk, recommended that the United States organize an invasion by Cuban exiles to overthrow Castro.[5] Before long the CIA was recruiting hundreds of Cuban expatriates in Miami, arming and training them, in clear violation of the Neutrality Act, the charter of the Organization of American States (OAS), and specific U.S. laws against arming foreign agents. Article 15 of the OAS charter states that "no State or group of States has the right to intervene, directly or indirectly, for any reason whatever, in the internal or external affairs of any other State. The foregoing principle prohibits not only armed force, but also any other form of interference. . . . " Nonetheless a command post was established in suburban Coral Gables for an invasion of Cuba. The exiles were given training in the Florida Everglades and Keys and lectures in Miami hotels. U.S. military bases in Florida's

Opa-locka were made available to them.[6] All of this was certainly against the law and everybody in the American government knew it.

The illegality, however, did not stop; it was compounded. In May 1960 the CIA shipped exile recruits to a secret base in Retalhuleu, Guatemala, for final training. In July the agency started building an airstrip to accommodate C-46s, C-54s, and B-26s, and trained pilots to fly them during the eventual invasion.[7] Again, this was a clear violation of international law, the United Nations' charter, and the American Constitution, which calls for a vote of Congress before engaging in warfare against another state. But having gone this far in flouting legal protocol, the National Security State did not hesitate to go a step further. On November 13, as luck would have it, a segment of the Guatemalan army rebelled against the regime of America's ally, Miguel Ydígoras Fuentes, and seized Puerto Barrios, a banana port on the Caribbean. Had the rebels succeeded, the secret training agreement with Ydígoras might have been canceled and the CIA's cover blown. Certainly there would have been a hue and cry back home in the United States over the planned invasion. To solve its dilemma the CIA dispatched American B-26s with Cuban and American pilots to bomb the airport at Puerto Barrios. C-46s were used to transport troops loyal to Ydígoras to the scene, and in short order the rebellion was suppressed. One illegality, therefore, was compounded by a second one; neither one was discussed with either Congress or the American people. And when some of these facts did come out after the Bay of Pigs disaster in 1961, no action was taken against the president or other high officials who had patently broken the law. After four decades of permanent war Americans have adjusted to a political regimen in which government officials can do almost anything under the cover of such code words as *national security* or *executive privilege*, without being held legally accountable. Even in the rare instances where they are brought to trial and convicted, they are judged and treated by a different standard.

Consider what happened—or didn't happen—to a top intelligence official when he was caught committing perjury. On February 7, 1973, Richard Helms, who had just left his job as director of the CIA to become ambassador to Iran, appeared before the Senate Foreign Relations Committee for a confirmation hearing. He was asked by Senator Stuart Symington whether the CIA, under his tutelage, had ever tried to overthrow the Allende government in Chile, or had ever had "any money passed to the opponents of Allende." To both questions Helms responded with a crisp "no, sir." He was confirmed without much ado.

But a year later, in April 1974, the new CIA director, William E. Colby, in the course of testifying before the House Armed Services Subcommittee on Intelligence, revealed that the CIA in fact had spent more than $8 million to keep Salvador Allende Gossens from being elected and then, once Allende was in office, on "destabilizing" his government. These actions, Colby confirmed, had been approved by the National Security Council's 40 Committee, headed by Henry Kissinger, Special Assistant to the President for National Security Affairs. Not only had Helms lied to Congress, but a former Assistant Secretary of State, Charles A. Meyer, had also lied under oath. When a *New York Times* correspondent, Pulitzer prize winner Seymour M. Hersh, brought all this to light, President Gerald Ford tried to explain that the money had been used to subsidize "opposition newspapers and electronic media and to preserve opposition political parties." In fact the money was used to assist a nationwide strike of 250,000 truck drivers, shopkeepers, and professionals which contributed to the overthrow of Allende, and for the murder of the top Chilean general, who was loyal to Allende, and similar ventures.[8]

At the 1973 confirmation hearing Helms had also been asked whether he knew that Army intelligence agents had infiltrated and reported on the antiwar movement in the late 1960s and early 1970s. "Do you know anything about any activity on the part of the CIA in that connection?" was the specific question. "We were not involved," was the clear-cut reply, "because it seemed to me that was a clear violation of what our charter was." But in June 1975 a White House commission, headed by Vice President Nelson Rockefeller, issued a report on CIA activities which disclosed that Helms had established Operation CHAOS to spy on the antiwar movement, to infiltrate and disrupt it. The CIA had also compiled a computer list of 300,000 names of individuals and organizations who opposed the war in Vietnam.

In due course Helms was brought to trial for perjury but there was resistance to it all the way, even by the new Democratic administration. President Jimmy Carter's CIA director, Admiral Stansfield Turner, told reporters that prosecution of Helms would cause serious problems for "national security"; the CIA would have to reveal damaging secrets. Neither Helms nor his apologists ever explained what secrets would have to be revealed if he admitted he had lied, or how anyone's life would be jeopardized—as Helms insisted—if he made an admission that had already been made by his successor, Colby. The words *national security* had taken on a special meaning, giving the leaders of the National Security State a privileged type of immunity. By the time Helms's lawyer, Edward Bennett Williams, was through, writes Richard Harris in *The New Yorker*, "he had convinced just about everybody in Washington that Helms had testified as he had to protect the national-security secrets he had sworn a CIA oath to protect." He had also sworn to uphold the laws of the *United States* which, presumably, is a higher entity than the CIA. Williams, however, did not dwell on that.

Helms's trial opened before Federal District Judge Barrington D. Parker on October 31, 1977, with no reporters present (the Justice Department in contravention of its usual practice had not informed the press), and the proceedings lasted only half an hour. According to an article in the *New Republic* the Justice Department and Helms's lawyer, Williams, had come to an agreement and jointly asked the judge—in his chambers—to impose a thirty-day suspended sentence, with no fine. The judge was furious. He postponed sentence for a few days, then levied a two-year suspended term against Helms and a $2,000 fine. Even so, Helms was delighted—he did not have to serve a day in prison. His friends took him out to a celebration party and chipped in the $2,000 to pay for his fine.

One of the more disquieting features of the Helms saga was that some of the nation's leading liberals came to the ex-CIA director's defense. The liberal *New York Times* praised the "adroit solution" of the Carter administration "in paying homage to both law and secrets" at the same time The *Washington Post* agreed that Helms should not "have been let off scot-free," but argued that neither should he "have been prosecuted more severely. He had, after all, sworn a prior oath to defend the integrity of the agency of which he was the director." Most surprising was a column by the *New York Times*'s liberal columnist, Anthony Lewis, who defended the "plea bargain" among other reasons because Helms's lawyer would "certainly have demanded masses of classified documents to prepare the case" and the prosecutors "might have been faced with a court order to produce something whose disclosure would arouse legitimate concern." By this logic no one working for the Pentagon or any of the government's intelligence agencies need ever be brought to account for any crime because his lawyer might subpoena secret documents "whose disclosure would arouse legitimate concern."[9]

Early in the permanent war many liberals demanded that the CIA either be dissolved or at least divested of its covert action assignments. Such proposals are no longer heard. Complaints are voiced over this or that excess committed by the CIA and on two or three occasions there have been official investigations of those excesses, but the need for an agency that regularly engages in unlawful activity both at home and abroad is seldom contested. Nor has there been any recent demand that the 1949 law which gave the Agency the right to keep secret what it spends—in direct contravention of the Constitution which demands that spending by all agencies be a matter of public record—be rescinded. The public has been conditioned to accept the principle that the government has a right to commit such illegal acts as arming foreigners to invade a sovereign country, the commissioning of perjury and burglaries, on the theory that there is a superior law to the one we have been living under for two centuries—the law of national security.

The corrosion of legal and moral values during the period of permanent war has been accompanied by a corrosion of basic tradition. The most compelling impact on the American way of life since World War II has been the reversal of the two-century-old traditions against imperialism and militarism. "For Americans," notes historian William Appleman Williams, " 'imperialism' has always been a dirty word."[10] The United States has not hesitated to claim or seek additional territory—its appetite in fact has been voracious—but its expansion during the first century and a quarter of its existence was limited to the North American continent and, in rhetoric at least, the United States was committed to the right of nations to self-determination without outside interference. But there was nothing approaching global imperialism in the American saga. The Monroe Doctrine, whatever its more devious purpose may have been, defended the right of Latin American states to be free of foreign occupation. Here and there the anti-imperialist tradition was sullied by such acts as the seizure of Puerto Rico and the Philippines in the Spanish–American war, the domination of Cuba through the machinery of the Platt Amendment, the occupation of Haiti, the Dominican Republic, and Nicaragua for periods of time. Point 3 of the Atlantic Charter, signed by President Franklin D. Roosevelt and the British Prime Minister Winston Churchill four months before Pearl Harbor, described one of the Allies' postwar goals as "the right of all peoples to choose the form of government under which they will live," and the restoration of "sovereign rights and self-government . . . to those who have been forcibly deprived of them."

Antimilitarism too seemed to be an absolute law for American leaders, many of whom realized that a militarist society would inevitably become an authoritarian society. Except for the effort by Colonel Lewis Nicola in 1782 to enlist General Washington in an attempted coup that would have established a monarchy in the United States—with Washington as king—the military by and large has played little role in American politics. The United States, it is true, has engaged in many wars—as of 1924 six major and 104 minor ones—but until the present time it has always been opposed to large standing armies and large military establishments.[11] At the end of the Revolutionary War, Washington dissolved the national army and sent it home, leaving defense entirely to the ragged and inept state militia. Less than six months after he resigned his commission and returned to Mount Vernon, the Continental Congress stated the nation's views on militarism in plain terms: "Standing armies in time of peace are inconsistent with the principles of republican governments, dangerous to the liberties of a free people, and generally converted into destructive engines for establishing despotism."[12]

Years later when President Washington asked Congress to establish a regular army consisting of four regiments of infantry and one of artillery—a total of 2,631 men—"to awe the Indians, protect our trade, prevent encroachments," he conceded that "a *large* standing army in time of peace hath ever been considered dangerous to the liberties of the country."[13] His only justification was that a "few troops" would be "safe." Congress, however, did not agree. Admittedly the Constitution did authorize a standing army, but James

Madison, in defending the provision, subsequently made the same sort of apology as Washington. An army on a small scale, he said, "had its inconveniences," but on "an intensive scale its consequences may be fatal." Clearly for most of the founders of the country military preparedness was a dangerous drug to be taken in small doses at best. That tradition was little challenged until after World War II. Prior to each war military forces were relatively small, and though they were substantially enlarged during hostilities, they always contracted when the fighting had ended. As of 1845, just before the Mexican War, the military contingent stood at a meager 9,000 officers and men; as late as 1904 at a relatively small 53,000; and in 1939, as World War II was about to begin in Europe, 185,000—less than a tenth of its present size.[14]

The antimilitarist and anti-imperialist traditions, however, were decisively breached after World War II. The United States had surplus money and surplus military equipment to offer its friends; it traded them for economic concessions and military bases. For instance, in return for a $100 million lend-lease loan to Saudi Arabia Franklin Roosevelt was able to secure oil concessions for American companies that otherwise might have gone to British firms. A similar pattern was evident in the acquisition of military bases. Except for a few refueling stations the United States had no foreign bases before World War II. But the spreading tentacles of its power invited establishment of military bases on every continent.

In September 1940 Roosevelt gave fifty destroyers to Britain and, in return, Britain granted the United States the right to build bases in Canada, Bermuda, and the West Indies. As its army and navy spread across the planet, the United States soon acquired an empire of bases. By 1961, at the peak of this development, there were 450 major and 2,208 minor bases. "No nation since the days of ancient Rome," wrote Merlo J. Pusey, associate editor of the *Washington Post*, "has maintained a military presence in the world comparable to that of the United States in the 1950s and 1960s." Not even Great Britain in its heyday had "stood astride the globe in the dominant posture that the United States assumed after World War II."[15]

The armed forces had played a negligible role in American affairs in all other postwar periods. One generation after 1939, however, Washington was spending $80 billion a year on its military machine (about 150 times that of 1939), had troops stationed in 119 countries, and had formed military alliances with forty-eight nations (contrary to George Washington's dictum of "no entangling alliances"). The net worth of the Department of Defense (DoD) in 1962 was conservatively estimated by the *Statistical Abstract of the United States* at $164.8 billion. The Air Force exceeded in wealth the resources of the fifty-five largest American corporations combined.[16]

For the first time in American history the military overwhelmed the civilian powers. While it was never able to grab the absolute control it sought, the military, nevertheless, had not only become a tolerated but a respected, even revered senior partner in running American society. A 1948 report by a committee of the Commission for the Reorganization of the Executive Branch of government, headed by ex-President Herbert Hoover, stated that "the military have picked up the ball of national policy and are running down the field with it." Congress, it asserted, "was practically helpless." In 1951 Senator Ralph Landers, a Vermont Republican, was equally pointed: "we are being forced to shift the American way of life into a pattern of the garrison state. . . . Our wealth, our standard of living, the lives of our young people and our institutions are under the control of the military." A decade later President Eisenhower, in an acclaimed farewell address, sternly warned of the "military–industrial complex."

> Until the latest of our world conflicts, the United States had no armaments industry. American makers of plowshares could, with time and as required, make swords as well. But now we can no longer risk emergency improvization of national defense; we have been compelled to create a permanent armaments industry of vast proportions. . . . We annually spend on military security more than the net income of all United States corporations. This conjunction of an immense military establishment and a large arms industry is new in the American experience and is felt in every city, every statehouse, every office of the federal government.

He warned of the "grave implication" on "our toil, resources . . . livelihood . . . and the very structure of our society. . . . The potential for the disastrous rise of misplaced power exists and will persist."[17]

The military, supported by the industrialists, had already tried to seize control of the economy during World War II. Donald Nelson, head of the War Production Board, records in his *Arsenal of Democracy*, that "from 1942 onward the Army people, in order to get control of our national economy, did their best to make an errand boy of the WPB." *The United States at War*, a Bureau of the Budget document published in 1946, says that the Army tried to gain "total control of the nation, its manpower, its facilities, its economy," and when Roosevelt or Nelson blocked their efforts temporarily, "the military leaders took another approach to secure the same result. . . . " Since war expenditures accounted for more than one of every three dollars of gross national product in 1945, the War Department felt it had a legitimate right to run the economy.

This view was reinforced by business leaders in and out of government—for instance James Forrestal of Dillon, Read (later Secretary of Defense) and Charles E. Wilson of General Electric. What the nation needed, said Wilson in January 1944, was "a permanent war economy." He proposed that every large company choose a liaison with the armed forces (to be commissioned as a colonel in the reserves), because military preparedness "must be, once and for all, a continuing program and not the creature of an emergency." Under his scheme Congress would be "limited to voting the needed funds," while the military and big business would determine how to spend it. The argument had questionable cogency during hostilities but it certainly had no validity at all for the postwar period when the nation presumably was to be at peace. This difficulty was surmounted, however, by pointing to a new enemy. In 1968, Fred Cook quoted Col. William H. Neblett, national president of the Reserve Officers Association, as saying: "The Pentagon line was that we were living in a state of undeclared emergency; that war with Russia was just around the corner."[18]

It is axiomatic that any institution (or any nation) will seek to enlarge its power if given the opportunity. The American military had that opportunity during World War II when it was the fulcrum of national survival and, though it never quite achieved the full control over American society it wanted, it had enough of a base to retain and extend that power in the postwar period. For the first time in American history the role of the military did not contract once hostilities ended; there was now a new enemy to point to and, therefore, new opportunities to expand its influence.

If the military did not gain full control of the economy during the war—mostly because of Roosevelt's resistance—it did ensconce itself in key positions and it formed a permanent alliance with big business that endures to this day. When the war ended, the officer class was favorably placed in a number of government posts relating to industry. Colonel John R. Alison was appointed Assistant Secretary of Commerce for Aeronautics; Major General Philip B. Fleming became head of the Federal Works Agency and director of the Office of Temporary Controls; Vice Admiral William W. Smith was appointed chairman of the Maritime Commission; Major General Robert M. Littlejohn headed the War Assets Administration; General Graves B. Erskine was chief of the Retraining and Re-employment Administration. "There were scores of lesser fry in lesser posts and missions," *Time* noted (January 20, 1947).

Of greater consequence was the fact that military officers ruled a number of countries, in whole or in part: General Douglas MacArthur ruled Japan, Lieutenant General Lucius D. Clay ruled the American sector of Germany, and Lieutenant General Geoffrey Keyes the American sector of Austria. It didn't seem amiss therefore (in fact it seemed only natural) that the State Department be turned over to the military. Thus General of the Army George C. Marshall was appointed Secretary of State, and ten of the twenty executive officers in the department were transferees from the military services. On the diplomatic side, Lieutenant General Walter Bedell Smith became ambassador to Moscow, Admiral Alan G. Kirk ambassador to Belgium, and Lieutenant General Albert C. Wedemeyer was assigned to head a special mission to China. "Today," boasted the *Army and Navy Bulletin* (January 8, 1947), "the Army has virtual control of foreign affairs. . . . The chain of control in diplomatic hot spots, both in the execution of basic policy and in the formulation of ad hoc arrangements, lies almost totally in the hand of the military authorities." In 1953 nine Army generals and 58 colonels, on leave or retired, were working for civilian agencies of government. In 1957 the numbers had increased to 200 generals and admirals, plus 1,300 colonels or Navy officers of similar rank and 6,000 of lower grade.

When a senator asked George Marshall in May 1951 whose side the president took in disputes between the State Department and the Department of Defense he replied: "I can recall no occasion where Mr. Truman has acted adversely to the Chiefs of Staff and the Secretary of Defense in relation to the State Department."[19]

Already suffused with power as the war ended, the military had no intention of relinquishing it. It obviously had to reduce its manpower and much of the economy that served it was destined to be returned to civilian purposes. With might and main, however, it tried to assert sovereignty over the nation's youth and the foreign service. Except for the Civil War and World Wars I and II, the United States had never conscripted men into the armed forces—certainly never in peace time. From 1944 to 1955, however, the generals mounted a campaign for universal military training (UMT) more far-reaching than the wartime draft. Service in the armed forces would no longer be *selective*, with men deferred for a variety of reasons, but *total*—all youth reaching the age of eighteen, except the handicapped, would be required to take military training for a period of years and then placed in the reserves to continue their training a few nights each month, and every summer.

Many members of the Congress couldn't understand why we needed so many troops when we had atom bombs that could kill 75,000 or 100,000 people at one fell blow. But as Major General F.O. Bowman, a commander at Fort Knox, explained later, more than military necessity was involved: "We have these young men while they are young and fresh. Their minds have not been cluttered up by worldliness. They make wonderful subjects for Army training." Presumably civilian schools do not offer the right approach to citizenship, for as Assistant Secretary of Defense Anna Rosenberg explained it in 1952, "a large part of the training as envisaged . . . is citizenship training, literary training, training in morale, and training in the things that young people ought to have." The military's own idea of good citizenship was attested to by the questionnaire draftees were required to fill out—to prove they were "reliable, trustworthy, of good character, and of complete unswerving loyalty to the United States."[20] They were also asked whether they had ever been members of one of the 300 organizations on the Attorney General's subversive list, including of course the Communist Party, and such esoteric groups as People's Drama, Inc. and the Chopin Cultural Center.

The military did not win its war for UMT. It had to settle for second best, *selective* service. But the campaign the military mounted and the allies it enlisted indicate the extent of its influence. A congressional committee branded the campaign as an outright violation of "section 201, title 18 of the United States Code." Congressman Forrest A. Harness, head of the committee, charged that "the War Department is using government funds in an improper manner for propaganda purposes." In 1948 alone, the Department enlisted the support of 370 national organizations "including the U.S. Chamber of Commerce and the American Legion; it . . . contacted 351 mayors in the principal cities of the land; it . . . promoted at least 591 articles and editorials in the press." The Boy Scouts were prevailed on to distribute fact sheets on UMT and the American Legion was induced to print 600,000 copies of a brochure titled "You and the Army Reserve."

The continued, even escalating, power of the military in American life wrecked the antimilitarist tradition and paved the way for a reoriented and remodeled America. One of the grievances that had been levied against King George III by the authors of the Declaration of Independence was that "he has affected to render the military independent of and superior to the civil power." Woodrow Wilson made a similar observation about militarism a century and a quarter later: "So long as you have a military class, it does not make any difference what your form of government is; if you are determined to be armed to the teeth, you must obey the only men who can control the great machinery of war. Elections are of minor importance."[21] As summarized by history professor Stephen E. Ambrose of Louisiana State University, the military after World War II "was deeply involved in, and had an incalculable impact on, every aspect of American life, including foreign policy, the economy, the allocation of resources, college and university programs and funding, the black revolution, civil disorders, the environment, basic education of millions of non-high-school graduates (and thousands who had graduated), and most of all the general tone and quality of contemporary life."[22]

The other tradition that was demolished in the postwar period was the anti-imperialist tradition. Like every well-placed nation–state the United States has always been ambitious to expand. As early as 1778, Samuel Adams, leader of the left wing of the Revolution, proposed to his compatriots that they set their sights beyond the thirteen original colonies toward the acquisition of Canada, Nova Scotia, and Florida. His cousin, future president John Adams, stated that "the unanimous voice of the continent is Canada must be ours; Quebec must be taken." George Washington referred to the United States in March 1783 as a "rising empire," and Thomas Jefferson wrote in 1786 that "our confederacy must be viewed as the nest from which all America, North and South, is to be peopled." He prayed that the Spaniards would hang on to their colonies long enough "till our population can be sufficiently advanced to gain it from them piece by piece." Meanwhile "we must have" some of their territories around the Mississippi—this is all we are prepared as yet to receive."[23]

In the course of expansion, the United States did not impose colonial status on the territories it bought or wrested from Spain, France, the Indians, Mexico, and Britain. The territory north of the Ohio River and west of the Mississippi, which was deeded to the United States by the treaty of 1783, could have been converted into a dependent colony by the founders. They chose, instead, to give this territory the same status as the original thirteen states. Under the Northwest Ordinance of 1787, the territory was to be divided into three to five potential states and once these divisions had attained a population of 60,000, they were to be admitted to the Union "on an equal footing with the original states in all respects whatsoever." The same type of disposition was made for the states carved out of the Louisiana Territory, the former Spanish and Mexican possessions, and the Oregon Territory. None was reduced to the level of colony. Indeed, had the United States tried to make them into dependencies the result would have been catastrophic, for there was no way of policing such immense areas against secession and revolution. They could only be held together by the fervidness of nationalism.

Contiguous territorial expansionism, however, was supplanted by outright colonization when the United States annexed Hawaii, 2,100 miles from San Francisco, toward the end of the nineteenth century, then acquired the Philippines and Puerto Rico as a result of the Spanish–American War, and established a protectorate over Cuba. In the ensuing years "dollar diplomacy" and "banana imperialism" brought the whole Caribbean area into the U.S. sphere of influence, though none of the states was formally annexed. But it was a modest empire. It was not on a par with those of Britain or France, and while the empire excited sharp protest from the Anti-Imperialist League and such men as former president Grover Cleveland, William Jennings Bryan, and author Mark Twain, it only defiled the anticolonialist and anti-imperialist tradition to a limited extent.

World War II, however, drove the United States to adopt a policy of global imperialism in which most of the world was to be tailored to the American measure. At war's end the United States was suddenly master of a vast empire. To be sure, it only added small pieces of territory to its suzerainty—Micronesia, Okinawa, for instance—but its control of the "free world" was exercised in three other ways. Japan was now directly occupied by General MacArthur's troops and the general was busy recasting its political structure to conform to the American pattern. One zone of Western Germany and a sector of Berlin were under a U.S. military government. Second, many countries were tied to Uncle Sam through grants and loans. The significance of these funds was noted by Howard K. Smith who wrote in his *The State of Europe*, "the economic veins of a large part of the world have been connected to America's pumping industrial and agricultural heart. Many of them depend on America not merely for aid without which they would be worse off; they depend on the heart's regular pumping for naked survival. By a decision on whatever grounds to reduce or cut off the flow, America could stop factories, cause riots and upheaval, break governments."[24] Third, the United States had replaced Britain as master of the seas, including even the eastern Mediterranean. It was ensconced in four hundred major, and a couple of thousand minor, naval and air bases throughout the world so that existing empires and existing trade depended on American sufferance. "For America," Smith concluded, "becoming 'imperialist' is as easy as rolling off a log. With this preponderance of power, and most of the rest of the world in a crisis of scarcity, there need be no crude conquests; they can be carried out gently, invisibly, by the almost surreptitious means of wealth, by investments that bring silent control, and by aid-grants accompanied by polite hints regarding the direction of the receiving nation's policy." The new imperialism soon proved itself not quite as effete as Howard K. Smith pictured it, but it certainly was as wide-ranging.

America seized the reins of global imperialism for much the same reasons that Britain had a century earlier. Britain filled the void left by the disintegrating Turkish, Mogul, Chinese, and other empires. The United States was now called upon to fill the void left by the disintegrating and impoverished British, French, Dutch, Belgian, German, Italian, and Japanese empires. Not only was the opportunity there, but the only way to avoid global imperialism was to stand by quietly while most of the world turned to socialism.

The U.S. national income had more than doubled between 1940 and 1945 and as a result of this wartime prosperity, the U.S. need for foreign markets was more critical than at any time in history. According to the National Planning Association, the capital equipment industry was "nearly twice the size which would be needed domestically under the most fortuitous conditions of full employment and nearly equal to the task of supplying world needs."[25] America, a market economy, needed outside markets to keep its great economic machine in operation. Under a different kind of social system, Assistant Secretary of State Dean Acheson told a congressional committee in 1944, "you could use the entire production of the country in the United States," but under the present free enterprise system the government "must look to foreign markets" or "we are in for a very bad time." Donald M. Nelson, head of the War Production Board, and President Roosevelt argued in the same vein. To gain such markets the United States would have to organize the world in its own image. Otherwise, unemployment levels might reach those of the Great Depression—15, 20, 25 percent of the work force—with all the attendant social consequences.

Franklin Roosevelt understood this all too well. He planned for a postwar world in which the United States would exercise global domination—and he saw nothing sinister in this. In his schema the United States, unlike the British and French imperialists of the past, would fashion a *benign* imperialism. In short, Roosevelt envisioned a partnership between the United States and its client states. American business would enjoy a quantum jump in foreign trade and investment, protected by an American navy and army that would guarantee the overseas stability required by such ventures. But there would be no need, he felt, for the terrorism that the older imperialists had used against their colonies. "Roosevelt," observes Richard Hofstadter, "appears to have believed that the ruthless imperialism of the older colonial powers might be replaced by a liberal and benevolent penetration that would be of advantage both to the natives and American commerce."[26]

The Roosevelt team was preparing for this mission even as hostilities proceeded. A War and Peace Studies Project of the Council on Foreign Relations, which included top government planners and a sprinkling of the foreign policy elite with ties to big business, held discussions on what America's economic objectives should be after the war. Though their conclusions were not formal government decisions, they carried decisive weight with the administration. The Project concluded that "the British Empire as it existed in the past will never reappear and . . . the United States may have to take its place." The United States therefore "must cultivate a mental view toward world settlement after this war which will enable us to impose our own terms, amounting perhaps to a Pax-Americana."[27] If we were to prosper under the present system, it stated we would have to control at least the economic life of the Western Hemisphere, the former British Empire, and the Far East.

After Roosevelt's death the architects of the new imperialism—men like Dean Acheson and John J. McCloy—proceeded along this line, thinking of themselves not as cruel enslavers but as human benefactors.[28] They felt that they were introducing a system of worldwide stability and laying the groundwork for an enduring peace. World War II, in their opinion, had resulted from an excess of economic nationalism. By establishing a strong world economy with a sound dollar as the international medium of exchange, free trade as the guiding principle of commerce, and a large American military force prepared to police the world against disorder, the new imperialists believed they were creating the precondition for a warless world. Capitalism and peace, some of them believed, were synonymous. In a March 1947 speech at Baylor University, President Harry Truman argued that freedom of speech, press, and religion was impossible without "free enterprise"—capitalism—and free enterprise could survive in the United States only if it became a world system. Only the

United States had the military might, economic resources—and overriding need—to establish such a system.

In time it became apparent that *benign* imperialism was not possible in an age of revolution, nor was it possible to retain the democratic society at home while protecting and expanding U.S. power abroad. The United States soon found that traditional democracy at home could not be sustained while conducting a permanent war in pursuit of imperialist goals abroad. The process of forging the new imperialism tilted American society toward the authoritarianism it claimed to be fighting overseas.

To rule an empire America had to maintain a vast military machine and institutions such as the CIA and the NSA which operated under a blanket of secrecy. The public was increasingly excluded from the decision-making process. The American system was soon transformed from government by consent of the governed to government without the consent of the governed. The pernicious feature in all this was not only the expansion of military influence into civilian areas from which it should have been excluded, but the injection of the militarist élan throughout our society—a constant pressure directing American life toward the reactionary. As defined by a conservative expert, Samuel P. Huntington of Harvard, military values are exactly the opposite of "the Lockeian liberalism that has predominated in American society." Whereas the nation was built on the philosophical "ideals of liberty, democracy, equality, and peace," the basic military principles are "authority, hierarchy, obedience, force, and war."[29]

To paraphrase Abraham Lincoln in his famous 1858 speech to the Illinois Republican convention, the U.S. government is now part democratic and part totalitarian. Just as in 1858 it was impossible for the nation to "endure permanently half slave and half free," this generation too has reached a crossroads. In the process of massive rearmament, the postwar American governments have set a course toward despotism as the founders of the nation had foreseen two centuries ago. "Perhaps it is a universal truth," James Madison wrote to Thomas Jefferson in 1798, "that the loss of liberty at home is to be charged to provisions against danger real or pretended from abroad."[30]

2

The Second Government

It soon became apparent that the policy of benign imperialism would not work as expected. America did forge a great empire, but it did not occupy the countries under its control as the British, French, and others had done in the nineteenth century, and its hold on client states—exercised through economic aid, military aid, and puppet armies—in many instances was tenuous. Some countries seceded from the American sphere, most notably China, while others—Madagascar, Algeria, Indonesia, Kenya, Indochina—were plunged into internal and civil wars when the old colonial powers refused to leave. The "partnership" Roosevelt had hoped for with former colonies and the world stability he had banked on as the cornerstone for benign imperialism did not eventuate as planned. More and more then the American government took to paramilitary and military action to defend its empire; in tandem with this development, America fashioned a new set of institutions, a second government, to coordinate and direct the permanent war.

The initial problem for Washington was that the Soviets refused to become part of the American system. Roosevelt had expected that if Moscow were offered a measure of security and material aid, it would evolve a *soft* communist line directing discontent around the world into reformist rather than revolutionary channels. This was not as far-fetched as it sounds today for the socialists of the Second International had frequently defended the empires of their "bourgeois governments." The communist parties around the world had also unexpectedly muted their criticism of capitalist regimes after 1933–34 when the foreign policies of those regimes meshed with that of the Soviet Union—when Roosevelt, for instance, tendered diplomatic recognition to the Soviet Union and, again, when Leon Blum of France signed the Franco-Soviet pact. It was not inconceivable, then, that the communists could be transformed into good social democrats and live as a left opposition *within* the established system. "We really believed in our hearts," stated Harry Hopkins, Roosevelt's closest advisor, "that this was the dawn of the new day we had all been praying for and talking about for so many years. . . . The Russians had proved that they could be reasonable and far-seeing, and there wasn't any doubt in the minds of the President or any of us that we could live with them and get along with them peacefully for as far into the future as any of us could imagine."[1]

America's divergence with Moscow after the war did not begin over revolution but, rather, over the shape of the postwar world. The fires of revolution had long since burned themselves out in the Soviet Union. The Russians wanted economic aid to rebuild the 70,000 villages and cities that had been partly or wholly destroyed and they were willing to pay a price for that aid in the form of a moderate political policy. The issue of revolution did eventually drive a wedge in relations between the United States and the Soviet Union, but not at the beginning. Moscow tried with might and main to stifle popular revolt. "Near the end of the war," writes historian D. F. Fleming, "Stalin scoffed at communism in Germany, urged the Italian Reds to make peace with the monarchy, did his best to induce Mao Tse-tung to come to terms with the Kuomintang, and angrily demanded of Tito that he back the monarchy, thus fulfilling his [Stalin's] bargain with Churchill."[2]

It is ironic that both France and Italy might have succumbed to communism if it were not for Stalin. Two leaders of the Communist Party of France, André Marty and Charles Thillon, had been urging since 1944 that their party—the largest force in the French Resistance—seize political power. In Italy the communists had formed a partisan movement known as the *Garibaldini*, and in March 1944 had conducted a general strike in the northern part of the country which historian Hugh Seton-Watson described as "the most impressive action of its kind that took place at any time in Europe under Hitler's rule."[3] In both France and Italy, on the morrow of liberation, armed resistance fighters seized the factories. With their stockpile of arms they might have gone further—to seizure of political power—as Marty and Thillon had proposed.

The crisis was only averted because Joseph Stalin was not favorable to revolution just then. His primary interest was in getting economic help from the United States to rebuild his devastated country. General Charles de Gaulle took a plane to Moscow, talked with Stalin, and the French communists evacuated the factories and disarmed their partisans. Instead of revolution, they entered the "bourgeois government" with their leader, Maurice Thorez, serving as vice premier. Another word from Moscow and the Italian communists took a similar tack, disarming their followers, leaving the occupied factories, and accepting a leading role in government for their chief, Palmiro Togliatti. Stalin, on the whole, played a moderate role during this period.

The Russian leadership was willing to contain the fires of revolution where it could, but that did not satisfy the Truman administration which insisted that it go further. American leadership wanted Russia to become a subordinate part of the American system, to adopt Washington's own blueprint for the postwar world. The Soviet Union, however, could not accept this schema and still remain a communist or socialist nation. This was the basic point at which there was divergence. Each nation was motivated differently, with opposite approaches as to how to achieve recovery and prosperity.

The United States needed a considerable expansion of international trade to avoid a depression. As Dean Acheson had stated, America "must look to foreign markets" or "we are in for a very bad time."[4] The American problem, as Stephen E. Ambrose and James A. Barber, Jr. have noted, was that "much of the proposed market place was closed, nationalized, or both. Americans feared that their manufacturers would be unable to compete with foreign industries that had all the resources of the state behind them." In other words, Russia could subsidize her industries to undersell American goods.[5] Unless the United States met this challenge, it would have no place for its wares and would suffer the pains of overproduction and depression—a return to unemployment rates equal to those of the 1930s. Free trade—a relaxation of barriers such as quotas and tariffs, along the lines of the British empire system—were indispensable for American economic health. The whole world must adopt the American system of free trade, President Truman said in March 1947, if the American system itself was to survive. The United States could undersell any country in virtually any manufactured commodity, but only if it had access to the market.

The problem was solved in a unique way. The United States gave its allies and friends many billions of dollars in grants and loans to revive their battered economies. They, in turn, used the money to buy American goods. Most of these dollars (about 90 percent) came back to the United States as payment for machinery, foodstuffs, and equipment. Therefore, while the Marshall Plan and other aid programs were considered generous—they did in fact stimulate economic recovery in Europe, Japan, and other parts of the world—they were not entirely eleemosynary. In return, each recipient had to agree to certain conditions. One was to accept the American dollar as the international medium of exchange which gave the United States advantages in international finance that no other nation had. More important, they had to accept the open door principle: free—or freer—trade. As a result, tariffs were lowered on numerous commodities, three-quarters of the quotas on foreign goods were dropped, and Britain was forced to give up the empire preference system which favored goods coming in from empire nations such as Canada over goods coming in from nations outside the empire, such as the United States. There were also some special requirements. One of the conditions for a loan to Britain, for instance, was that the Rockefeller interests be permitted to buy 600,000 shares of Tanganyika Concessions, the largest financial holding company in sub-Sahara Africa.

Given such conditions American business was able to penetrate the world market as never before. It had such a wide margin in efficiency and productivity that it could undersell virtually anyone—providing there were no trade barriers. The results proved the point. From 1950, the year that stability was assured for Western Europe, to 1965, American exports to Europe grew from less than $3 billion to $9.5 billion, and direct private investment of American entrepreneurs in Europe rose from almost $2 billion to almost $14 billion. In Britain the figure in 1950 was less than $1 billion, in 1965 more than $5 billion; in France a mere $217 million and fifteen years later more than $1.5 billion; in Germany $204 million in 1950, almost $2.5 billion in 1965. "Foreign aid," John F. Kennedy observed, "is a method by which the United States maintains a position of influence and control around the world. . . ."[6]

The United States also provided military aid to its friends. From the spring of 1949 to January 1953, it shipped 4 million tons of war material to its NATO allies alone, including 503 planes and 82 warships. From 1945 to 1965 Europe received $16 billion in military gifts, and the world as a whole received twice that much. But the purpose of military aid was to shore up the "American way," to guarantee that governments friendly to the U.S. system of free trade could defend themselves against revolutionary rivals and remain in power. This focus was clearly expressed by an interdepartmental committee of the American government which stated that the purpose of military aid to the NATO countries was "first to protect the North Atlantic Pact countries against *internal* aggression inspired from abroad"—leftist revolutions, in other words—and only secondly to "deter aggression" (emphasis added).[7] Tenuous governments such as those of Greece, Turkey, Pakistan, Indonesia, and others could not have retained power if it were not for that military aid. But that was not an end in itself for Washington; the goal was to buttress the worldwide economic pattern the American government was pursuing.

In accord with this objective, the United States was willing to include the Soviet Union and its satellite states in its program. At various times during and after the war it considered loans to Moscow of $10 billion, $1 billion, $6 billion, but only on condition that the Soviets agree to free trade. In other words, they were to give up the government monopoly of foreign commerce and allow the free market to determine imports and exports. The Soviets, however, could not fit themselves into this pattern without dire results. For the United States, the acquisition of world markets was imperative to avoid a depression and unemployment. For the Soviet Union, the open door to all trade would have been a catastrophe. Naturally the Russians sought to sell their goods to the West, in exchange for machinery, construction materials, and other items needed for recovery. But since their system guaranteed everyone a job as a matter of political principle, they did not depend on world trade as the United States and other capitalist states did. If trade were minimal and Soviet national income low, the Russian system provided for spreading the work and lowering the nation's living standards.

In effect, the Russians shared a common misery while they waited for times to get better and without American aid, the Soviet economy, and both its people and those of the nations under its control suffered immensely: some died, and all the while political repression increased. The Soviets exploited their satellite states—by paying, for instance, below-market prices for Polish or Czech goods, while charging those countries above world-market prices for Russian goods. Whether this method of survival was a virtue or a vice, the fact is that Moscow was not under the same kind of compulsion as the United States to find world markets.

On the other hand, to accept the conditions for aid demanded by Washington would have meant the end of communism in Russia. Under the Soviet system the state holds a monopoly of foreign trade, in part to keep out cheaper goods from abroad. Thus if an American steel mill can sell a ton of steel for $500, whereas a less efficient Soviet steel mill must charge $800, the Soviet ministry of foreign trade protects its home industry simply by refusing to buy American (or German, or Japanese, or French) steel. The Soviets have a *closed* economy, not an open one, operating on the same principle as the United States did after the Civil War when it imposed large tariffs on foreign imports to protect less efficient American manufacturers. If the foreign trade monopoly in the Soviet Union were to be breached, as the United States wanted, and the door opened without restriction to Western imports, American corporations would easily undersell their Russian counterparts and drive them out of business. (The East European nations, with the possible exception of Czechoslovakia, would be even more vulnerable.) The Soviet Union in the end would have to deindustrialize and become a second-rate nation relying primarily on the sale of raw materials. Soviet specialists told an American in London that the American free trade proposal was merely a means "to hold the market for manufactured goods" for American corporations. They also argued that "protection was necessary for the industrialization of Eastern European countries and their industrialization was necessary to free them from economic domination by the capitalist countries."[8]

In the absence of United States sympathy for the Soviet problems, this divergence of economic policies was one of the major causes of the permanent war. The two systems could not coexist unless the American government was willing to be tolerant of Soviet economic principles. Unfortunately it wasn't. On the contrary, almost all American leaders in 1945 were convinced, as Henry Luce of *Life* magazine had put it, that this was to be "the American century," that the wartime victory would make it possible for the United States to dominate world affairs for decades, if not centuries. America was determined that the Soviet Union would not stand in the way. Bernard Baruch, presidential advisor and financier, expressed the mood with remarkable forthrightness: "America can get what she wants if she insists on it. After all we've got it—the Bomb—and they haven't and won't have it for a long time to come."[9] James F. Byrnes, soon to be Secretary of State, told Truman in April 1945 that the Bomb (which had not yet been tested) "might well put us in a position to dictate our own terms at the end of the war."[10] Secretary of War, Henry L. Stimson stated that the United States held "a royal flush and we mustn't be a fool about the way we play it." The Secretary recorded in his diary that day, May 14, 1945, that the Soviets "can't get along without our help and industries. . . . "[11]

There was a general feeling then and in the ensuing years that continued pressure on Moscow would force the Kremlin into "the American system." Byrnes in fact felt confident that the Russians could be made to give up most of the sphere of influence that had been deeded to them in the wartime meetings between Roosevelt, Churchill, and Stalin. With the Bomb in our possession, Byrnes was confident the Soviets could be forced to "retire in a very decent manner" from Eastern Europe, and could be kept from playing a serious role in the Far East. If the Russians proved surly—by refusing to evacuate East Germany, for instance—the United States would have to "make it clear to all that we are willing to adopt those measures of last resort [i.e., nuclear war] if, for the peace of the world we are forced to do so."[12]

American leaders were not worried about communist philosophy per se—in ensuing years they achieved friendly relations with communist Yugoslavia, communist Rumania, communist Hungary, and in the last decade communist China. But the very existence of the Soviet Union was a challenge to American geopolitical ambitions. Revolutionary governments that opposed the open door trade policy were frowned on by Washington, which often tried to overthrow them. The Soviet Union, on the other hand, proceeding from the age-old political thesis that "the enemy of my enemy is my friend," gave aid to such governments and groups. It wasn't that Moscow was in any sense revolutionary, but the fire of national interest remained. In a bipolar world the United States considered it necessary to exert unrelenting pressure on Moscow, to "contain" it, and ultimately force it to change its communist system. On the Soviet side, the reactive defense was to assist those who sought to secede from the American system.

It is not surprising, then, that American leaders tended to be "tough." There was talk of war and preventive war against the Soviet Union almost from the day the war against the Axis powers ended. In October 1945, just two months after Japan surrendered, General George S. Patton delivered a speech urging the nation to remain "armed and prepared" for an "*inevitable*" new war.[13] A month later General Henry H. (Hap) Arnold, of the Air Force, proposed a policy of "offensive readiness." "We must use our most brilliant scientists," he said, "to develop better weapons more quickly and more effectively. We must take advantage of the bases we now have to be closer to an enemy's vital points with our weapons than he is to ours. We must use the most modern weapons of all kinds so that we can beat any potential opponent to the draw."[14] There could be no question against whom such talk was directed; the only nation in the world capable of challenging the United States even to a limited extent was the Soviet Union.

That it wasn't just the military brass talking is indicated by the fact that a few months later, in 1946, presidential assistant Clark M. Clifford prepared a secret report for Harry Truman titled "A Summary of American Relations with the Soviet Union." The 62-page document was based on conversations with the Secretaries of State, War, Navy, the Attorney General, the Joint Chiefs of Staff, Fleet Admiral William D. Leahy, and the director of Central Intelligence, among others—all of whom, according to Clifford, expressed "a remarkable agreement." After listing a compendium of Soviet sins, from espionage to seeking control over most of the world, the Clifford report argued that America must maintain whatever military forces are necessary "to confine Soviet influence to its present area." It ought to dangle a carrot before the Russians so that they "can earn their dividends, among other ways, in American trade," but the carrot should go with a nuclear stick. "The U.S.," Clifford wrote, "with a military potential composed of highly effective weapons [i.e., the atomic bomb] should entertain no proposal for disarmament or limitation of weapons." Instead it "must be prepared to wage atomic and biological warfare." There "must be constant research in both offensive and defensive weapons" to enhance American capabilities in that direction.[15]

Beyond the Soviet challenge which stirred men like Clifford in 1945–47 was that of national revolutions, impelling the American establishment to take measures it had not intended to take and to establish government institutions for fighting a permanent war it had not planned on fighting. Such revolutions shook the rafters in Madagascar in 1943–44, Greece in 1944, Algeria, Tunisia, Morocco in 1945, and were in various stages of gestation or development in the Philippines, Indochina, Indonesia, China, and elsewhere during the 1945–47 period. There was concern in high places in Washington that the victory won after four years of war and hundreds of thousands of casualties was in danger of being undone. Should large parts of Europe and the Far East break from the "American system," the wartime victory would turn hollow.

Typical of the dilemma facing the United States was what happened in the Philippines. In line with its anticolonialist protestations and the promises of the Atlantic Charter, the United States granted independence to the islands on July 4, 1946, amid pomp and ceremony, and with an assurance of $380 million in aid to rebuild the new nation's war-torn economy. There were certain qualifications to this American divestiture which in effect retained the Philippines as an economic dependency. Both independence and aid were conditional on acceptance of the Philippine Trade Act, passed by the U.S. Congress. Under section 341 of that act, the Filipinos were required to grant American businesses the same rights as native entrepreneurs. Moreover, the Philippine constitutional provision denying foreigners the right to own more than 40 percent of any local company was changed so that it did not apply to capitalists from the United

States. The Trade Act also tied Philippine currency to the dollar until 1974 and allotted export quotas to American firms that had been in foreign trade before the war.

In practice, all this meant that some Filipinos would have greater say in their own political affairs but American corporations would still dominate the economy. Undersecretary of State William L. Clayton conceded that the Trade Act deprived "the Philippine government of a sovereign prerogative. . . . "[16] *Business Week* referred to independence as "nominal." Still, it did fit the parameters of "benign" imperialism, and this undoubtedly was the pattern that the American government wished to establish everywhere—economic control of dependent countries, without the necessity of costly and dangerous physical occupation by its own troops which was neither feasible nor desirable after World War II. As the Pentagon explained it to the Senate Committee on Foreign Relations in February 1969, "U.S. options in military situations" were a pyramid in which the United States began by offering "military advice and assistance to the country's military establishment" as well as "training by American officers" and material aid to deal with its own "insurgency situations." Only in those rare cases where the native forces were unavailing would the United States give "direct support by U.S. forces" and, finally, as the last step, institute "unilateral U.S. operations against the insurgents."[17] The hope was always to avoid direct American intervention by leaving it to American-trained puppet police and armies to control native peoples. Few Americans anticipated that such policies would eventually lead to American landings in Lebanon or the Dominican Republic, and "little" wars like the one in Vietnam. Those who had anything to do with formulating strategy were convinced that client armies were adequate to the task of maintaining the law and order needed for stable economic relations.

The flaws in this approach became evident, however, in the first experiment at "benign" imperialism, the Philippines. Not surprisingly, the conditions of the Philippine Trade Act were approved by an administration of questionable credentials. President Manuel Roxas, whose election *Business Week* had called a "political farce," had played a double role during the war, collaborating with the Japanese while spying for the United States. After the war, he displayed that same capacity for survival by agreeing to the Trade Act and granting the United States ninety-nine-year leases for various military bases. It is doubtful whether the United States would have concluded such favorable arrangements with more radical elements. We need only envision George Washington granting Great Britain military bases in New York City after the Revolutionary War and agreeing to a favored trade position to realize how incongruous such a position is for genuine nationalists.

But having entered into a partnership with Roxas and similar elements, the Truman administration found itself on the horns of a dilemma. While Roxas had been collaborating with the Japanese during the war, the communist-dominated Hukbalahap (National Anti-Japanese Army) was waging guerrilla war against Japan, and receiving U.S. aid for its efforts. After General Douglas MacArthur returned to Manila, the Huks disarmed themselves and agreed to partake in normal political activities. In the 1946 elections their Democratic Alliance won six Congressional seats in Central Luzon, by wide margins, and though the Alliance was a minority party nationally, it held the balance of power in the Legislature. Roxas, confronted with this challenge by the left, used his army (still commanded by American officers) to suppress the movement, remove the six congresspeople from office, and outlaw Huk-controlled labor and peasant organizations. As might have been expected, the radicals returned to guerrilla warfare. At the peak of their effort, according to Lieutenant Colonel Tomas C. Tirena of the Philippine Air Force, they commanded 15,000 men, plus "80,000 HMB's [National Army of Liberation], with a mass support of 500,000."[18]

Faced with a popular revolution, the United States was forced to take a position. Theoretically Truman could have remained neutral, but the United States was too involved in Philippine affairs to stand aside. It could have taken the side of the Huks, assuring their victory, but that would have cut off the United States from business and conservative friends of long standing. It also would have jeopardized the very favorable economic arrangements that had just been negotiated. Perhaps if someone at the State Department had made the appraisal that this was one of scores of nationalist revolutions soon to take place around the world, Washington might have adopted a different course. But the United States, like the West generally, had had a long history of imposing its will on weak countries such as those in the Caribbean. It did not seem to American leaders in 1946 that something radically new was happening or that there were any long-term risks in siding with Filipino reactionaries against the communist-led Huks. The Joint U.S. Military Advisory Group (JUSMAG) therefore equipped, trained, and advised 54,000 government troops and a similar number of "civilian guards" in their campaign to defeat the Huks.

The legality of this intervention is murky at best. Does a sovereign government have the right to call on another sovereign government to help it suppress a domestic insurgency? If so, the United States was on tenuous ground when it criticized the Russian government for invading Czechoslovakia in 1968 at the request of a newly installed Czech government which obviously had no mandate from the Czech people; or when it criticizes Angola for calling on Cuban troops to help it against the UNITA rebels and South African forces which have invaded the southern part of the country. Whether legal or not, the actions by President Roxas certainly were morally questionable by international standards, and very much at odds with American tradition. For the first time, we were manifesting a knee-jerk reaction whereby any movement with communist, neo-communist, neutralist, or "third camp" tendencies immediately elicited our opposition—regardless of the rights and wrongs of the particular situation. Our intervention in the Philippines locked us into a civil war for many years, during which we embraced—with one or two exceptions—one dictatorial regime after another.

The United States was also involved in at least three other revolutionary or prerevolutionary tempests in the Far East at approximately the same time. Intervention in Indochina was even more brazen than in the Philippines for, while the Huks represented only a minority in their country, the Vietminh of Indochina undoubtedly articulated the aspirations of the vast majority. When Japan seized Indochina toward the end of World War II she was met by a guerrilla band of 10,000 men, determined, in their words, to smash both "French imperialism and Japanese fascism." The most forceful of the two guerrilla groups was the Vietminh (national front), a coalition led by the communists and Ho Chi Minh. According to Ellen J. Hammer in *The Struggle for Indo-China*, Vietminh was "a broad national movement uniting large numbers of Vietnamese regardless of their politics." On March 6, 1946, France recognized the Vietminh regime as part of the French Union, but refused to relinquish authority over the army, diplomatic functions, currency, and the economy. The usual incidents occurred as popular wrath mounted. At Haiphong on November 23, 1946, the French cruiser *Suffern* fired on the Vietnamese section of town, killing between 6,000 and 30,000 people. This was the signal for the French seizure of all of Indochina and the installation of a discredited former emperor, Bao Dai—who had also been the puppet for Japan—as the head of government. Before long guerrilla warfare broke out again as Vietminh General Vo Nguyen Giap mobilized 70,000 irregulars to fight 166,000 French troops.

The Truman administration might have remained neutral or sided with the rebels in this instance, but contrary to the promises of the Atlantic Charter, the United States asserted that it "recognizes French sovereignty over Indochina" and began shipping supplies to the French which by 1952 reached 100,000 tons. As of 1954 it was paying 78 percent of French military costs. In fact, that year the United States offered France three atom bombs, one to be dropped on China near the Indochinese border, and two to be used against the Vietminh at Dienbienphu where they had the French surrounded.[19]

The third Asian civil war in which the United States played a role in that early period was in China. As of V-J Day the United States was within an eyelash of what was potentially the greatest of all imperial prizes—the addition to its empire of the most populous state in the world, China. With the defeat of Japan and the enervation of Britain, the United States had an open field. The civil war in China, in abeyance during the common defense against Japan, was once again aflame. The Chiang Kai-shek regime was by general consensus corrupt and tyrannical—according to General Joseph Stilwell it was "a one-party government supported by a Gestapo. . . ."[20] Roosevelt had demanded that Chiang introduce reforms. Truman's emissary, General George Marshall tried for thirteen months to edge the Kuomintang and the Communists into a coalition, but in vain. The landlords and businesspeople who supported Chiang felt they did not have to make any concessions to Mao's Communists or the people of China because Truman had no choice but to support Chiang. Truman, after all, could not seek to organize the world in the American image and permit China to fall to communist guerrillas.

Washington gave Chiang $3 billion in aid—a very large sum at the time—plus weapons from a million disarmed Japanese soldiers, as well as other help. But of the 4 million men in Chiang's army, 1,690,000 defected or were otherwise lost between July 1946 and November 1947 alone, and mountains of American weapons fell into rebel communist hands. In its crusade against communism, the United States again had intervened on the unpopular and losing side.

A fourth U.S. intervention eventually led to the fifth most costly military engagement in American history. Korea had been annexed by Japan in 1910. An agreement at the end of World War II gave the Russians the northern, industrial half of the country—above the 38th parallel—while the United States received the more agricultural segment below. All kinds of revolutionary committees emerged to greet the liberating forces, many led by communists—but only a few under noncommunist leadership. Two days before General John R. Hodge landed to assume command of the American sector, Committees of Preparation for National Independence held an assembly and formed a national government for *all* Korea. The People's Republic was headed by a much respected noncommunist. His regime, according to *New York Times* reporter Foster Hailey, "was as representative of Korea as any group that could have been quickly organized."[21] The United States, however, refused to recognize the unified government. Instead, it installed a seventy-year-old exile, Syngman Rhee, and in August 1946 declared South Korea an independent, separate republic. Less than two years later, the two segments of Korea were in a civil war and Truman was sending scores of thousands of American troops to fight on their terrain.

As the problem of civil war and revolution grew in significance, and as tensions with the Soviets mounted, Washington turned from ad hoc responses and put in place a machinery, ideology, and mystique for waging a permanent war.

One of the first requirements of the National Security State was further research, development, and production of the one weapon—Truman had called it "the greatest thing in history"[22]—which the administration believed would assure the United States of military supremacy for a long time to come. In this way, the National Security State—the second government—and the impulse toward authoritarianism was born.

In a message to Congress less than two months after Hiroshima, Truman proposed the establishment of an Atomic Energy Commission (AEC). This seemed indispensable if America were to brandish the atomic stick, as it did, for instance, when Truman gave Soviet ambassador Andrei Gromyko an ultimatum for the Red Army to evacuate two provinces of Iran or suffer a nuclear attack on the Soviet Union itself.[23] Many years later, in 1981, the author of the containment strategy, George F. Kennan, conceded that "the nuclear bomb is the most useless weapon ever invented. It can be employed for no rational purpose."[24] But in 1945–46 Truman considered it the fulcrum of American power and he urged that the "secret" of how to make it be kept secret at all costs. The AEC, he proposed, "should be authorized to establish security relations governing the handling of information, material, and equipment under its jurisdiction. Suitable penalties should be prescribed for violating the security regulations. . . . "[25] The regulations subsequently embodied in the McMahon–Douglas Atomic Energy Act of 1946 contained punitive sections more severe than any peacetime act in history. Under the old Espionage Act, the death penalty could be imposed only in time of war. The Atomic Energy Act, however, provided for the ultimate punishment in peacetime as well if, in the opinion of a jury, the theft of an atomic secret was done with the deliberate intent of injuring "defense." The act was so sweeping that it punished even carelessness and indiscretion, including the dissemination of "restricted data" that a scientist might discover independently in his own laboratory, without government aid or supervision. The effect, wrote Alan Barth, an editorial writer for the *Washington Post*, was "to make perilous the very interchange of ideas and information indispensable to scientific progress." Secrecy became so phobic that of the 308,000 reports in the AEC files as of 1949, all but 10 percent were marked secret, unavailable to the public.[26] To indicate how far afield this protective tendency went, on one occasion AEC ordered General Electric to refuse bargaining rights at an atomic energy installation to the United Electrical Workers Union (UE) on the grounds that its leaders were suspected of being procommunist and might betray atomic secrets. (The Wagner Act of 1935 granted collective bargaining rights to any union that could show it represented a majority of the employees involved, but the AEC, on its own motion, scrapped this provision for atomic plants without bothering to have Congress amend or scrap the old law.)

In a nation ever poised for war, the government obviously has a right to protect military information. But it is hardly credible that 270,000 or 275,000 documents out of 308,000 all contain "secrets" that might help a potential enemy. Testifying before the Moorehead subcommittee in 1971, William Florence, an expert on classification, stated that 99.5 percent of all "classified" documents held by the Department of Defense (and presumably also by AEC) could be declassified without harm to national security.[27] Former Supreme Court Justice and Ambassador to the United Nations, Arthur Goldberg, told the same subcommittee: "I have read and prepared thousands of classified documents. In my experience, 75 percent of these documents should never have been classified in the first place; another 15 percent quickly outlived the need for secrecy; and only about 10 percent genuinely required restricted access over any significant period of time."[28] Had Thomas Paine been alive he might have questioned the government's right to hide from the public even 10 percent of its documents. "There is not place for mystery . . . in the representative system," he said. "The reason for everything must publicly appear. Every man is a proprietor in government, and considers it a necessary part of his business to understand."[29]

The determination to keep so many facts from the public—and to impose such harsh punishment for dissemination—can only be explained as an attempt to create a mystique of fear and conformity. The Russians of course had something to gain from spies and from cribbed documents—they certainly benefitted from the information supplied by the German-born scientist Klaus Fuchs who spied for them while working on the Manhattan Project in Los Alamos. But whether the cure was worse than the disease is another matter. The "secret" that was to be safeguarded was not as impenetrable as most Americans believed. The Russians were only a few steps behind the United States in atomic research, having begun their efforts in the late 1920s and having separated uranium 235 (the material for bombs) from ordinary uranium in 1942. In a report for the House

Committee on Foreign Affairs (August 1972), Leneice N. Wu of the Library of Congress stated: "Soviet development of atomic energy had proceeded quite well until World War II. In terms of the quality of research, the Soviet capability at that point has been estimated to have been on a par with that of the United States." The Russians abandoned their research after the Nazi attack in 1941, but when they resumed in 1944 they made headway almost as rapidly as the United States had done. By late 1947, they had a nuclear reactor in operation and, by 1949, a bomb. "Secrecy," Wu points out, "cannot long delay the independent acquisition of scientific and technological information."[30] The "secret" was of so little value that on September 11, 1945, Secretary of War Henry L. Stimson (with the support of three other members of the cabinet) proposed to Truman an "atomic partnership" with the Soviet Union. The alternative, he said, would be "a secret armaments race of a rather desperate character"—which he implied no one could win.[31]

The AEC's campaign to prevent the *Progressive* magazine from publishing an article in 1979, "The H-Bomb Secret" illustrates how far afield the secrecy policy took them. The author, Howard Morland—a college graduate with nothing more than the usual undergraduate course in physics—assembled enough material from interviews, unclassified documents, and articles to explain how an H-Bomb could be made. On hearing that the article was to be published, the government invoked the Atomic Energy Act of 1954 which gave it the right to suppress all information (not just its own "secrets" but even public information) about weapons and materials. A judge in Milwaukee granted the government motion to restrain publication in March of that year, and it took six months to get the article into print—and only then because another U.S. publication had already published it and others were threatening to do so. The government offered to allow publication if Morland would delete certain sections, and even liberal newspapers such as the *Washington Post* urged the author to do so voluntarily. When a copy of the article surfaced in Australia, two Energy Department officials flew there to prevent publication. The piece was finally printed in November 1979, and contrary to the dire government predictions neither the Mafia nor any nonnuclear country used it to produce H-bombs. The secret it turned out was no secret at all.

And an important side issue was that to actually build a bomb—including engineering facilities, plutonium, and many other things—would not only be difficult but impossibly costly.

The Atomic Energy Commission was a prototype of the institutions that the National Security State was putting in place. Increasingly, the American government was ranging into activities that were legally or morally questionable, such as secret subsidies to German and Italian Christian Democratic parties or direct interference in the internal affairs of a half-dozen countries. Another set of American institutions—separate from the traditional ones—was needed to organize such activities, plan them, and conceal them from the public. Although established by a federal law, the AEC nonetheless operated as if its mandate was self-granted. It participated in or made earth-shaking decisions without discussing them with the public, or seeking a vote of Congress.

In the years 1948 and 1949, by way of example, the government was called upon to respond to three defeats—the victory of the Communists against the Beneš regime in Czechoslovakia, the victory of the Chinese Communists against the U.S. ally, Chiang Kai-shek, and the Soviet testing of its first atomic device. This was a traumatic moment in American history, calling for a prolonged discussion of where we were going. Many leading figures had urged that we drop our fixation on the atomic bomb as the instrument of our security. Stimson, Henry Wallace, and others had urged Truman to make this change as early as 1945. A number of generals, including Eisenhower, had opposed use of the atomic bomb over Hiroshima and Nagasaki. Innumerable scientists who had worked on the Bomb wanted it shelved. But, in answer to the 1948–49 setback Truman decided to put another military chip in the pot, the hydrogen bomb—or the Super as it was then called. The National Security Council, not Congress, made the secret decision to proceed with this weapon, a thousand times more powerful than the A-bomb. The nine top scientists (headed by J. Robert Oppenheimer) who constituted the General Advisory Committee of the AEC wrote a report urging that the new weapon not be produced, but the government and the AEC went ahead anyway. Here was a weapon destined to change the course of American and world history, but the National Security

State did not deem it necessary to go beyond its own inner circles to decide whether and when to produce it.

The "second government" clearly did not operate on the principle of checks and balances, nor did it overly concern itself with the legality or illegality of its actions abroad or at home. The goal was to checkmate the Soviet Union and abort the revolutions which the Kremlin allegedly was promoting. You did that any way you could, with whatever weapons were at hand, and with a "damn-the-torpedoes-full-speed-ahead" spirit. As the saying goes, you fought fire with fire. The question of legality was incidental.

To wage a permanent war the American government needed on the one hand an ideology and mystique that would guarantee against popular resistance to its policy and, on the other, the more concrete institutions to coordinate and carry out the strategy for "victory." The ideology was provided by Truman in his historic address to Congress on March 12, 1947. The nations of the world, said the president, were divided into two groups, which practice two diametrically opposite ways of life. One, he said, "is based upon the will of the majority and is distinguished by free institutions, representative government, free elections, guarantees of individual liberty, freedom of speech and religion, and freedom from political oppression." The other "is based upon the will of the minority forcibly upon the majority. It relies upon terror and oppression, a controlled press and radio, fixed elections and the suppression of personal freedom."[32] This simplistic counterposing of democracy and communism was to be repeated tens of thousands of times in ensuing years by pundits as well as politicians, and became the raison d'être of the permanent war.

A central strategy of that war—which still obtains though its author long ago repudiated it—was supplied by the director of the Policy Planning Staff of the State Department, George F. Kennan. In a 1947 article for *Foreign Affairs*, published under the pseudonym "X," Kennan argued that aggressive tendencies inherent in communism required "long term, patient but firm and vigilant containment." The United States must apply "counterforce at a series of constantly shifting geographical and political points, corresponding to the shifts and maneuvers of Soviet policy." The United States should "promote tendencies which must eventually find their outlet in either the breakup or the gradual mellowing of Soviet power."[33] In other words, the United States would use political, economic, and military pressures to "contain" Moscow and its allies until the Soviet Union was finally forced to change its political system. At the time, Kennan thought it would take a maximum of ten to fifteen years. Columnist Walter Lippmann considered the "X" article and the Truman Doctrine a call for "unending intervention in all countries that are supposed to 'contain' the Soviet Union."[34]

Along with the ideology and strategy came a new mystique, one which exaggerated the power of the adversary (the communists were viewed as if they were "ten-feet tall," cynics said) and produced a mood of constant danger and emergency. Ideas or persons associated with communism, the Soviet Union, leftism generally, or dissidence, must be shunned, its promoters punished. General Douglas MacArthur described it aptly when he told the Michigan State Legislature on May 15, 1952 "that our country is now geared to an arms economy which was bred in an artificially induced psychosis of war hysteria and nurtured upon an incessant propaganda of fear."[35]

The hysteria and fear were indispensable if the permanent war—and the arms race it inspired—was to be pursued. There was, however, serious opposition to the militarization of America from both the left and right. A Win-the-War conference early in 1946 and a Conference of Progressives, a few months later, included not only radicals such as singer Paul Robeson, but a federation of labor, the CIO, two former members of Roosevelt's cabinet, Harold Ickes and Henry Morgenthau, Jr., former Vice President Henry A. Wallace, James Patton, president of the National Farmers Union (NFU), Walter White, secretary of the National Association for the Advancement of Colored People (NAACP), and many similar figures. Both conferences directed their darts against "British imperialism," while urging a modus vivendi with the Soviets. As a gauge of its strength, the "Progressives" were at that time about twice as large as a rival liberal group, the Americans for Democratic Action (ADA), which eventually slipped into the anticommunist pattern. On the right, many old-line Republicans like Robert A. Taft were determined to cut both the budget and taxes. They reacted unfavorably in 1947 to Truman's request for $400 million aid to Greece and Turkey to "fight communism." Republican Arthur Vandenberg, who was more sympathetic to Truman's position, warned the president that if he wanted these funds he would have to "scare the hell out of the country."[36]

That, indeed, has been the establishment's approach ever since. Before the Soviets had acquired or even tested their first atomic device, for instance, Lieutenant General Leslie R. Groves—who had headed the Manhattan Project which produced the first Bomb—warned that in the first five hours of a nuclear attack 40 million Americans would be killed. General Carl A. Spaatz cautioned that it would be too late for defense after the atomic bombs started falling. The Bomb was ominous enough but given the state of the art at that time, such statements were gross exaggerations. Nevertheless, by drawing this ominous picture the military was able to win approval for an $11 billion budget in fiscal 1948. In 1956 military spokesmen and the CIA talked of a "bomber gap" which predicted that by the end of the decade, the Soviet Union would have 600 to 700 long-range bombers—twice as many as the United States. In fact, as of 1961 the Soviets had less than a third that number, 190, whereas the United States had 600. In his last State of the Union message on January 12, 1961, President Eisenhower admitted that "the bomber gap of several years ago was always a fiction." Nonetheless in his election campaign of 1960, John F. Kennedy made much ado about an alleged "missile gap." The Russians, he said, were acquiring missiles so rapidly that by the early 1960s they would have three times as many as the United States. As it happened, there was never a "missile gap," any more than there had been a "bomber gap." The administration later admitted that instead of 600 to 800 missiles, as claimed by the Air Force, the Soviets had only 50 to 100.[37]

Ronald Reagan has brought the mystique of fear and emergency to its present apogee. "Let's not delude ourselves," he told the *Wall Street Journal* a few months before the 1980 elections, "The Soviet Union underlies all the unrest that is going on. If they weren't engaged in this game of dominoes, there wouldn't be any hot spots in the world."[38] In his fiscal 1983 report, Secretary of Defense Caspar Weinberger charged that the Soviet Union "poses a greater danger to the American people than any foreign power in our history."[39] The Reagan administration relies on an attenuated fear psychology—like its predecessors but somewhat more intense—to gain popular support for its militaristic policy. It tells the nation that the Soviets have far outspent us in recent years and have not only achieved parity, but are forging ahead. We are simply trying to catch up, in order to overcome "the severe inadequacies in the realm of strategic and other nuclear weapons." This claim has been disputed by such men as former Defense Secretary McNamara, who charge that the Pentagon has consistently exaggerated Soviet advances. Once a nuclear strategist for the Pentagon, Rear Admiral Gene R. LaRocque now heads the Center for Defense Information. He has stated that "the Soviet Union does not have military superiority over the U.S. The U.S. and its NATO allies have outspent the Soviet/Warsaw Pact military forces for many years—$215 to $175 billion in one year alone. . . . Today we can explode 12,000 nuclear weapons on the Soviet Union, while they can explode 7,000 on us. Neither we nor the Soviets can build a defense against nuclear weapons, no matter how much we spend."[40] But Reagan was able to induce Congress (and the American people) to schedule outlays of a trillion and a half dollars on the military machine. The anticommunist mystique had done its work. Thousands of writers, journalists, scholars, think-tank theorists, and others have been drumming the anticommunist message ("you can't trust the Russians") into American consciousness for four decades, to the point where the overwhelming majority of people believe that we must expand militarily to prevent the Soviet Union from pulverizing our land.

The mystique also has been implanted in the national consciousness by more direct, and punitive, means. The menace of communism and the consequent need to keep our "secrets" secret has been used as justification for exacting conformity from the American people. Secrecy has become an obsession. It is used as a tool against the Russians—whom it only inhibits minimally—but mostly, secrecy is used against the people of the United States. Three months after the Atomic Energy Act became law, Truman issued Executive Order 9835, providing for the investigation of the "loyalty" of "every person entering the civilian employment of any department or agency of the executive branch of the Federal Government." Prior to 1939 a federal employee took an oath to defend the Constitution; that was deemed a sufficient test of his loyalty. A civil service rule, going all the way back to 1884, prohibited the government from asking employees or prospective employees about their "political or religious opinions or affiliations."

But now a whole machinery was put into place—with the Federal Bureau of Investigation (FBI) as its linchpin—to inquire into the "loyalty" of applicants for federal jobs. Loyalty was now defined in terms of beliefs and associations—not actions. A man who believed it was necessary to overthrow the government by force and violence, but did nothing to implement that belief, would previously have been immune from government sanctions. Now he was not hired and if already employed, was fired. The Attorney General compiled an arbitrary list of organizations which he considered "totalitarian, fascist, communist, or subversive," and anyone who appeared to be linked to one of them was punishable. The accused was given an opportunity to appear, but the government did not have to produce the informer, and the victim, consequently, had no opportunity to confront his accuser. Without trial and with no chance of defending himself, he could lose a government job, and worse still, would probably be blacklisted elsewhere. In the first five years after Truman's order the FBI, according to J. Edgar Hoover, investigated and processed 4 million applications for government jobs. Some of the discharges "for security reasons" were ludicrous. James Kutcher, a war veteran who had lost both his legs in the 1943 Battle of San Pietro in Italy, was fired from a minor clerk's job at the Veterans Administration because he was a member of a small Trotskyist group—even though there were obviously no "secrets" in the Veterans Administration that the Russians or anyone else would use for devious purposes. (The loyalty question on federal job forms nonetheless survived until mid-1976 when the American Civil Liberties Union won two court decisions to remove them.)

The militarist elan of conformity and orthodoxy had a tendency to spread outward. The Attorney General of the United States, Francis Biddle, prepared a list of 200 "subversive" organizations, many defunct, as a guide to checking the loyalty of federal employees. When the Dies House Un-American Activities Committee (HUAC) made that list public, it became the "bible" for ferreting out "subversives" in occupations as well. Soon there was a cascade of measures to check "loyalty" in strange places. A million tenants in government-financed homes had to sign loyalty oaths that they were not commu nists; some were evicted for failing to comply. Before long loyalty oaths were being required of teachers in public schools and professors at universities, maritime workers, and workers in defense industries. In Indiana, prizefighters and wrestlers had to sign loyalty affidavits in order to fight or wrestle. The *Harvard Law Review* of April 1972 reported that 14 million civilian workers were subject to "loyalty qualifications"—one-sixth of the total work force. According to Mark H. Lynch, at the end of 1982, two and a half million civilian and military employees had security clearances, plus one and a half million contractors, 15,000 CIA, and 68,000 employees in the National Security Agency. Clearly, a very large number of people had to watch what they said and did lest their security status be questioned and their jobs or profits jeopardized.

Supreme Court Chief Justice and former Republican candidate for president, Charles Evans Hughes, stated in 1912 that, "It is the essence of the institutions of liberty that it be recognized that guilt is personal and cannot be attributed to the holding of opinion or to mere intent in the absence of overt acts. . . . "[41] The loyalty program, of course, mocked this definition of democratic rights. But in an era of permanent war, this program was not deemed sufficient to exact the necessary conformity. To supplement it, the Army had already instituted what was called a "security risk" program in 1940, and by 1947 the State Department, the AEC, and CIA followed suit. Under the "security risk" program the government didn't have to prove disloyalty, only that there was a "risk" that the employee *might* become disloyal because he was, say, a homosexual and might as a result be a target of blackmail. The Magnuson Act was approved providing that merchant seamen and specified longshoremen be cleared for "security." State and local governments took over where the Federal Government left off: hundreds of thousands of teachers, professors, and other employees were required to sign affidavits that they were not communists or "subversives." Under the 1947 Taft-Hartley law, union officials were obliged to execute affidavits swearing they were noncommunists or lose the right to represent their union before the National Labor Relations Board. Applications for passports were screened, and leftists or former leftists were denied the right to travel. The House Un-American Activities Committee, the Senate Internal Security Subcommittee, and later Senator Joseph Mc-

Carthy's Government Operations Committee used their facilities as a means of punishing dissidents. Hiding behind congressional immunity, these committees publicly stigmatized alleged "subversives" (including *former* leftists), and in hundreds of instances caused them to be discharged. In addition, of course, such committees functioned as blacklisting institutions: HUAC admitted in 1948 that it had compiled dossiers on 300,000 individuals; a year later the figure was a million. Using these files, the committee furnished inquiring employers with derogatory information concerning 60,000 individuals and 12,000 organizations.

How much the loyalty-security programs dampened the spirit of dissent amongst millions of scientists, soldiers, workers, civil servants, and Department of Defense employees has never been scientifically measured, but it is safe to say that innumerable persons were constrained to be silent on controversial issues, or at least to moderate their views. So fearful did the public become of being associated with communists that Steve Nelson, a communist leader in Pennsylvania, indicted under the Smith Act, had to "sound out" 152 lawyers, according to *Nation* editor Victor Navasky, before finding anyone to represent him.

The loyalty-security campaign certainly had its effect for the propaganda of fear continues to this day. A 1983 poll, summarized by the *New York Times*, revealed that 88 percent of the American people consider the Soviet Union hostile to us, and 71 percent believe it intends to make war on us. This is grist to the mill of the National Security State. The Communist Party which once had 80,000 to 100,000 members lost nine-tenths of its adherents, and an equal or larger percentage of its 1 to 2 million sympathizers. It also lost its hold on the unions, where at one time it controlled organizations with one-third the membership of the CIO. "If communism is an issue in any of your unions," CIO president Philip Murray told an executive board meeting of the CIO in July 1947, "throw it to hell out . . . and throw its advocates out along with it." In 1949 the CIO expelled eleven national unions charged with being communist-dominated. From then on the road for the Communist Party was steadily downhill. So was that of other leftist forces, such as the Trotskyists and later the Maoists. Only single-issue leftist organizations, such as the civil rights movement and the antiwar movement made episodic progress, and even they were negatively affected by the anticommunist mystique.

In addition to mystique, ideology, and strategy, the National Security State of course established a set of institutions to coordinate and actually execute the permanent war. Their most salient characteristics were a tendency to seek greater powers and operate outside popular control. And such was the nature of American society in the postwar era that even in the few instances when the national security institutions were censured as a result of a public outcry, they almost always regained—and often expanded—their lost "rights." Thus, the CIA, which some people believed would lose its mandate to conduct covert operations after the ill-fated Bay of Pigs invasion of 1961, recovered to the point where its 1982–84 operations in Nicaragua were openly admitted.

Rights lost by the CIA and FBI vis-à-vis illegal break-ins and surveillance of domestic leftists were quietly restored by executive orders under the Reagan administration.

A command and operational center for the worldwide confrontation with the Soviet Union and revolution was mandated by the National Security Act of 1947. The bill, handiwork in large part of Ferdinand Eberstadt, a friend and former partner of Navy Secretary James Forrestal in the Wall Street investment firm, Dillon, Read, created a "National Military Establishment" under a single civilian Secretary of Defense and gave legal sanction to the Joint Chiefs of Staff. Under this unified structure it was expected that rearmament and intervention (as in Korea and Vietnam) could be more effectively systematized. The "security" act also created a National Security Council charged with coordinating "domestic, foreign, and military policies." The National Security Council (NSC) played a different role under each president, in some instances more important, some less, but it was the critical force in developing policy. Its role was so overriding that Dean Acheson, in his memoirs, downgrades the role of the Cabinet in favor of the NSC. "The Cabinet," he wrote, "despite its glamour, is not a major instrument of Government; the National Security Council, properly run, can and should be."[42] Since the Council met secretly it was not subject to control by Congress or the public. "The American people cannot challenge its thinking directly," wrote Blair Bolles. "Decisions which it makes are never attributed to it."[43]

On the operational side, the Act provided for a Munitions Board under the Secretary of Defense to orchestrate and evaluate military procurement. A Research and Development Board was also established to perform a similar function in the scientific and engineering field. A National Security Resources Board was charged with planning industrial, military, and civilian mobilization for war—a central theme of the National Security State, after all, is the integration of military with civilian functions. Under another bill passed the same year, the Armed Services Procurement Act, procedures were laid down for the acquisition of armaments. Included were sixteen "exceptions" to the system of bidding which, in effect, freed most defense contracts from competition. This, of course, had the effect of consolidating the military-industrial and the military-academic relationship and producing what Irving Louis Horowitz called a class of "civilian militarists." Congress also saw to it that the military machine had available to it basic scientific research which in due course could be converted into military hardware. A National Science Foundation Act, approved in 1950, created a foundation to promote and fund basic research and scientific education, including grants for graduate students. At the request of the Secretary of Defense it was charged with undertaking "specific scientific research activities in connection to matters relating to the national defense."

A particularly ominous aspect of the dual government was the provision in the 1947 law establishing a Central Intelligence Agency. No institution of the second government revealed the tendency to enlarge its area of activity more than the CIA. Nowhere in the National Security Act, for instance, was there any provision for covert action. While the CIA's functions were specified as coordination, development, and analysis of *intelligence*, there was nevertheless a vague section of the act (102d) which authorized the CIA "to perform such other functions and duties related to intelligence affecting the national security as the National Security Council may from time to time direct."[44] The "other functions" specified in the law clearly are "related to intelligence"—not covert action. Nonetheless, the NSC stretched the CIA mandate to include covert acts unrelated to intelligence, such as the overthrow of a government. The members of Congress were never told by the Truman administration that it intended for the CIA to play such a role; on the contrary, they were led to believe the opposite.

According to the 1976 Senate Select Committee on Intelligence, the CIA's own general counsel conceded in a memorandum soon after the passage of the Act that there was "nothing to show that Congress intended to authorize covert action by the CIA."[45] Nonetheless the National Security Council stretched the CIA mandate to include such action: by 1953 the CIA was conducting major covert projects in forty-eight countries and its Clandestine Services were consuming three-fourths of its budget. It was financing foreign churches, foreign labor organizations, foreign civic groups, foreign political parties such as the Italian Christian Democratic party, and guerrilla movements in Albania, Poland, the Ukraine. From covert activities abroad it was a natural step to conduct illegal activities against Americans at home. This was an explicit violation of the 1947 Act, which prohibited the CIA from exercising "police, subpoena, or law-enforcement powers or internal security functions."[46] This provision had been written to appease fears that the CIA might become an American Gestapo, a secret police. But it took on secret police functions anyway and justified this practice on the grounds that its domestic activities were only ancillary to its foreign activities. For instance, the CIA hired Cuban refugees in Miami to spy on neighbors on the tenuous ground that this was necessary for counterintelligence against Fidel Castro. Fidelista spies were not uncovered and "it soon became domestic snooping plain and simple," a Cuban told George Volsky of the *New York Times*.[47]

On the same theory, the CIA began to intercept mail by Americans to addresses in the Soviet Union and other communist countries. It spied on newspeople and infiltrated such organizations as the Congress of Racial Equality (CORE), the War Resisters League, the Washington Ethical Society, Women Strike for Peace. Further, the CIA compiled files on 7,000 Americans and 1,000 American organizations, funded a large part of the budget of a student association, trained local police red squads in techniques for spying on leftists, and paid for the publication of many books.

Since the Central Intelligence Act of 1949 exempted the CIA from making its expenditures public, it could do as it wished with few restraints. The CIA did not have to report to Congress, except to small watchdog committees which were required to keep the reports secret. Periodically there was a public outcry by liberals, and the administration or Congress conducted hearings to allay public opinion—but the CIA excesses continued.

Despite the Church Committee revelations of 1976, for instance, Presidents Ford, Carter, and Reagan all issued executive orders permitting the same abuses to continue with minor modifications. All of these men authorized secret searches (break-ins) of the homes of Americans if the Attorney General approved them; all allowed for infiltration of domestic political organizations; all permitted the opening of mail under some circumstances. Reagan's Executive Order 12333 specifically permits the CIA to conduct domestic surveillance. Given the fact that the second government does not feel itself accountable to the public, it is not surprising that authoritarian agencies like the CIA show remarkable longevity.

A similar expansion of authoritarian functions was manifest in other areas of the National Security State—some of them carryovers from the prewar era, such as the FBI. The FBI had been precluded from political intelligence from 1924 until Roosevelt instructed it on the eve of World War II—by executive order again, not legislation—to monitor "subversive activities." Passage of the Smith Act in 1940 which made it a crime to advocate violent overthrow of the government also gave the FBI a legal handle to pursue leftists. It went far beyond that, however, and soon became an integral and pivotal part of the National Security State. The FBI compiled dossiers on public officials for the purposes of political harassment; investigated radical organizations; sent agents into such respected organizations as the NAACP, the American Friends Service Committee, and SANE; recruited 5,000 spies; drew up a list of many thousands of "dangerous" people to put in concentration camps in times of crisis; and conducted the counterintelligence program (COINTELPRO) which disrupted radical organizations, burglarized their offices, and played havoc with individual members.

The FBI engaged in exactly the kind of dirty tricks the CIA was practicing abroad and, like the CIA and the rest of the National Security State, it was constantly trying to enlarge its prerogatives. In

March 1983, Attorney General William French Smith announced new "guidelines" for the FBI which would permit it to infiltrate and spy on organizations *before* it had a "reasonable indication of criminal activities," and investigate anyone with an "apparent intent to engage in crime." These guidelines, Smith said, were not subject to congressional review.[48]

With the FBI and CIA involved in such behavior the spirit caught on with other agencies. The Department of Defense (DoD) opened up a "war room"—400 feet long, 250 feet wide—in the basement of the Pentagon. The room was complete with data processing machines, closed circuit televisions, and "war maps" and it was designed to control and suppress domestic protests. The army, using 1,500 nonuniformed agents, compiled dossiers on hundreds of thousands of U.S. citizens. The list of its illegal activities, such as spying on prominent citizens like Reverend Jesse Jackson, indicates how far afield the military's concept of "national security" goes. Would it also include, in time of emergency, the seizure of civilian powers by the military? While this sounds far-fetched at the moment, once our society loses its checks and balances there is no telling how far the armed services will go. The machinery of national security has been turned against millions of the same American citizens it is supposed to be defending.

No agency reveals this turning inward of the anticommunist crusade more than the NSA. It has many thousands of employees and spends hundred of millions a year, yet its very existence was not known for five years. Established in 1952 by a top-secret order of President Truman, the NSA's purpose was "communications intelligence" which included the breaking of foreign government codes as well as the protection of American codes and equipment. One of its known programs, SHAMROCK, provided for the interception of all private cables dispatched abroad from the United States. Another program, called MINARET, concentrated on reading electronic messages by people or organizations on a "watch list" provided by other agencies. Needless to say, this was illegal—a specific violation of the Communications Act of 1934 (U.S.C.605) which provides that no company (or individual) that transmits or receives foreign messages may "divulge the existence, contents, substance, purport, effect or meaning thereof. . . . " When the Army Signals Security Agency asked RCA, Global, ITT, and Western Union to continue giving the government access to international cables after the war, the cable companies agreed only on condition that the attorney general give them assurance against criminal prosecution and lawsuits.

Under the SHAMROCK program the NSA was intercepting 150,000 messages a month. Not even the president, however, may have known about this practice. The Senate Select Committee on Intelligence reported that no president since Truman knew of the program. Needless to say, in the course of reading so many messages, the NSA learned quite a bit about 75,000 American citizens from 1952 to 1974. This information was then processed by the NSA's Office of Security and provided to the CIA and other agencies. Although the Office of Security files were destroyed in 1974, the practice of reading electronic messages by American citizens continues.

There were other agencies and departments put in place or, if already in place, enlarged by the National Security State. Concurrently there was a fundamental change in America's relations with foreign countries that prepared the United States for fighting open or secret wars against any nation on earth. In the fall of 1947 the United States concluded a security agreement with nineteen Latin American republics pledging joint military action against any outside power which attacked any of them. The Rio Pact, as it became known, was the first such treaty approved by the U.S. Senate since the Revolutionary War—a 180-degree reversal of Washington's policy of "no entangling alliances." Two years later the State Department concluded another security agreement, this time with fourteen Western European nations and Canada—the North Atlantic Pact—and by 1955 had entered into seven other such arrangements. The major capitalist states, therefore, were united into a common military alliance, led by the United States, against the Soviet Union.

All the treaties included a provision that an attack on one would be considered an attack on all, requiring each to come to the aid of the others, and virtually all underscored America's commitment to help allied governments restrain native revolutionaries. The security treaty with Japan, for instance, provided for the United States, if so requested, to use its army "to put down large-scale riots and disturbances, caused through instigation or intervention by an outside power or powers." To cement these alliances the United States began selling or giving away arms to its allies. As of 1964 it was supplying weapons to sixty-nine nations, half the sovereign states in the world, and training most of their armies. It also had "contingency" agreements—often signed by American generals or ambassadors and never submitted to the Senate for ratification—committing the United States to join another country in war or for joint military action against "mercenaries." Such a secret pact was signed, for instance, with Thailand in 1965 by Lt. Gen. Richard G. Stillwell. According to the then U.S. ambassador, this treaty committed American troops to "die, if necessary, to defend the current government in Bangkok. . . . "[49] In effect, as political analyst Amaury de Riencourt has observed, the U.S. assumed a "protectorate" over dozens of nations, and forged them into an alliance for U.S. control of the planet.

In the interests of a new imperialism, the machinery of the United Nations which the United States helped organize in 1945 to preserve world peace was bypassed in favor of its own unilateral, very often illegal policies, just as the American Constitution was often bypassed in order to veil the domestic and international illegality of the National Security State.

3

The President's Wars

The militarization of America has brought in its wake many abuses of power. Nowhere has it been so blatant or so threatening to national existence, however, as the assumption by our presidents that they and they alone have the right to wage war, even nuclear war, without public or congressional consent. The founders of the United States designed a democratic system whereby no single person, including the president, could jeopardize the lives of our troops and our people on his own motion. Though the president was assigned the task of conducting a war, he could not do so unless and until Congress, under Article 1 Section 8 of the Constitution, declared war against another country. This was a logical extension of the principle of checks and balances which permeates the Constitution. Having had an execrable experience with King George, the founders were well aware of the vicissitudes of one-man decision making. They were also aware of the preciousness of human life, which they listed as the first "unalienable" right in the Declaration of Independence, even before "liberty" and the "pursuit of Happiness."

The president, it was generally conceded, did have a right to use limited military force in special situations. Congress enacted legislation in 1819, for instance, authorizing the president to order the Navy to take action against pirates. In 1862 the Navy was also authorized to work out procedures for rescuing American citizens held by foreign governments, and on many occasions actually did rescue Americans held in captivity. The president, it was generally agreed, could take action against invaders, smugglers, cattle rustlers, marauders, and others. As historian Arthur Schlesinger, Jr. has correctly noted, this was "something different from warfare against organized governments."[1] Fighting Indians, who were deemed to have no legal rights other than those conferred by the United States, was also considered an exception to the rule of congressional authorization for war.

Presidents, it is true, stretched their prerogatives time and again by arguing they were taking defensive action, or that there was no time or means to consult Congress. Thus, in 1818, President Monroe ordered General Andrew Jackson to chase Seminole Indians back into Spanish Florida. Once there Jackson made the unilateral decision to fight the Spaniards as well—an act which made Secretary of War John C. Calhoun consider having him court-martialed. In more recent times presidents have gone a few steps further. In 1893 U.S. Marines were landed in Hawaii to help the revolutionary Committee of Safety overthrow the native regime. In 1900 American troops joined other Western forces to put down the Boxers who had seized Peking, China. In 1903 U.S. forces intervened to help a province of Colombia secede and establish the independent nation of Panama, which then granted the United States the right to build a canal across the isthmus. In the ensuing years there were interventions in a half-dozen Caribbean nations—sometimes just to collect debts owed American banks—and there was the intervention of the United States, Britain, France, and a dozen other countries against the Soviet Union in 1918–20 in a vain effort to oust the Bolsheviks. In most of these instances Congress was never consulted, but almost always the government used a legalistic pretext of some sort for its action—usually that it was protecting American lives and American property. The *principle* of congressional power to declare war was seldom questioned.

So strong was that principle that both the courts and the executive branch conceded that authorization for military action must be secured from Congress not only in "general" wars but in "limited" ones. In 1801, Chief Justice John Marshall, in ruling on the nature of the "undeclared" war with France, stated that "the whole powers of war being, by the Constitution of the United States vested in Congress . . . the Congress may authorize general hostilities . . . or partial hostilities." President John Adams did not in this instance call for a declaration of general war, but he did call Congress into special session "to consult and determine on such measure as in their wisdom shall be deemed needy for the safety and welfare of said United States."[2]

Thus, whatever the transgressions and abuse of powers from time to time, there was virtually unanimous opinion throughout most of our history that the right to make war against another sovereign state, or even to take warlike actions, rested with Congress, not the president. Even so executive-minded a figure as Alexander Hamilton was definitive in his opposition to a "single man" deciding on the issue of war. As Arthur Schlesinger, Jr., notes, in the seventy-fifth *Federalist* Hamilton wrote: "The history of human conduct does not warrant that exalted opinion of human virtue which would make it wise to commit interests of so delicate and momentous a kind, as those which concern its intercourse with the rest of the world, to the sole disposal of a magistrate created and circumstances as would be a President of the United States." James Madison, as quoted by Schlesinger, was more specific. In a letter to Jefferson in 1798 he wrote that "the Constitution supposes, what the history of all governments demonstrates, that the executive is the branch of power most interested in war, and most prone to it. It has accordingly with studied care vested the question of war in the legislature."[3]

During the Mexican War, Abraham Lincoln wrote to a colleague: "allow the President to invade a neighboring nation, whenever *he* shall deem it necessary to repel an invasion . . . and you allow him to make war at pleasure." Suppose, he said, that a president "should choose to say he thinks it necessary to invade Canada, to prevent the British from invading us, how could you stop him?" It was because of concerns of this sort, Lincoln wrote, that our constitutional convention "resolved to so frame the Constitution that *no one man* should hold the power of bringing this oppression [war] upon us."[4] Lincoln subsequently departed from these fine words during the Civil War, but the principle he asserted that "no one man" should have the power to take the nation into war was universally accepted. Only in rare instances did anyone argue the opposite. In the three general wars that the United States waged from 1898 to 1945, no president sought to circumvent Congress; all deferred to it.

In a message to Congress on April 11, 1898, President William McKinley listed grievances against Spain for its behavior in Cuba, and asked for authority "to use military and naval forces" against the ancient colonial power. He made it very clear that "the issue is now with Congress. . . . Prepared to execute every obligation imposed upon me by the Constitution and the law, I await your action."[5]

Nineteen years later, on April 2, 1917, Woodrow Wilson, in an address to the joint session of the two houses of Congress, opened his talk with this comment: "I have called the Congress into extraordinary session because there are serious, very serious, choices of policy to be made, and made immediately, which it was neither right nor *constitutionally permissible* that I assume the responsibility of making. . . . In unhesitating obedience to what I deem my *constitutional duty*, I advise that the Congress declare the recent course of the Imperial German Government to be in fact nothing less than war against the government and the people of the United States; that it formally accept the status of belligerent which has thus been thrust upon it. . . ."[6] (emphasis added).

On December 8, 1941, President Franklin D. Roosevelt appeared before a joint session of Congress, gave a brief report on what everybody already knew, namely that the Japanese Navy had bombed the American fleet at Pearl Harbor a few hours before, and asked "that the Congress declare that since the unprovoked and dastardly attack by Japan on Sunday, December seventh, a state of war has existed between the United States and the Japanese Empire."[7] This statement reveals a fundamental change in the way military action has been initiated. Almost no one in high places now questions the president's right, *without Congressional approval*, to wage limited or total war on his own initiative. The tragic irony in all this is that the stakes are now much higher. It is conceivable in certain circumstances that the whole nation can be destroyed and most of its people killed, exactly as the founders feared, by the unilateral action of "one man."

In the Spanish-American War the United States lost 385 men on the battlefield; in World War I, 53,402 lives were lost; in World War II, 291,557. If one were to add the number of people wounded and deaths from other causes, the total casualties in all three conflicts was about 1,400,000. By contrast, during the October Missile Crisis of 1962—when according to President Kennedy the United States and the Soviet Union would have suffered "150 million casualties in the first eighteen hours" if hostilities had actually broken out—no effort was made to seek congressional sanction as Roosevelt, Wilson, and McKinley had done. Kennedy acted, his counsel Theodore Sorenson notes, "by Executive order, Presidential proclamation and inherent powers, not under any resolution or act of Congress."[8] Had a full-scale war broken out—no matter which side pressed the nuclear button first—almost everything the United States had worked to build in 300 years would have been destroyed in less than a day. Kennedy said, "Even the fruits of victory would be ashes in our mouth." But in the face of this impending catastrophe, which might have taken place even before the American people became aware of this crisis, the Kennedy administration insisted that the president alone had the right to make the decision. Harvard professor Graham T. Allison, though conceding that "there was time for Congress to pass a resolution authorizing or endorsing whatever actions Kennedy felt necessary to take," feels he was nonetheless right in bypassing Congress and the people. "There could be only one hand at the nuclear trigger. . . . Although the Constitution assigned to Congress the authority to declare war, technology and time have, it appears, amended the Constitution. Kennedy's ExCom [Executive Committee, of the National Security Council, a group of thirteen to eighteen advisors who met regularly for twelve days] served as a partial equivalent of the constitutional intent." Allison, like many others, is troubled by his conclusions. "Lincoln," he notes, "has written that 'no one man' should have the power to involve the nation in war." Yet this case must serve as an exception—"the need for unity, secrecy, flexibility, and dispatch—made congressional consultation impractical."[9]

Historian Arthur Schlesinger, Jr., who generally is opposed to wide presidential prerogative, also argues that in this case it was justified. "Time was short, because something had to be done before the bases became operational," he writes. "Secrecy was imperative. Kennedy took the decision into his own hands. . . . " Schlesinger is reassured because Kennedy did not make the decision "in imperial solitude. The celebrated Executive Committee became a forum for exceedingly vigorous and intensive debate. . . . Though there was no legislative consultation, there was most effective executive consultation." While Schlesinger bemoans the fact that the October Missile Crisis "which should have been celebrated as an exception, was instead enshrined as a rule," he feels that "even in retrospect" it was "an emergency so acute in its nature and so peculiar in its structure that it did in fact require unilateral executive decision."[10]

One of the most extreme apologies for presidential power in war crises has been made by Richard E. Neustadt, author of a book on the subject. "Technology," he writes, "has modified the Constitution: the President, perforce, becomes the only man in the system capable of exercising judgement under the extraordinary limits now imposed by secrecy, complexity, and time."[11] This is certainly an exaggeration, but if true it would seem incumbent on our presidents to seek an immediate amendment to the Constitution vesting *all* warmaking power with them and divesting it from Congress and the public. The reason this has never been done, we suspect, is that Americans would balk at specifically granting the same kind of rights to their president that absolute monarchies used to allow their kings.

It is unfortunate that such noteworthy scholars can find excuses for allowing the president to engage in something so critical as nuclear war on his own motion. Why was it necessary to keep this conflict secret? Why couldn't the American people have been told about it on the day President Kennedy learned that the missiles were being emplaced in Cuba, or a day or two later? According to Schlesinger and Allison, secrecy was needed to formulate a strategy that would force the Soviets to retreat, it was hoped without confrontation. But the administration verified that the Soviets were shipping nuclear missiles to Cuba—forty-two of them, it was later determined—on October 15. They would not be operational for two weeks—in other words by October 29, if there were no hitches in their emplacement. From October 15 to 22 the Ex-Com was debating strategy, concluding that the choice was between a "surgical strike" by American planes against the missiles and their sites, and a naval blockade, with a majority tending toward the latter. These and other alternatives could have been discussed publicly in that week before Kennedy made the issue public. He could have received the approval of Congress for his blockade strategy—an act of war—at least a week before the missiles became operational.

But the real problem for Kennedy was that public discussion would have raised serious doubts about the wisdom of his position.

He certainly could not have mobilized the near-unanimity he engendered by springing the issue on the public suddenly (on October 22) and withholding innumerable facts which might have tilted many people in another direction. Here was a young, popular president threatening action which might cause the United States to lose everything in the course of one day. Yet, according to Theodore Sorenson, Kennedy's counsellor and closest advisor next to Robert Kennedy, the missiles did not make a substantive difference, only a difference in "appearances." "To be sure," he writes, "these Cuban missiles alone, in view of all the other megatonnage the Soviets were capable of unleashing upon us [from the Soviet Union itself], did not substantially alter the strategic balance *in fact*. . . . But that balance would have been substantially altered *in appearance;* and in matters of national will and world leadership, as the President said later, such appearances contribute to reality."[12] In other words, the stationing of a few dozen missiles in Cuba would not materially improve Russia's nuclear capability—it would not add to the number of people Moscow could kill in a nuclear attack—but it wouldn't look good to our allies and our enemies if we allowed those weapons 100 or 150 miles from our shores and did nothing about them. Our allies might conclude that we were weak, that we lacked will. Perhaps. But if Kennedy had not waved the military stick, he could have worked out a diplomatic compromise with little difficulty. The facts which have been revealed long after the crisis confirm this view.

A major reason that Castro wanted the nuclear weapons on his soil was because the United States, despite its defeat at the Bay of Pigs, was still trying to undermine the Fidelista regime. Many in the United States regarded the Bay of Pigs only as a temporary setback. Richard Nixon, whom Kennedy had defeated in the 1960 elections, urged the president to "find a proper legal cover and . . . go in." Senator Kenneth Keating of New York proposed a naval blockade and a trade embargo to "isolate Cuba and reduce Castro's military machine, his iron grip on the Cuban population—to impotence."[13] Kennedy seemed to be following this course. His embargo on shipments to the Caribbean island (joined by our Latin American allies)—which included everything but food and drugs—had badly crippled the Cuban economy which had previously been so overwhelmingly dependent on the United States. Washington also continued a $2.4 million a year subsidy to the Cuban Revolutionary Council, tolerated air drops to anti-Castro guerrillas, as well as sabotage, infiltration, and boat raids which either originated in Florida or were directed from there. As late as September 1962 a group of exiles known as Alpha 66 attacked three ships along the Cuban coast. The following month they conducted another foray which was said to have resulted in the killing of twenty Cubans and Russians.

To add fuel to the fires, Kennedy's Secretary of Defense, Robert S. McNamara had unsheathed a counterforce strategy in a speech early that year—the threat of a surprise attack on missile silos in the Soviet Union. According to Castro, the Soviets and Cubans agreed to place Russian nuclear missiles on the island *as a deterrent* to American aggressiveness. Castro told French newspaperman Jean Daniel, that he received "an accumulation of information" warning of a new CIA invasion. Castro did not believe it at first until he received a report of a meeting between Kennedy and Khrushchev's son-in-law, Alexei Adzhubei, in which the president said that the situation in Cuba was "intolerable." Kennedy reminded Adzhubei that the United States hadn't interfered when the Soviet Union intervened in Hungary in 1956—an unsubtle hint for the Russians to return the favor if the United States were to do the same in Cuba. It was after the Adzhubei interview, Castro said, that Cuba and the Soviet Union decided on the missiles.

There was plenty of room it seems for deals and compromises in this crisis, plenty of room to allay the tensions. For instance, Kennedy might have agreed to curtail the illegal activity of the Cuban exiles in Miami in return for withdrawal of the missiles, or to the withdrawal of U.S. missiles in Turkey. Eventually he agreed to both—but only *after* the crisis. In return for removal of the missiles, Kennedy could also have lifted the embargo. The embargo's only accomplishment after twenty-five years has been to slow down the improvement in Cuban living standards. It has not succeeded in forcing Castro out of power or even weakening his hold on the Cuban people to any significant extent.

Had Kennedy asked Congress for a war vote it probably would have given it to him. An extended discussion, however, would have brought out the fact that Kennedy didn't believe that the Cuban missiles really altered the strategic balance but, rather, that their primary effect would be on "appearances." He could not come to the American people and tell them "many of us may have to die within one day in order for this country to retain its appearance of strength." The longer such a discussion went on, the more the president would have lost support at home. In due course, the people would have learned what Sorenson admitted in his book on Kennedy years later, that the president "was concerned less about the missiles' military implications than with their effect on the global political balance."[14] Obviously, there was little additional threat to American lives—the threat was to Washington's status in the world's political balance. It is doubtful that many Americans would have been willing to die for so flimsy an objective.

In a sense Professor Neustadt is right—technology did put pressure on the Constitution. A missile from Moscow, traveling at 16,000 or 17,000 miles an hour can hit targets in the United States within thirty minutes. If launched from a nuclear submarine near our Atlantic or Pacific shores, the missile can make contact in just a few minutes. In such an emergency there would obviously be no time to assemble Congress to discuss or vote on anything. There are only three solutions to this problem. One is to liquidate the nation-state, the source of conflict leading to war. That idea was proposed after World War II by such notable thinkers as Walter Lippmann, Albert Einstein, Robert Maynard Hutchins, Bertrand Russell, and others who urged that the United States, Britain, and the Soviet Union use their might to establish a single world government.

Another solution, urged by Secretary of War Henry L. Stimson in 1945, was that the United States and the Soviet Union form a "partnership upon the basis of cooperation and trust" to "control and limit the use of the atomic bomb. . . . " To the objection that the Russians might not be trustworthy, Stimson replied that "the chief lesson I have learned in a long life is that the only way you can make a man trustworthy is to trust him; and the surest way to make him untrustworthy is to distrust him and show your distrust."[15] Stimson's proposal for an "atomic partnership" was supported by three other members of Truman's cabinet, Secretary of Commerce Henry Wallace, Secretary of Labor Lewis Schwellenbach, and Postmaster General Robert Hannegan. The third solution was to amend the

Constitution, withdrawing from Congress the right to declare war and placing it entirely in the hands of the president.

Given the conservative mood of the nation immediately after World War II, the American people were not too likely to opt for world government or atomic partnership; it would take considerable education to prepare them for such severe modifications to political habits. The third alternative would unquestionably have been rejected hands down. The prospect of allowing a single man to determine whether a whole nation lives or dies was chilling. Given a democratic vote the American people unquestionably would have rejected it; and that is probably why it was never put to the American people or Congress for a vote. Successive presidents preferred to disregard Article 1 Section 8 and to operate as if they had the unilateral right to make war, without bothering to ask for a formal change in the Constitution.

American presidents from Truman on have taken the same attitude toward nuclear weapons that Truman did during World War II, namely that it was just another weapon—though admittedly with much greater firepower—and that its use or nonuse was to be determined exclusively by the chief executive. The exclusion of the people and Congress from decision-making powers on nuclear matters became apparent with the first atomic test. In retrospect it has a frightening import.

On July 16, 1945, as leading scientists stood in the desert at Alamogordo, New Mexico, awaiting the test, there was serious concern that they might not be able to limit the chain reaction of the nuclear fuel to the test site. Stephane Groueff records in her 1967 book on the Manhattan Project that Enrico Fermi—often called "the father" of the Bomb—"was making bets with his colleagues on whether the Bomb would ignite the atmosphere, and, if so, whether it would destroy only New Mexico—or the entire world."[16] J. Robert Oppenheimer, scientific chief of the project, and Arthur Compton of the University of Chicago, had already discussed their fears about what the chain reaction might do to "the hydrogen in seawater. Might not the explosion of the atomic bomb set off an explosion of the ocean itself? Nor was this all that Oppenheimer feared. The nitrogen in the air is also unstable, though less in degree. Might not it, too, be set off by an atomic explosion in the atmosphere?" Such a result, Compton felt "would be the ultimate catastrophe. Better to accept the slavery of the Nazis than to run the chance of drawing the final curtain on mankind."[17]

Tortured by such questions Compton ordered a recalculation of the possibility of such accidents. Novelist Pearl Buck, who later discussed the incident with Compton, reveals that he intended to have the test scrapped "if it were proved that the chances [for a runaway chain reaction] were more than approximately three to one million." Scientists today discount the idea that a chain reaction can be so continuous as to destroy the planet, but in 1945 they weren't so sure. One can only speculate whether the American citizenry—had they known the odds Compton was talking about and the fears expressed by Fermi, Oppenheimer, and others—would have given their assent to the atomic test.

But this was a time of war in which decisions were made by the executive, not the people. It may not even have occurred to the scientists, to the chief of the project, Leslie Groves, or to President Truman (assuming he knew of the scientists' misgivings that morning) that American citizens had any right to be consulted. One can only wonder, however, what would have happened if the Alamogordo test had caused a few thousand deaths or if the October Missile Crisis seventeen years later had resulted in an actual nuclear war, what the reaction of the American people would have been. Secretary of War Stimson had told an "Interim Committee" he called together on May 31, 1945 that the atom bomb must not be viewed "as a new weapon merely but as a revolutionary change in the relations of man and the universe."[18] The question still remains to be answered whether a president has the right to deal with "a revolutionary change in the relations of man and the universe" exclusively by his own executive decision or whether, in a democracy, he is duty bound to open a national debate on the issue and seek a popular mandate.

As might be expected when great events are planned in the shadows, the decision to drop the Bomb on Hiroshima and Nagasaki (and originally on two other targets, Kokura and Niigata) was by executive order and it was made in secret. Should the Bomb have been used in August 1945? Truman later argued that it saved many thousands of lives, yet the Japanese had already made two overtures to surrender and a group of U.S. experts who visited Japan in 1946 concluded that the enemy would have surrendered prior to November 1 "even if the atomic bombs had not been dropped, even if Russia had not entered the war, and even if no invasion had been planned or contemplated."[19] There is certainly no room for argument, however, about the president's curtailed power in peacetime—the right to decide on war is the exclusive prerogative of the legislature. Nevertheless, from then to now, no president has ever asked Congress to approve any policy, strategy, or planned action involving nuclear weapons. They have all been made by one man—the president who was in office at the time.

On at least a dozen occasions that have come to light in recent years, presidents have threatened or contemplated the use of nuclear weapons. In none of these instances was the public ever consulted. For example, in 1946 Truman called in Soviet ambassador Andrei Gromyko and gave him an ultimatum: unless the Soviet Union immediately evacuated the Iranian province of Azerbaijan which she had occupied during the war by agreement with Britain and the United States, the United States would drop bombs on the Soviet Union itself. The Russians yielded in this instance, but if they had called Truman's bluff, world war would have ensued. While the Russians did not have atomic bombs as yet, it is by no means certain that the United States could have won such a war. The United States had enough atomic warheads at the time to wreak havoc on the Soviet Union, but not destroy it. And, as the French correspondent Raymond Aron of *Le Monde* observed, "United States superiority over the Soviet Union in the nuclear field was offset . . . by Russian superiority in conventional arms and by the Red Army's continued ability to overrun Western Europe in a matter of days. . . . "[20] A secret report of the National Security Council in April 1950 (NSC-68) confirmed this estimate. "The Soviet Union and its satellites," it said, had the capability "to overrun Western Europe, with the possible exception of the Iberian and Scandinavian Peninsulas." A United States victory was out of the question. "A powerful blow could be delivered upon the Soviet Union," said NSC-68, "but it is estimated that these operations alone would not force or induce the Kremlin to capitulate."[21] Had the Russians decided to reject the ultimatum, we might have had a world war with millions dead on both sides. The

American president, however, had become so accustomed to executive autonomy that he proceeded on his own anyway. Again, success was its own justification.

On at least two other occasions the nation was brought close to nuclear war with the Soviet Union by executive decision. One was the October Missile Crisis of 1962. The other occurred eleven years later in the Middle East as a result of a war involving three other nations. On October 6, 1973—the Jewish Day of Atonement, Yom Kippur—100,000 Egyptian soldiers crossed into the Israeli-held Sinai Peninsula. For the next two-and-a-half weeks the fighting between Israel on the one hand and Egypt and Syria on the other was indecisive. Finally the United States and the Soviet Union arranged a cease-fire between the hostile forces. Unfortunately the Israelis were slow to put it into effect. They had surrounded a large Egyptian force in the Sinai and they felt that within a few days they could win the war rather than have it end in a stalemate. The Russians were angry. On October 24 Leonid Brezhnev told President Nixon over the hot line: "If the Israelis are not going to adhere to the cease-fire, let us [both] work together to impose a cease-fire, if necessary by force." The United States rejected this suggestion and the Soviet Union, subsequently, sent a ship loaded with nuclear weapons to Alexandria, Egypt. Egypt already had Soviet-made "Scud" missiles capable of delivering nuclear bombs, and for fifteen hours the world faced yet another missile crisis. No one except the inner circle of the American and Russian governments knew what was happening. At 11 P.M. that night, after Henry Kissinger had called together an emergency meeting at the White House, the United States declared a worldwide DefCon 3 alert. (DefCon means Defense Condition. DefCon 5 is the normal condition of peace, DefCon 1 is war, DefCon 3 is midpoint between war and peace.) An aircraft carrier was dispatched at full speed to the Mediterranean. The Strategic Air Command—in charge of bombers and nuclear missiles—was placed on an advance alert, and the Sixth Fleet—patrolling the Mediterranean Sea—was put on DefCon 2, just one step away from a nuclear war.[22]

Before things could get out of hand, Israel halted its offensive and the Soviets withdrew their ship with the nuclear bombs. The crisis ended almost before Congress or the American people learned there had been a crisis. Once again, however, the president had placed

America's very existence in jeopardy exclusively on his own authority, in clear violation of the established principles set by our forebears.

In addition to these three instances of near confrontation directly with the Russians there have been other plans for nuclear attacks on Soviet allies, none of which were taken up with Congress. At a press conference in 1950, President Truman threatened to use nuclear bombs against North Korea. President Eisenhower tells us in his memoirs that he contemplated atomic warfare against China to force it to end the Korean war. As we have already noted, in 1954 Secretary of State John Foster Dulles offered three nuclear bombs to France for use in the Far East. In 1958 the Joint Chiefs of Staff told Eisenhower that the islands of Quemoy and Matsu could not be held by Chiang Kai-shek unless the United States was prepared to use nuclear bombs. That year Eisenhower ordered secret nuclear preparations during the Lebanon crisis. In 1961 Kennedy let the word out to the Pathet Lao that he would order the use of nuclear bombs on Laos unless the Pathet Lao joined a tripartite government. Again in 1961 he contemplated the use of superbombs when the Russians threatened to blockade Berlin. Seven years later President Johnson queried the chairman of the Joint Chiefs, General Earle Wheeler, about the possible need for nuclear weapons to hold the besieged Marine base at Khe Sanh in Vietnam. That same year President-elect Nixon, implementing what he called "the madman theory" (that he was a "madman" on the issue of communism), sent word to Hanoi through intermediaries that he would use nuclear weapons on Vietnam by the end of 1969 unless the communists came to terms.[23]

Once the floodgates of one-man decision making were let loose, it was all but inevitable that the principle would apply not only to contemplating or threatening nuclear war against foreign countries but to downgrading the value of life generally, including the life of American citizens. Consider the attitude taken toward radiation. The U.S. government was unquestionably surprised by the extent of deaths from radiation when the first atomic bomb fell on Hiroshima. General Groves's staff at Los Alamos sent him a telex on August 24, 1945, expressing concern "about Japanese broadcasts claiming murderous delayed radioactive effects at Hiroshima in view of [U.S.] press release that activity would be small."[24] Despite such warnings, however, the United States sent Marines into Hiroshima and Nagasaki a month later to clean up some of the damage—about a thousand of them to Nagasaki. Thirty-four years later dozens of these young men, most of them in their fifties now, had filed claims for diseases they believed were contracted as a result of their clean-up duty in 1945. The claims included confirmed cases of leukemia, blood diseases, and bone marrow cancers. The Veterans Administration granted none of the fifty requests for compensation at first, claiming that the radioactivity was "below the hazardous limits."[25] The government certainly was not deliberately consigning soldiers to their death, but there was a callous attitude toward the dangers that were unquestionably part of the psychology of permanent war. When the choice was between a risk and a military benefit, the latter tended to prevail.

From 1945 to 1963 the United States conducted 193 nuclear tests in the atmosphere, even though responsible scientists warned that thousands might die from radiation-induced cancer. Scientists who had developed the bomb pleaded that the tests be suspended. Nobel laureate Linus Pauling estimated in June 1957 that 10,000 people had already perished or were destined to perish as a result of those tests. The following year he asserted that the carbon 14 released by the tests "will ultimately produce about one million seriously defective children and about two million embryonic and neonatal deaths, and will cause many millions of people to suffer from minor hereditary defects."[26] Atomic Energy Commission scientists by contrast argued that these were all exaggerations, and made no effort to prevent a quarter of a million members of the armed forces from taking part in atomic tests. Some soldiers were stationed in trenches slightly more than a mile from ground zero. Others were marched to ground zero soon after the explosions. Dr. Donald S. Frederickson, chairman of the radiation research committee of the National Institutes of Health, was asked years later by Senator Alan K. Simpson of Wyoming whether "some 40,000 cancer deaths could be predicted to occur in the 250,000 participants." The doctor replied that "the figure is fairly accurate."[27]

The deaths were all "invisible" in the sense that they didn't take place until ten, twenty, or thirty years after the event. Nor could they be linked with mathematical certainty in each case to nuclear radiation. Most Americans, including their presidents, therefore, felt few pangs of conscience. But in effect massive numbers of people were being executed or punished without due process of law—merely by the decision of the military and the presidency. Individual presidents no doubt were concerned about such matters when it came to their attention, but in a choice between America's "national security" and deaths that would occur decades later, they opted for the former and disregarded the latter. In war, after all, one must expect casualties.

A similar attitude was taken toward troops during the Vietnam war. One of the impediments to American troops in that engagement was the heavy jungle. Chemical companies soon provided the military with defoliants to destroy the greenery, and the U.S. Air Force sprayed 20 million gallons of it on 6 million acres of land in Vietnam. One of the most toxic of these chemicals contained the deadly poison dioxin and was dubbed Agent Orange because it was stored in orange drums. Before long there was an epidemic of birth defects in part of South Vietnam, and the level of spraying was reduced. It was finally ended in 1971, but by that time many American fliers who had sprayed the herbicide or soldiers who had been in its path had contracted skin cancer, liver disorders, and circulatory problems.

When Harry Truman decided to go ahead with the hydrogen bomb, a weapon many times more powerful than the Hiroshima atom bomb, he did it on his own motion, without seeking legislation. He did, of course, have to seek funds from Congress for the new weapon, but that is not the same thing as a public debate on its strategical value or need. "Thus," writes Robert Borosage, "by 1950 the President possessed the power to procure, disperse, and use atomic energy without Congressional approval. . . . Within the branches of government, a realignment of power took place. The executive preempted many of the legislative functions. In the area of national security, the executive became sovereign, the legislature, except for its powerful committee heads, who are satraps of the security bureaucracies, was rendered impotent."[28]

Within the last decade Congress has shown a small measure of independence: at President Carter's suggestion it shelved the B-1 bomber (on the ground that the cruise missile was better suited for that particular function), and it cut down the number of MX missiles requested by President Reagan (primarily because the planned basing system was too complex and costly). But the B-1 was reinstated under the Reagan administration and the Pentagon was given limited approval for fifty MX missiles. The whole system of procurement, then, is weighted toward presidential decision. The president, based on secret initial probing at the Pentagon and in the defense industry complex, may designate a certain category of technology for deeper research—say, the technology for evading radar interception. Based on such research, the president and Defense Department might, for example, suggest specific research on a "stealth" bomber. Each step suggests the next one, with few people in Congress willing to challenge the president or Pentagon, particularly since they have little access to the secret research and development. Except in the rarest of exceptions, therefore, the president's requests are honored without much ado.

Even more important is the president's delineation of strategy and, especially in our day, nuclear strategy. Here congressional intervention is virtually nonexistent. From "massive retaliation" to "mutual assured destruction" to "flexible response" to "limited counterforce" to "graduated response" to "protracted nuclear war" and, ultimately, under Reagan to "strategic defense initiative"—or star wars—the strategies were proclaimed by presidential ukase, often at private meetings rather than in Congress. The "massive retaliation" scheme—which threatened instant retaliation with all American "strategic" power should the Soviet Union commit any further "aggression"—was announced by Secretary of State John Foster Dulles at a Council of Foreign Relations meeting. The "counterforce" strategy, which called for nuclear attacks on silos, airports, and other military facilities rather than population centers, was a severe change from "massive retaliation," but it was first put forth publicly at a University of Michigan commencement on June 16, 1962. "Flexible response," which gave the president *all* options, from a CIA operation to a counterforce nuclear attack and everything in between, was never debated beyond a small group of experts and specialists. Secretary of Defense James Schlesinger described it to reporters as merely "a change in targeting strategy as it were."[29]

It is interesting that upon leaving office, many officials point out the futility of relying on nuclear weapons. "We are rapidly getting to the point that no war can be *won*," Eisenhower wrote Richard L. Simon, president of Simon and Schuster in April 1956. "War implies a contest; when you get to the point that contest is no longer involved and the outlook comes close to destruction of the enemy and suicide for ourselves . . . then the arguments as to the exact amount of available strength as compared to somebody else's are no longer the vital issue."[30] Yet Eisenhower never put his Secretary of State's "massive retaliation" strategy to Congress, though he evidently thought no strategy could result in victory by either side. Truman made similar statements in an unpublished 1958 article which came to light twenty-five years after he left office. Yet he did not feel his policies for accelerating the arms race or his strategy of containment merited a decision by Congress. Certainly the war issue was of greater consequence to our lives than the repeal of prohibition or the many laws relating to taxes. Yet no postwar president has initiated a national debate or sought a specific mandate of Congress on any strategy. And Congress, immobilized by anticommunist fears, afraid to be labeled "soft on communism," has been content not to challenge one-man rule.

It is now generally accepted that the president alone has the right to press the nuclear button—but no one in high places has yet come forth to propose that Article 1 Section 8 of the Constitution be amended to give him that right *legally*. On the contrary, the tendency is to challenge anyone who disputes presidential power. Thus when Jeremy J. Stone, director of the Federation of American Scientists questioned whether President Reagan has the right to order first use of nuclear weapons—"the President is not our king and this country is not his kingdom to risk or not as he wishes"—he received a sharp reply from the Defense Department's general counsel Chapman B. Cox. "We do not agree," Cox wrote. If the president were required to ask congressional approval it would "tend to undermine" NATO's defense and "threaten NATO's ability to deter Soviet aggression."[31]

The men of power, as C. Wright Mills called them, eschew a public discussion of the nuclear issue for fear it will raise anxieties and increase sentiment for disarmament. Similarly, fears prod them to take unilateral and arbitrary action vis-à-vis nonnuclear (i.e., conventional) war. The Truman Doctrine, proclaimed in 1947, was, as columnist Walter Lippmann put it, a call for "unending intervention in all countries that are supposed to 'contain' the Soviet Union,"[32] yet it was never submitted to congressional vote. Another document, NSC-68, drafted in 1950 and possibly the most important strategy paper in American history, was a blueprint for the permanent war but was kept secret—except for a favored few and judicious leaks to the press—until parts were published in a book twelve years later and the document was, finally, declassified by Henry Kissinger in 1975. NSC-68 called for a rapid rearmament policy and the use of other pressures to "foster a fundamental change in the nature of the Soviet system." It certainly merited a national debate.

In theory there are four restraints on the use of military force by the president. One, as noted above, is the war powers clause of the Constitution, Article 1 Section 8, which gives Congress alone the right to declare war and "to raise and support armies." The second is the Neutrality Act, which makes it a crime to take hostile military action against a foreign country with which the nation is at peace. The third is the War Powers Resolution, passed after the Vietnam war, which limits the use of armed force by the president unless Congress approves it within sixty days. And the fourth involves laws that provide that select congressional committees shall be "informed" of covert actions (but not have the right to approve or disapprove, or to inform their colleagues in Congress or the public). Every one of these restraints has been blithely bypassed since 1945.

When Truman sent troops to fight in Korea, Secretary of State Dean Acheson told a Senate Committee that Congress had no say in this matter. The president, he said, has "the authority to use the Armed Forces in carrying out the broad policy of the United States and implementing treaties. . . . It is equally clear that this authority may not be interfered with by Congress. . . ."[33]

President Lyndon Johnson's justification for sending a half-million troops to Vietnam was the Tonkin Gulf Resolution. On August 2, 1964 three North Vietnamese PT boats allegedly attacked two American destroyers, the *Maddox* and the *Turner Joy* in the Tonkin Gulf, which lies between China and North Vietnam. Actually the *Maddox* had fired the first shots, claiming that the PT boats were racing toward it. There were no American casualties and all the *Maddox* had to show for this great battle was a machine-gun bullet in its hull. Two days later, on a dark night, the two destroyers reported they were under "continuous torpedo attack." *Turner Joy*'s sonar had heard no torpedoes, but it fired away for four hours. Later reports indicated that all twenty-one torpedo reports were made by a single sonarman on the *Maddox*. "In retrospect," writes David Wise, former Washington bureau chief for the *New York Herald Tribune*, "both the captain of the *Maddox* and the commander in charge of both destroyers concluded that virtually all of the 'torpedoes' reported by the *Maddox* were actually the sound of her own propellers." He also notes that "regardless of whether any attack took place, the messages between Washington and the Pacific that day demonstrate that *at the time* neither the President nor McNamara was certain that an attack had occurred."[34]

Four years later, Senate investigators found a cable from a *Maddox* officer which said: "Review of action makes many recorded contacts and torpedoes fired appear doubtful. Freak weather effects and over-eager sonarman may have accounted for many reports." The cable urged "complete evaluation before any further action." Disregarding the advice, President Johnson appeared on TV, even while the Pentagon was trying to sort out what had happened, to paint an incident which, at best, was what John L. Lewis would have called "small potatoes." But with the public kept in the dark as to the truth it was enough to dragoon the whole nation into a sense of crisis. Three days later Congress passed the Tonkin Gulf Resolution authorizing the president to "take all necessary measures to repel any armed attack against the forces of the United States and to prevent further aggression." The vote in the House was unanimous, in the Senate 88 to 2, with only two Senators, Wayne Morse of Oregon and Ernest Gruening of Alaska having the courage to oppose Johnson.

No one outside the administration, however, believed that the Tonkin Gulf Resolution was anything resembling a carte blanche to send a half-million troops to Vietnam, particularly since Johnson had said over and over again during the 1964 campaign that "we are not about to send American boys nine or ten thousand miles away from home to do what Asian boys ought to be doing for themselves." Nonetheless the troops were sent and Nicholas de B. Katzenbach, Assistant Attorney General, put forth the amazing argument that the president didn't need a war declaration because the Tonkin Gulf Resolution was the "functional equivalent" of a declaration of war.[35]

Later the administration argued that it had the constitutional right to wage the Vietnam war without the Tonkin Gulf Resolution, purely on its own. The extravagant use of presidential power in this instance prompted Alexander Bickel of the Yale Law School to comment that "if this decision was not for Congress under the Constitution then no decision of any consequence in matters of war and peace is left to Congress."[36]

The abuse of power almost invariably breeds further abuse. As one of the spinoffs of the illegal war in Vietnam, the next president, Nixon, ordered the secret bombing of Cambodia, a nation with whom we were formally at peace, and constantly denied that such bombing was taking place. In the fourteen months after February 9, 1969, the United States conducted 3,630 B-52 raids on this unhappy land, presumably to destroy Vietnamese communist bases. The bombing continued even after Cambodia's head of state, Prince Norodom Sihanouk had resigned and the United States had withdrawn its troops from Vietnam, and it continued despite the fact that Congress included in every military appropriation bill a provision specifically forbidding such action. When the bombing was eventually discovered in 1973, Nixon and Henry Kissinger insisted that it was done with Sihanouk's approval (although he never confirmed it) and that it was directed at unpopulated areas occupied only by North Vietnamese troops. At his confirmation hearings for Secretary of State Kissinger said "it was not a bombing of Cambodia, but it was a bombing of North Vietnamese in Cambodia." This too was untrue, as a memorandum of the Secretary of Defense himself showed: all fifteen areas to be bombed included hundreds of Cambodians (in one instance 1,640). Nixon, in reality, was waging a secret war not only without congressional sanction but in direct violation of a prohibition against such action.[37]

It is interesting that Nixon was forced out of office for covering up a 1972 burglary at Watergate, but that an Article of Impeachment presented by Representative John Conyers accusing him of "false and misleading statements concerning the existence, scope and nature of American bombing operations in Cambodia in derogation of the power of Congress to declare war . . . " was defeated in the House Judiciary Committee by a vote of 26 to 12.[38] As this instance shows, one of the most disturbing features of the National Security

State has been the Congress's voluntary (sometimes eager) acceptance of its own emasculation.

When President Ronald Reagan ordered the invasion of Grenada, a small island of 110,000 people, in 1983 congressional opposition was muted to the point of being insignificant. There is always a pretext for illegal action, and the one used by Reagan was that the lives of American medical students on the island were in jeopardy because of the assassination of the prime minister, Maurice Bishop. There was serious doubt about this contention, since no student had been threatened, let alone hurt, and the government had offered to allow all to be flown to safety outside the country. Nonetheless, in what was Reagan's most "successful" military action of his first term in office, American troops invaded and occupied the island.

The War Powers Resolution of 1973, adopted as a reaction to the abuses committed by the presidency during the Indochina war, allowed the president to initiate military action when he saw fit, but required him to report the beginning of hostilities within forty-eight hours and to terminate the action within sixty days (subject to another thirty days extension). Under this new law the president was required to report on the progress of every undeclared war at least every six months, and Congress could decide whether to continue or end hostilities within sixty days of the report. Understandably, President Nixon declared that the resolution was "clearly unconstitutional" and would "seriously undermine the nation's ability to act decisively. . . . " President Ford claimed the bill "has the potential for disaster." It is worth noting, however, that the heart of the bill had already been emasculated. Under the Senate version, rejected by the House, the president could engage in hostilities *only* when one of four situations obtained: to repel or forestall a direct attack on the United States and its possessions; to repel an attack on U.S. troops abroad; to protect American citizens while they were being evacuated from hostile territory; and "pursuant to specific statutory authorization." In other words, a direct vote by Congress would be needed to authorize the hostilities. Senator Thomas Eagleton correctly argued that the compromise version granted the president "unilateral authority to commit troops anywhere in the world for 60 to 90 days." Once a president has initiated military action for sixty or ninety days it is hardly likely that Congress would repudiate him while American men were fighting and dying on foreign soil. Graham T. Allison is undoubtedly correct when he says the Resolution would not have "prevented the massive Americanization of the [Vietnam] war that occurred in 1965. . . . It seems fairly certain that, if President Johnson had reported to Congress as required by the Resolution shortly after the initiation of sustained United States combat troops in the South, Congress would have speedily authorized a continuation of the war."[39]

Vietnam and Korea were the two big wars that the United States has engaged in since 1945, but we have been involved militarily in innumerable internal and external wars, without the sanction of anyone but the president and his National Security Council. Summarizing the situation some years ago the Senate Foreign Relations Committee observed that "the executive, by acquiring the authority to commit the country to war, now exercises something approaching absolute power over the life or death of every living American—to say nothing of millions of other people all over the world. . . . The concentration . . . of virtually unlimited authority over matters of war and peace has all but removed the limits to executive power in the most important single area of our national life. Until they are restored, the American people will be threatened with tyranny and disaster."[40]

4

The Secret Wars

In an attempt to urge the United States to respect a decision of the World Court, Senator Daniel Patrick Moynihan of New York noted that "we are, when we have our wits about us, a law-abiding nation. It is in our interests that others should be. If, for example, the Soviets are not, then that is their problem. If, because the Soviets are not, we cease to be, then that is their victory."[1] By this definition the Soviets, in fact, have won, because the demands of the permanent war have driven our leadership to adopt the very illegal and immoral methods ascribed to them.

Our traditional-type wars, such as Vietnam and Korea, have been undertaken without legitimate authority, and the other facet of the permanent war, covert and paramilitary action, is patently illegal by any international standard (that, in fact, is why it is "covert"). As a spin-off of our illegal behavior in world affairs, moreover, our government repeatedly breaks the law in dealing with its own citizens at home. The justification for this mammoth illegality is that we are "at war" and that what is illegal in peacetime is "legal" in wartime.

The essence of the present morality is expressed by the 1954 Hoover Commission Report on government organization:

> It is now clear that we are facing an implacable enemy whose avowed objective is world domination by whatever means and at whatever cost. There are no rules in such a game. Hitherto acceptable norms of human conduct do not apply. If the U.S. is to survive, long-standing American concepts of "fair play" must be reconsidered. . . . We must learn to subvert, sabotage and destroy our enemies by more clever, more sophisti-

> cated and more effective methods than those used against us. It may become necessary that the American people will be made acquainted with, understand and support this repugnant philosophy.[2]

Since we are at war in what former Secretary of State Dean Rusk called "the back alleys of the world," we must use the same nasty tactics as do those we consider to be our adversaries.

The Hoover report is wrong when it ascribes to the Soviet Union alone the objective of "world domination"; in fact *both* superpowers have such a goal (as all superpowers throughout history have had). Leaving that aside, however, what the report says is that democratic principles cannot be effective against totalitarianism and that, consequently a democratic society must adopt the authoritarian principles of its adversary. That is what has been happening for four decades. Worse still, the National Security State has created an institutional framework for the subversion of the system of checks and balances on which the nation was founded. This is something new in American life. While pre-World War II governments had frequently violated democratic principles, it was only in the postwar period that an institutional framework was created to legitimize subversive government behavior.

It wasn't intended to be that way; no one sat down to formulate a blueprint for unlawful conduct. On the contrary, the one institution that was established during World War II to carry on covert and paramilitary action within the Axis nations, the Office of Strategic Service (OSS), was dissolved on October 1, 1945. In its place President Truman established the Central Intelligence Group (CIG), but its sole purpose was to gather intelligence. It conducted no psychological warfare (though it had that capability), performed no "dirty tricks" against foreign governments. What stiffened American policy and channeled it into covert action was that the section of the world under U.S. overlordship showed signs of foundering. There was fear, first of all, of a new depression at home. The unemployment rate from 1931 to 1940 had never fallen below 14 percent, and in four of those years it ranged above 20 percent. Unless the government could find markets for the greatly enlarged capacity of American factories, there was a distinct possibility of another depression in the postwar era. There was also fear of social unrest—even revolution—in the industrial countries that comprised the Western alliance, such as France, Italy, even Britain. "It is now obvious," said William Clayton, Undersecretary of State of Economic Affairs, "that we have grossly underestimated the destruction to the European economy by the war."[3]

To make matters worse, in January 1947 a great snowstorm—the worst since 1894—hit Britain like an avalanche, leaving as much as twenty feet of snow in some places and, after a thaw, blocks of ice. By February more than half the factories were out of production. Conditions elsewhere were even worse. France was producing only half as much iron and steel as before the war. Germany lay in rubble: its major cities—Cologne, Essen, Berlin, Frankfurt, Hamburg, Munich, Mannheim—immobilized. Food was scarce, money almost worthless. There were no apartments to be had and few jobs. Unless something was done and done quickly to "save Europe," disaster was imminent. The communists might absorb a disoriented Europe, and with it Asia and Africa as well. It would not be a matter of Soviet "expansionism" but an unavoidable coefficient of social decay.

There was also the tidal wave of unrest throughout the developing world—in Asia and Africa, and to some extent in Latin America—that could cause a wholesale break from the "American way." The situation in the Philippines, where the Huks again had taken to guerrilla warfare, was perhaps an augury of things to come. So were the festering events in China, North Africa, Vietnam, Indonesia, and the renewed civil war in Greece which triggered the promulgation of the Truman Doctrine.

Neither Truman nor Roosevelt before him had anticipated that social insurgency would be the problem it turned out to be. Roosevelt had faith in his program of "benign" imperialism and was confident, in addition, that Stalinist communism would help him contain unrest. Stalin had turned moderate toward the United States in the 1930s after Roosevelt tendered diplomatic recognition to Russia. It was not, therefore, inconceivable that the communists could be converted into leftists of a moderate hue, like the Labour Party in Britain or the SFIO in France. Truman had less faith in the Kremlin, but he was convinced that Moscow was in no condition, with its wartime losses—20 million dead, fifteen large cities, 1,710 towns, 7,000 villages partly or wholly destroyed, a million buildings demolished, 10,000 power plants ruined—to foment social upheavals. And with the United States in sole possession of the Bomb, the Soviets would be careful about ruffling American feathers. As it turned out the policy of "benign" imperialism did not work and revolutions broke out here, there, and everywhere without—as in China and Yugoslavia—Soviet encouragement.

With increasing frequency the American government was being called upon to choose sides in civil wars and civil conflicts. (In May 1966, Defense Secretary McNamara told a group of newspaper editors that there had been "149 serious internal insurgencies" around the globe in the previous decade.)[4] Unfortunately the U.S. government approached this problem with distressing rigidity. America found herself increasingly in league with notorious tyrants, and to hold on to this or that bastion of empire was forced to defend them by the means suggested in the 1954 Hoover report: illegal, immoral, or at best unfair. As Victor Marchetti, a former high official of the CIA, and John D. Marks observe in their book *The CIA and the Cult of Intelligence*, the CIA "gradually drifted into a posture whereby its paramilitary operations were in support of the *status quo*. The agency, in pursuit of 'stability' and 'orderly change,' increasingly associated itself with protecting vested interests. . . . [It] always seemed to work against legitimate social and political change. . . . "[5]

Illustrative of this tendency was the bailout of the Christian Democratic government in Italy in 1947–48. Toward the end of 1947 it became obvious that the regime headed by prime minister Alcide de Gasperi was in danger of collapsing. James Forrestal had recorded in his diary (in September of that year) that there was a danger of the "formation of a Communist republic in the north." De Gasperi pleaded with the American ambassador in Rome that "without your help we have only a few weeks to last. . . . " The ambassador dispatched an "urgent" cable from Rome warning that the communists "are now preparing for action by force," and urging that the United States send secret military aid to the Italian government at once to deal with the problem. After looking into the situation the National Security Council (NSC) concluded that the communists intended to come to power either by winning the elections of April 1948—where by all accounts their chances were quite good—or by a general strike or armed insurrection. The NSC debated whether to use strong economic, political, and military measures to prevent such an eventuality. George Kennan, then a top State Department official, suggested that the Italian government be urged to outlaw the Communist Party and risk a civil war that would give the United States the pretext for reoccupying the Foggia Fields and other territory. This would result in considerable violence, of course, but Kennan observed that "it might well be preferable to a bloodless election victory . . . which would give the Communists the entire peninsula at one coup. . . . "[6]

The American government here was not only discussing an internal dispute which was the exclusive province of Italians, not Americans, but elaborating a strategy to help one side defeat the other. While lawyers who specialize in international law might argue the legality or illegality of such interference into the affairs of another state, there is no question that the United States would never have tolerated such interference into its own affairs. If the Soviet Union were to offer sub rosa aid to one candidate against another in a presidential election, for instance, or if it were to supply millions of dollars to the United Steelworkers of America to provoke a national steel strike, the level of outrage in the United States would very likely force a break in relations. The proposals of Kennan and other presidential advisors were certainly a violation of accepted standards of international behavior. We were trying to shape the government of another nation, exactly as we would have done if we had won a war against it with airplanes and tanks. For the Truman administration, and the ones that followed, there seemed to be nothing wrong in that.

Truman did not go quite as far as Kennan had proposed, but his activity on behalf of the Christian Democrats ranged from promises to return Trieste to Italy, a gift of twenty-nine merchant ships and the return of gold taken from Italy by the Nazis, to the threat that Italians who voted Communist would be denied the right to emigrate to the United States. A campaign, encouraged by the administration, was undertaken amongst Italian-Americans to send 10 million letters and telegrams to friends and relatives in Italy, urging them to vote against the Communists. Extra wheat was shipped to Italy to prevent a further cut in the bread ration. Richard Barnet, a former State Department official now a writer on international affairs, reports that special radio programs were beamed at Italy a few days before the voting, subtle threats were made that a Communist victory would imperil the tourist trade, and a CIA agency spread liberal sums of money to noncommunist parties. A top CIA agent, James Jesus Angleton, "forged documents and letters purporting to have come from the Communist Party that suggested that Italians would soon be suffering the fate of the Czechs and the Poles."[7] From 1948 to 1968 the CIA contributed $65 million to parties challenging the Communists in Italian elections, and another $6 million (approved by Gerald Ford) during the June 1976 balloting.

According to a report by the Senate Select Intelligence Committee, since the early postwar days when Washington was trying to arrange or rearrange political power in Italy, the Philippines, and Greece, the American government has engaged in literally thousands of such covert, disruptive activities. Only a few dozen of them have involved the overthrow of governments—as in Iran, Guatemala, and Chile. Other CIA activity is less sensational but equally pernicious. It includes pay-offs ("subsidies") to prominent individuals who are willing to accept CIA advice and counsel; financial help and technical assistance to political parties the CIA considers friendly; covert propaganda and financial assistance to unions, business firms, cooperatives, and the like; covert propaganda (for instance by paying off a newspaper editor or reporter to publish slanted articles). The idea is to use these "assets," as the CIA calls them, to penetrate the power center of foreign countries and—in the words of Richard Bissell, the CIA clandestine chief who managed the ill-fated Bay of Pigs invasion in April 1961—to "influence the internal affairs of other nations—sometimes called 'intervention'—by covert means."[8]

The story of CIA lawlessness is ultimate proof of the contention of the founders of the United States that without "checks and balances" democracy atrophies. As John Adams put it 200 years ago, "arbitrary power sits upon her brazen throne and governs with an iron scepter."[9]

The establishment of the CIA in 1947 was a secondary feature of the National Security Act. Most of the act centered on proposals by Secretary of the Navy James Forrestal and his friend, investment broker Ferdinand Eberstadt, for unification of the armed services into a new Department of Defense (DoD). The act also provided for a National Security Council to coordinate military and civilian policy in the conflict with the Soviet Union. But the provision for a Central Intelligence Agency (CIA) was almos· an addendum made to satisfy Truman's wishes for a civilian, rather than a military, agency to take charge of intelligence. As we have already mentioned, neither publicly nor in private discussions did members of Congress conceive of the Agency as the initiator of covert or parliamentary action.

According to the Church Committee, "a memorandum by the CIA's general counsel, written after the passage of the [1967] Act, concedes that the legislative history contains nothing to show that Congress intended to authorize covert action by the CIA."[10] George F. Kennan, who originally favored a covert capability for the agency, recalls that "We had thought that this would be a facility which could be used when and if an occasion arose. . . . There might be years when we wouldn't have to do anything like this."[11] Years later, in 1963, Harry Truman recorded in the *Washington Post:* "I never had any thought . . . when I set up the CIA that it would be injected into peacetime cloak and dagger operations. Some of the complications and embarrassment that I think we have experienced are in part attributable to the fact that this quiet intelligence arm of the President has been removed from its intended role. . . . "[12] Harry Howe Ransom, a specialist in CIA affairs, observes that "probably no other organization in the Federal Government has taken such liberties in interpreting its legally assigned function as the CIA."[13]

Whatever the intent of the legislators, however, there was need for a new institution to deal with the second "enemy" in the permanent war—the revolutionary, communist, socialist, or "third force" nations and movements which challenged the "American system." The CIA was suited for this purpose. In another time the United States might have considered occupying some of the countries (e.g., Greece or the Philippines) which it was integrating into its sphere of influence, just as Britain, France, and other imperialist nations had done in the nineteenth century. But occupation of dissident countries was no longer feasible. Britain may have been able to seize most of India in the nineteenth century with 50,000 troops and France most of Indochina with only a few thousand soldiers, but it was evident after World War II that many times these numbers were needed for an imperialist power to have even the remotest chance of annexing India, Indochina, or Algeria. Thus, apart from the fact that old-fashioned imperialist occupation was generally alien to the American temperament, it was also not practical, especially on a global scale. The only real alternative was either to form an alliance with liberated former colonial peoples, or manipulate events and people inside these countries through covert, and if necessary, paramilitary measures.

The CIA was the most obvious candidate for this role. Its roots went back to the wartime Office of Strategic Services (OSS) which had performed similar functions, and some of its personnel came from the same source. The only problem was that the CIA and its parent organization, the NSC, had no specific mandate for intervening in the internal affairs of other countries. Because American tradition is against intervention, Congress, if asked, would certainly have turned down any demand for such a mandate. The only option therefore was to go ahead without legal authorization from Congress. The executive branch of government had become accustomed to doing that anyway under the hundreds of "emergency" laws passed after 1933 and during the war. According to a 1973 Senate Special Committee, those laws gave the president the right to "seize properties, mobilize production, seize commodities, institute martial law, seize control of all transportation and communications, regulate private capital, restrict travel. . . . "[14] They reinforced the wartime, and now the postwar mood that the executive had the right to do almost anything on its own without congressional or judicial restraint. In any case, covert activities were initiated by the CIA only a few months after the National Security Act was passed in 1947 and they continued to expand despite efforts to contain them in the next four decades.

In December 1947 the State Department informed the NSC that Soviet covert activities were becoming an ever greater menace and urged the NSC to counter it with a campaign of its own. At the Council's very first meeting, on December 19 that year, it issued a directive, NSC-4-A, ordering the Director of Central Intelligence (DCI) to begin covert psychological activities. The following year an autonomous Office of Policy Coordination (OPC) was formed within the CIA to carry out psychological and other covert actions approved by the NSC. In its first few months the CIA's activities in this area were confined to spreading false information, operating "black" radio programs, subsidizing publications favorable to the CIA viewpoint. Directive NSC 10/2 superseded NSC-4-A in June 1948 and added three other functions to the CIA repertoire—political warfare, economic warfare, and "preventive direct action." In other words, direct aid was now provided to guerrillas, saboteurs, and front organizations "fighting communism."

A milestone of sorts was reached in 1949. By then the "cold" war had heated up considerably, and though Congress had failed to give the NSC or CIA a mandate for covert actions, it now gave them a mandate for effectively concealing such actions. The Central Intelligence Act authorized the Agency to hide its expenditures within the budget of other departments so that they would not be known to "the enemy," or the American public. On the theory that intelligence sources had to be kept secret, the CIA was also exempted from the provisions of any law that required disclosure of the "organization, functions, names, official titles, salaries, or numbers of personnel employed by the Agency." And just to complete the process of removing the CIA from public control, the Agency was authorized to spend money on "objects of a confidential, extraordinary, or emergency nature . . . solely on the certificate of the Director."

This was an immense boost to CIA fortunes. As David Wise, former Washington bureau chief of the *New York Herald Tribune* observes, "the way was open for the CIA to engage in special operations on a large scale." Speaking to a university audience years later, the former CIA Deputy Director for Intelligence, Robert Amory, noted that "we went in through the NSC-CIA act because that was the only way we could get unvouchered funds."[15]

Given this unprecedented power the CIA became virtually a law unto itself. Dean Acheson was constrained to warn President Truman that "neither he, the National Security Council, nor anyone else would be in a position to know . . . what it [the CIA] was doing or to control it."[16]

Directive NSC 10/2 was superseded by NSC 10/5 in October 1951, authorizing worldwide covert operations—again expanding the CIA's role. Meanwhile the agency was enlarging its activities anyway, operating far beyond the original parameters of black radio stations or contributing a few thousand dollars to the London-based anticommunist magazine *Encounter*. For example, from 1949 to 1953, Albanian guerrilla squads were sent into their homeland by land, sea, and air on eight occasions to try and overthrow the government and detach Albania from the Soviet sphere of influence. According to British author Nicholas Bethell, who reviewed British government papers on the subject, thousands of people died in these abortive campaigns. Attempts to establish guerrilla movements in the Ukraine around the same time, and for the same purpose, were similarly abortive. "Almost none of the agents, funds, and equipment infiltrated by the agency into those two countries were ever seen or heard from again," report Victor Marchetti and John D. Marks.[17]

They also report that an attempt to establish "a vast underground apparatus in Poland for espionage and, ultimately, revolutionary purposes," not only failed but the network was co-opted by the Polish secret service along with the millions of dollars in gold the CIA sent in to support it. There was no public outcry in the United States against all this only because it was unknown. We were committing acts of war against the Soviet Union and two of its client states, but neither the CIA, the NSC, nor the president felt the American people were entitled to know about them, let alone give their assent. In the ensuing years the executive branch established a host of instrumentalities for political control and coordination of CIA activities, including the 10/5 and 10/2 Panels, the 5412 or Special Group, the 303 Committee, and the 40 Committee. Neither Congress nor the public, however, were ever allowed to play a determining role in the process.

The Korean War, which began in June 1950, accelerated CIA activity. Under Defense Department prodding the Office of Policy Coordination (OPC) allocated large sums of money for guerrilla and propaganda operations in China and other areas considered part of the Soviet orbit; OPC's manpower almost tripled in size. By 1953 the CIA was engaged in major covert projects in forty-eight countries.

Two of them, in Iran and Guatemala, were prototypes for the future, and are particularly interesting because they reveal the criteria used by the CIA and the National Security Council for determining who is an "enemy" and who is a "friend." The ink was hardly dry on the pact which ended the Korean War when the NSC decided to topple the government of Prime Minister Mohammed Mossadegh in oil-rich Iran. The Iranian leader's transgression, it seems, was not that he was a communist or a dictator (he was neither) but that he had nationalized the British-owned Anglo-Iranian Oil Company and the large refinery in Abadan.

Oil was the economic lifeline of Iran, but despite the revenues from petroleum, the nation remained backward beyond belief. Eighty percent of Iran's population was agrarian, almost 25 percent tribal. A United States Point Four official revealed that nine-tenths of the peasants lived at subsistence level, fifty percent of the population suffered from trachoma and other diseases generally associated with extreme poverty, and the infant mortality rate was three hundred for every thousand births. In Teheran, water ran in open *jubes* along the streets and was used not only for washing and toilet purposes but for drinking. Neither Britain, which had occupied most of Iran during World War II, nor Shah Reza Pahlevi, whose father had made overtures to the Nazis, had done anything to remedy these conditions. The people were understandably waiting for someone who would.

Mohammed Mossadegh, leader of the National Front and ideologically a democratic socialist, was appointed prime minister by the Iranian parliament in 1951, and entrusted with the task of remedying matters. Mossadegh concluded that there could be no progress in his country without land reform (dividing land among the landless peasants), and no true land reform was possible unless there was money for roads, cooperatives, credits, electricity, and dams. The only place where such money could be found was in the British oil concessions. Mossadegh nationalized them in the hope that he might sell 8 million tons of oil overseas and use the funds to build roads, reclaim thousands of acres of land, electrify the country, erect dams, and make credits available to the peasants.

Mossadegh could have appealed to the peasants to seize the land themselves—he informed an American writer in 1953 that he had contemplated it. But since the communist-controlled Tudeh (Masses) Party was strong in the villages he feared this would place the whole country in communist hands. He preferred to wait, meanwhile balancing himself between the communist and noncommunist forces, always hoping he might work out a modus vivendi with the West, especially the United States. To his consternation, however, Mossadegh found that where property rights were concerned the great powers would act in unison. A world boycott was declared on Iranian petroleum after the industry was nationalized, and Mossadegh was unable to find either tankers to transport his country's oil or customers to buy it.

The United States as yet had no stake in the oil fields but the Eisenhower administration was fearful that the virus of nationalization might become contagious. John Foster Dulles—a senior partner in the law firm of Sullivan and Cromwell and a long associate of big bankers—was now Secretary of State. His brother Allen W. Dulles, who had served as a supersleuth with the OSS during the war, had just been promoted to Director of the CIA. Under their guiding hands, the NSC not only decided to join the oil boycott but instructed the CIA to get rid of Mossadegh. The man placed in charge of this delicate task was the grandson of Theodore Roosevelt and a distant cousin of Franklin D. Roosevelt, Kermit (Kim) Roosevelt, then thirty-seven years old. Kim, like Allen Dulles, had served with the OSS during the Second World War and later had become a CIA Middle East specialist. With a half-dozen assistants and in collusion with Fazollah Zahedi—a six foot, two inch Iranian general suspected by the British of wartime collaboration with the Nazis—Kim began his operations from a basement office in Teheran. Also on the team was H. Norman Schwarzkopf, who had helped solve the Lindbergh kidnapping case in 1932 and had trained a police force for the Shah of Iran in the 1940s. He, too, was close to Zahedi, and according to Andrew Tully, a chronicler of CIA history, "supervised the careful spending of more than ten million of CIA dollars, as a result of which Mossadegh suddenly lost a great many supporters."[18]

The plans went poorly at first. On August 13, 1953, the pro-American Shah issued a decree replacing Mossadegh with Zahedi, but the aging prime minister arrested the colonel who brought him notice of the decree. Masses of people, friendly to the communist-dominated Tudeh, took to the streets. The thirty-three-year-old Shah and his queen, Soraya, fled to the safe confines of Baghdad, then to Rome. A few days later, however, Roosevelt's CIA money began to work its magic. Countermobs took to the streets, beat up demonstrators, and paved the way for Zahedi to seize the reins.

Even so Mossadegh might have prevailed if he had called on the communist masses for help. He refused, however, and consequently the CIA coup succeeded. The director of the U.S. Military Assistance Mission, Major General George C. Stewart, later noted that the coup was "about to collapse" when the United States began supplying "the [Iranian] army . . . on an emergency basis, uniforms, electric generators, and medical supplies that permitted and created an atmosphere in which they could support the Shah. . . . The guns that they had in their hands, the trucks that they rode in, the armored cars that they drove through the streets, and the radio communications that permitted their control, were all furnished through the military defense assistance program. . . . " He concluded that "had it not been for this program a government unfriendly to the United States probably would now be in power."[19]

Mossadegh was defeated and jailed, the oil properties were denationalized, and five years later American corporations reaped the bonanza. The British oil monopoly in Iran was superseded by a consortium in which an Anglo-Iranian corporation received 40 percent, five U.S. corporations—Gulf Oil, Standard Oil of New Jersey (now Exxon), Standard Oil of California, Texaco and Socony-Mobil—received another 40 percent, and the rest went to a British and a French firm. In the next decade the United States spent between $1 billion and $1.5 billion, in a nation of only 18 million people, shoring up the Shah's regime. Elections were held in September 1953, even while martial law was in effect, with Tudeh and Mossadegh's forces excluded, and only 11 percent of the electorate casting a ballot. Twenty-five years later the Shah's regime was overthrown in a massive rebellion led by a Muslim fundamentalist, Ayatollah Khomeini.

A second subversion of an "unfriendly" government engineered by the NSC and the CIA took place in Guatemala, a year after the events in Iran. Here, too, the adversary was a noncommunist regime which was trying to do something about widespread misery. The crisis traced back to 1944 when democratic revolutionaries overthrew General Jorge Ubico, who boasted of political kinship to Adolph Hitler and claimed that "I execute first and give trial afterward." After the overthrow, a former schoolteacher named Juan José Arévalo was elected president by a large margin and proceeded to legalize unions, raise minimum pay (to 26 cents a day), and reclaim the country's economy from the United Fruit Company and other foreign firms. When he introduced social security reforms that cost United Fruit $200,000 a year (bananas constituted about two-fifths of the nation's exports), the company reduced its production by 80 percent, and W. R. Grace and Pan American actively discouraged the vital tourist trade. After six years, Arévalo was succeeded by Jacobo Arbenz Guzmán, a general of leftist leanings who was not a communist but leaned toward communism more and more as American pressures on his regime increased.

Arbenz's most significant act was the passage of a land-reform bill (2 percent of the population owned 70 percent of the land) which distributed tracts to 85,000 peasant families. In the process, however, the regime seized 234,000 uncultivated acres from United Fruit. The company demanded $16 million for its lands, while the government offered $600,000 in twenty-five-year bonds. This was the setting when, in the words of a conservative Guatemalan, Miguel Ydígoras Fuentes, as quoted in Richard J. Barnet's *Intervention and Revolution*, "a former executive of the United Fruit Company, now retired, Mr. Walter Turnbull, came to see me with two gentlemen whom he introduced as agents of the CIA. They said that I was a popular figure in Guatemala and that they wanted to lend their assistance to overthrow Arbenz. When I asked their condition for the assistance I found them unacceptable. Among other things, I was to promise to favor the United Fruit Company and the International Railways of Central America, to destroy the railroad workers labor union; . . . to establish a strong arm government on the style of Ubico."[20]

Rebuffed by Ydígoras, the CIA fastened its hopes on Colonel Carlos Castillo Armas who had been trained in a military school at Fort Leavenworth. Within a few months Operation el Diablo was launched. The CIA established a headquarters for Castillo at Tegucigalpa, Honduras (much as it was to do for the Nicaraguan contras in the 1980s), and not long thereafter a training camp at Momotobito, a volcanic island belonging to Nicaragua, which was then ruled by the long-time American allies, the Somoza family.

Meanwhile Arbenz discovered the plot through intercepted correspondence between Castillo and Ydígoras, and applied to the Soviet Union to buy $10 million of small arms. A shipment of Czech weapons aboard a Swedish ship, *Alfhem*, in mid-May brought charges from Secretary Dulles that Arbenz might be planning to attack the Panama Canal a thousand miles away, and served as a pretext for more or less open support to Castillo's invaders. On June 18, 1954, the CIA-controlled colonel led a band of 150 exile mercenaries over the border from Honduras, while four P-47 Thunderbolts, flown by U.S. pilots, bombed the Guatemalan capital. The mercenaries settled six miles across the border, waiting for the planes to wreak enough havoc for Arbenz to collapse. Unfortunately, one bomber was shot full of holes and another crashed. And while the U.S. ambassador to Guatemala, Henry Cabot Lodge, was denying that any American planes or fliers were involved, Eisenhower made the decision to send in more. That was enough to tip the scales. Castillo never made it to the capital but, then, he didn't have to. Fearful of provoking a bloodbath and deserted by old friends in the army, Arbenz refused to distribute guns to the unions and peasant organizations which were clamoring for them. While he pondered, the bombing continued and on June 27 he simply gave up.

In the aftermath of the CIA-Castillo victory, United Fruit lands were promptly restored to the company and a tax on interest and dividends for foreigners abrogated, saving the company a tidy $11 million. All unions were temporarily disbanded (when allowed to function again they were harried to the point that membership declined from 107,000 to 16,000), the right to strike was abolished, and wage increases were held up. The 85,000 parcels of land distributed to peasants were returned to *finca* owners, some of whom went on a rampage, burning the crops of their serfs. In the next seven years the government distributed land to only 4,078 peasants, and this in a country where 70 percent of the rural population was landless. Upwards of 5,000 people were arrested by Castillo, and the election law was modified so that illiterates, who made up 70 percent of the population, were denied the ballot. In the one-candidate election that followed, Castillo was confirmed by what Eisenhower called "a thunderous majority."

Twenty-eight years later, Stephen Schlesinger and Stephen Kinzer, authors of a book on Guatemala, reported in the *New York Times* that "land ownership remains in the hands of the few. Social progress is severely limited for most people. Indians, who contribute more than half of the population of 7.2 million, have stayed poor, illiterate, landless. The economy has never recovered; by many measures the people are worse off today than they were under President Arbenz."[21]

Had the United States formally declared war on Iran and Guatemala, the Eisenhower administration would have been forced to make some embarrassing explanations. It would have had to explain why we were at war with Iran, a nation which had seized none of our citizens or property, which was in no sense a threat to our strategic interests, and which was not aligned directly or indirectly with the Soviet Union. It would have become evident that our sole reason for overthrowing a constitutional government was the quest for oil properties by our petroleum corporations and those of our allies. As for Guatemala, the American government would have had to explain why it was underwriting an invasion by a dissident force against a democratically chosen regime. Or, why it was berating the Soviets for fraudulent elections in Poland when the one-party elections engineered by the CIA in Guatemala were, if anything, even more crass. The attempt to overthrow governments that the National Security State didn't like has continued unabated. In May 1983, Stansfield Turner, a former CIA director under President Carter, told a *Baltimore Sun* correspondent that during his tenure the Agency tried to find ways to overthrow Iran's Ayatollah Ruhollah Khomeini, Libya's Moammar Khadafy, Cuba's Fidel Castro, and the Sandinistas in Nicaragua. "There is nothing morally wrong with trying to overthrow a foreign government by covert means. . . . " he said. "We should judge whether to overthrow any government not by abstract morality, but by which government is better, both for the United States and the country involved."[22] The same four states were targets for demolition by the Reagan regime, plus the governments of Afghanistan, Cambodia (Kampuchea), Chad, and perhaps others.

Periodically there has been sharp criticism of the CIA, and there have been investigations such as those by the Rockefeller Commission appointed by President Ford, and select committees of the House and Senate a year or so later. There has even been talk of curbing the Agency. Moreover, more rabid critics have on occasion, though not lately, suggested its dissolution. The CIA's illegal actions, nevertheless, have continued unabated. Even under presidents such as President Carter, who felt that the CIA had become something of a "rogue elephant," the Agency continued to carry out its misdeeds. Two administrations in fact discharged hundreds of employees of the CIA's covert action branch, in the hopes of reducing its scale of operations. No administration, however, has considered halting this activity entirely, and when Ronald Reagan came to office in January 1981 the Agency was endowed with a new spirit and an increased level of lawless assignments.

One of the most brazen covert actions began only a few months after Reagan was sworn in for his first term—brazen because so little attempt was made to hide it and because of the previous American record in Nicaragua. For all but a few months, American Marines had occupied and run Nicaragua from 1912 to 1933. When they were finally forced out as a result of the revolt led by Augusto César Sandino, they imposed on the small Central American state the dictatorship of National Guard chief, General Anastasio Somoza, and later, his sons. Now, in the wake of a truly popular revolution in 1979—in which all classes had originally participated, including the upper classes—the American government was intervening again. Under the auspices of the CIA small, armed groups were united into the Democratic National Front (FDN), with bases in Honduras. The Revolutionary Democratic Alliance (ARDE)—a lesser force based in Costa Rica—was originally led by former Sandinista, Eden Pastora. In due course the contras, as they were called (counterrevolutionaries) grew to about 15,000 or 20,000 men, including a group of Miskito Indians from the East Coast of Nicaragua. The Reagan administration at first justified its campaign on the grounds it was trying to interdict arms being sent by Nicaragua to leftist rebels in nearby El Salvador. There is probably an element of truth to this, though the level of Nicaraguan aid must have been small since the United States has never, as of this writing, been able to produce a single bullet sent by Nicaragua to the Salvadorean rebels.

But the shipment of arms to El Salvador was a negligible factor in this drama anyway; the true mission of the CIA was to overthrow the Sandinista government. That mission was carried out in a blatant manner: Congress was openly asked to vote funds for the contras, and the CIA dispatched Americans to secretly bomb port facilities and place mines in Nicaraguan waters. Thousands of people were killed as the contras made one foray after another into Nicaragua. According to reports heard in Honduras, where the CIA was directing the operation, the scenario called for the contras to occupy a slice of Nicaraguan land sometime in 1982. The United States would then recognize the contras as the legitimate government of the country and give them military and economic aid on a grander scale. Unfortunately for the CIA, the timetable could not be met, and, as the contras sloshed in futility, a large mass movement grew in the United States demanding that the Reagan administration withdraw. In increasing numbers, members of Congress voted to withhold funds for the covert war—which by now was totally overt—and Chairman Edward Boland of the House Intelligence Committee pushed through an amendment outlawing administration efforts to overthrow the Sandinista government. President Reagan, however, blithely ignored the "Boland amendment"; the House retaliated, for a time, by withholding funds from the contras. Many people were expecting an outright invasion, led by U.S. airpower and perhaps some U.S. troops. The significant point, however, is that the National Security State is so difficult to restrain, even when its illegality becomes evident to everyone.

The hidden wars conducted by the CIA relieved the American government of the necessity of telling the American people the truth. They had the great advantage that their parentage did not have to be admitted, nor their true objectives discussed publicly. An executive order by President Gerald Ford described covert intervention as an activity "designed to further official United States programs and policies abroad which are planned and executed so that the role of the United States *is not apparent or publicly acknowledged*" (emphasis added).[23] Our government could claim it was engaged in idealistic ventures to "defeat totalitarianism," to "check foreign (Soviet) aggression," to "prevent communist expansion," and the like, whereas in reality it was pursuing the age-old imperial objectives of economic and strategic gain. No different from what other countries had done previously except, of course, for the fact that they were carried out on a more extensive basis.

Few of the claims made by the National Security State have stood the test of close examination. It is not true, for instance, that we challenge communism as a matter of principle. As we mentioned earlier, if communism had been the enemy, the United States would not have allied itself with either the Soviet Union or the various guerrilla movements—the Maquis in France, the Garibaldini in Italy, the EAM in Greece, the Titoists in Yugoslavia, the Vietminh in Indochina—that were fighting against Germany, Japan, and Italy during the Second World War. If our antipathy to communism is a matter of principle, moreover, we would not have entered in friendlier-than-average relations with the communist governments of Yugoslavia, China, Hungary, or Rumania.

Nor is there any merit to the claim that the American establishment has an endemic hostility to dictatorship or totalitarianism per se. The evidence is quite to the contrary. The U.S. government since World War II has lived in unfortunate harmony with such totalitarian regimes as the monarchy, and later the colonels, in Greece, the Roxas and later Marcos regimes in the Philippines, the puppet regimes of France in Indochina and Algeria, the apartheid government in South Africa, with Batista in Cuba, Somoza in Nicaragua, Stroessner in Paraguay, Zia in Pakistan, the military governments of Indonesia, Thailand, Turkey, and so forth and so on. The claim that the permanent war is being waged against "communism" or "totalitarianism" as such is simply not credible.

The assistance given to Ramón Magsaysay in his campaign against the Huks in the Philippines during the early 1950s was also justified as aid to "fight totalitarianism," but there is little doubt that what weighed most in CIA and NSC deliberations were the American military bases in that country and the long-held financial investments. "Every time the Soviet Union extends its power over another area or state, the United States and Great Britain lose another normal market," observed William C. Bullitt, former U.S. Ambassador to the Soviet Union, in 1946.[24]

On the other side of the equation there were numerous instances of CIA intervention in which there was no "communist" issue by any measuring standard. The 1953 overthrow of Mossadegh in Iran and the 1958 attempt to oust Achmed Sukarno in Indonesia (which failed temporarily) were aimed against noncommunists. The parachuting of two CIA agents into Singapore in 1960 was a challenge to the anticommunist government of Premier Lee Kyuan Yew. The agency's expenditure of $20 million on the 1962 elections in Brazil and the overthrow of the neutralist President Joao Goulart in 1964 had nothing to do with communism; the communists were a negligible factor in that country. This was also the case in the Dominican Republic. The CIA, nevertheless, participated in the overthrow of democratic socialist Juan Bosch in 1963, and the dispatch of 22,000 American troops and a host of CIA agents to that country two years later to prevent a group of young Dominican officers from restoring Bosch to power. The communists, again, were a minuscule force in that country.

The CIA's help in suppressing a revolt against the government of Haile Selassie in Ethiopia in 1960, against the government of the Congo (now Zaire) in 1964, against the government of Greece in 1967, also had little or nothing to do with communism. Salvador Allende of Chile, whom the CIA helped defeat in the presidential elections of 1964 (at a cost of $6 million donated to his rival's campaign), was a socialist, not a communist, though he did have communist support. Even Fidel Castro was no communist when the Eisenhower administration decided to overthrow him, a point attested to by Deputy CIA Director C.P. Cabell. Testifying before the Senate Internal Security Committee on November 5, 1959, Cabell stated that the CIA's "information showed that the Cuban communists do not consider him [Castro] a Communist Party member, or even a pro-Communist. . . . The Communists consider Castro as a representative of the bourgeoisie. . . . We [the CIA] believe that Castro is not a member of the Communist Party, and does not consider himself to be a communist."[25]

The labeling of adversaries as "communists"—whether they were or not—had the same advantage for the American establishment and the CIA as did the labeling of adversaries of Christianity "pagan" or "anti-Christ"; namely, that any action against them, legal or illegal, moral or immoral, was automatically justified. It gave U.S. officials free rein to use whatever tactics they saw fit against "the enemy," just as in a traditional type of war. In the normal state of affairs a conflict with another nation would have to be resolved under the niceties of diplomacy and international law. Such tactics as assassination, even bribery, would be outside the pale. But the definition of "the enemy" as an outlaw force gave the CIA a blanket justification in its own mind for using whatever tactic was necessary. The CIA mood has always been confrontational, and either on the border of illegality or across it. By its very nature, then, the CIA could not reinforce democracy in any country; it could only undercut it.

Consider the plight of Ecuador after the Cuban revolution. When the United States broke relations with Castro in January 1961, the regime of José María Velasco Ibarra, a traditional conservative serving his fourth term as president, refused to go along. Later that year, according to Philip Agee, who was then with the CIA station in Ecuador, the CIA decided to mount a campaign against Velasco. By this time the Agency had a sizable number of assets whom it was paying to promote the CIA cause: prominent journalists, military figures, political elements, including the vice president of the country, the head of police intelligence, members of the cabinet, leaders of some of the parties, and most important, officials in the union and student movements. The CIA station's budget for bribes and expenses came to about $1 million a year, a very substantial sum for a country so small and so poor.

Although Velasco was under severe pressure from his cabinet and the military to abandon his policy vis-à-vis Cuba, he stood his ground. He was overcome by the vice president of the country, Carlos Julio Arosemena, who retained the same policy. Arosemena, for example, refused to follow the U.S. lead when the Organization of American States (OAS) voted to exclude Cuba from its ranks in January 1962. Ecuador stood fast with five other Latin American nations, but by April the pressure from within the country by all the forces bought and paid for by the CIA forced the leadership to break with Cuba. "President Arosemena didn't want to break relations but we forced him," Agee recalled in an interview with the *Washington Post*. "We promoted the Communist issue and especially Communist penetration of the government."

Agee's book, *Inside the Company*, written in diary form, is studded with entries such as these: "Quito, January 16, 1962. Our new campaign is off to a bang—literally." It seems that a national convention of radical youth was to have begun two days earlier but CIA supporters had exploded bombs in the doorways of two churches in the town where it was to be held and "public authorities then banned the URJE convention in order to avoid bloodshed." Or, "January 19, 1962. The campaign is back in full swing in Quito. Yesterday's rally against Cuba and communism was enormous. . . . Speakers attacked communism and Castro and called for a break in relations with Cuba while urging Ecuadorian support for a program of sanctions against Cuba at the coming Punte del Este Conference."[26] Democracy means that citizens and their representatives discuss an issue and freely vote on it; but how can there be a democratic discussion or vote when the key figures in the debate have already been bought off by the CIA? It is doubtful that the Ecuadoran people, left to their own devices, would have broken relations with Cuba. To begin with, their natural sympathy would have been with the Fidelistas if only because there is an endemic hostility to the Colossus of the North that goes back for generations. Second, it is doubtful that in a country with such pervasive poverty, a foreign policy issue such as Cuba would have taken precedence over domestic issues. But the CIA had enough Ecuadorans bought off to upset the democratic process and manipulate the course of events.

The essence of CIA covert action, and that of the NSC behind it, is that it arranges and rearranges power in foreign countries not to suit the wishes of the citizenry involved, but of the powers that be in the United States. Sometimes that is done through bribery and mendacity, sometimes by other criminal means, including assassination. "Thus, the United States came to adopt the methods and accept the value system of the 'enemy,' " the late Senator Frank Church told a Washington audience in December 1975. "In the secret world of covert action, we threw off all restraints. Not content merely to discreetly subsidize foreign political parties, labor unions, and newspapers, the Central Intelligence Agency soon began to directly manipulate the internal politics of other countries. Spending many millions of dollars annually, the CIA filled its bag with dirty tricks—ranging from bribery and false propaganda to schemes to 'alter the health' of unfriendly foreign leaders and undermine their regimes."[27]

Among the criminal acts Church attributed to the CIA was an attempt to assassinate former Prime Minister Patrice Lumumba in the Congo: "We sent a deadly toxin to the Congo with the purpose of injecting Lumumba with a fatal disease." Instructions for this assassination, incredibly, "were sent via diplomatic pouch, along with rubber gloves, a mask, syringe, and a lethal biological material. The poison was to be injected into some substance that Lumumba would ingest, whether food or toothpaste." The CIA-inspired assassination did not come off only because some of Lumumba's Congolese enemies got to him first.

The CIA had better luck with General René Schneider, commander-in-chief of the Chilean Army. As Senator Church describes it: "a military coup was organized with the CIA playing a direct role in the planning," to prevent Salvador Allende from assuming the presidency of Chile to which he had been duly elected.

> One of the major obstacles to the success of the mission was the strong opposition to a coup by . . . General René Schneider who insisted that Chile's constitution be upheld. As a result of his stand, the removal of General Schneider became a necessary ingredient in the coup plans. Unable to get General Schneider to resign, conspirators in Chile decided to kidnap him. Machine guns and ammunition were passed by the CIA to a group of kidnappers on October 22, 1970. That same day General Schneider was mortally wounded on his way to work in an attempted kidnap, apparently by a group affiliated with the one provided weapons by the CIA.[28]

On at least one occasion two assassinations occurred inadvertently as a result of CIA actions. "We participated in a military coup overturning the very government we were pledged to defend in Vietnam," Senator Church notes, "and when Premier [Ngo Dinh] Diem resisted, he and his brother were murdered by the very generals to whom we gave money and support." In another instance, the CIA was involved in the assassination of a rightist dictator, Rafael Trujillo in the Dominican Republic. According to a report by the Senate Select Committee, the dissidents who shot him were given "three pistols and three carbines" by American officials even though the United States was "aware that the dissidents intended to kill Trujillo." Trujillo's assassination was an exception to the general rule that the CIA directed its activities against people of the center and left. But like all the other efforts at killing foreign leaders it was "plausibly deniable." For although the guns, the poison, and the money were supplied by the CIA the Agency saw to it that someone else's hand was on the trigger or administering the poison. Morton H. Halperin, a former chief aide to Henry Kissinger, and three of his associates record in their book, *The Lawless State*, that "murder was viewed within the CIA as an important enough weapon that an assassination capability was institutionalized in 1961. The Agency . . . called the program 'executive action.' Preferring to keep the actual blood off their own hands, Agency officials hired people like mafiosos and an agent code-named WI/ROGUE to do the dirty work. WI/ROGUE is described in CIA documents as a 'forger and former bank robber'."[29]

No assassination campaign has been so sustained as the one against Fidel Castro of Cuba. The first one, in 1960, enlisted the Mafia, on the theory that the crime syndicate would like to have their Havana casinos returned to them. Three mafiosi, Sam Giancana, Santos Traficante, and John Roselli, designed an intricate plot to have someone close to Castro slip him a pill made by the Technical Services Division of the CIA that presumably would dispatch the Cuban leader slowly enough (24 to 48 hours) so that the assassin could escape. Unfortunately the designated murderer returned the pills to Roselli, stating that he no longer had access to Castro. Another effort, using the same kind of pills, was planned concurrent with the Bay of Pigs invasion a little later that year. In the confusion of arranging for the military attack, however, someone evidently forgot to pass the signal on to the would-be assassin. A third plan, this time under the direction of the Office of Naval Intelligence, involved two marksmen who were to be infiltrated into Cuba from the American naval base in Guantanamo, and whose mission was to shoot down both Fidel and his brother Raul on the revolutionary holiday, July 26. The killing was to be accompanied by a mortar shelling of Guantanamo, giving the United States a pretext for invading the island. The plot, however, was discovered in advance and frustrated. Another plot failed not long thereafter, one in which an underground network, named Amblood, was programed to do away with Castro with bazookas as he crossed the street from a stadium where he was speaking. Under Eisenhower, Kennedy, and Nixon, efforts to kill the Cuban leader continued—not only on Cuban soil but on that of other countries. One plan, to be executed by an exile group in Santiago, Chile, called for Castro to be shot by a gun hidden inside a camera when he appeared for a visit to Salvador Allende.[30]

The most far-reaching campaign of assassination ever conducted by the CIA was Operation Phoenix during the Vietnam War. Directed by a top CIA figure, William Colby, who later became director of the Agency, some 20,587 suspected members of the National Liberation Front were executed in a two-and-a-half year period.[31] The American people feel queasy about assassinations, and each time one of the CIA's efforts comes to light, the government disavows any role in it. Yet the idea of assassination continues to surface in CIA circles. During the 1984 presidential elections, a psychological-warfare manual, prepared by the CIA for the Nicaraguan contras, came to light. The most solemn bit of advice in this manual dealt with the "neutralization" of Nicaraguan officials. Though CIA's William Casey and President Reagan tried to dance around the meaning of the word "neutralization," there was no doubt in the minds of responsible journalists that it was in fact a mandate for assassination. Among other things the tract called for kidnapping, blackmail, the recruitment of criminals, and "neutralizing." In that context there could be no doubt as to its meaning.[32]

Toward the end of 1984 unnamed government officials admitted to the House Intelligence Committee investigating the CIA "neutralizing" manual that the CIA itself had engaged in military action in and over Nicaragua, action that not only violated international law but specific congressional decisions. On January 6, 1984 CIA helicopters attacked an arms storage facility at the northern Nicaraguan port city of Potosi. On March 7 of the same year—around the time that the CIA was mining Nicaragua's coastline at San Juan del Sur on the Pacific Coast—CIA helicopters joined those of the contras in shooting up the town—allegedly so that Latin American commandos operating for the CIA could withdraw. Thus we have the distressing situation of an American administration which claims that its only objective in Nicaragua is to preempt the flow of weapons to Salvadoran guerrillas, laying mines in a port, attacking facilities in two cities on either Nicaraguan coast, and offering cover for its own foreign commandos—none of which has anything to do with the stated purpose. In the course of violating international law the CIA of necessity compounds its crime by lying to the American people.

"The nation must to a degree take it on faith that we too are honorable men devoted to her service," CIA director Richard Helms stated in 1971. There is no question that CIA employees consider themselves patriotic, but whether they can be called "honorable" by objective standards is another matter. Operating on the thesis that the end justifies the means, they have no compunction about associating with unsavory people or undertaking criminal activities. Consider the issue of drugs. In the last few decades, the United States has been embarked on a crusade against heroin, cocaine, marijuana, and the like. Members of the military have even been required to take urine tests to prove they are not smoking pot or using cocaine. But in the interests of expediency the CIA has worked with, and covered up for, drug smugglers of various kinds. When Chiang Kai-shek fled to Formosa (Taiwan) from mainland China after Mao Tse-tung's victory in 1949, 12,000 of his troops, isolated near Yunan, were left to fend for themselves. They fled to the northeastern section of Burma where the CIA took them under its wing and directed their sporadic forays into their former homeland.

The exiles supported themselves in part with CIA money and in part by growing opium, which they sold lucratively on the world market. Andrew Tully reports in his book on the CIA that the Chinese exiles "not only took over the best land in Northern Burma, but they annexed all but a few acres of the state of Kengtung and organized their own squatter government."[33] The CIA winked an eye at the vices of its allies, on the theory that selling drugs and violating the sovereignty of a government friendly to the United States were lesser crimes than the communist system we were fighting in China. The CIA also displayed an affinity for opium-growers in Laos, where the 35,000 Meo tribesmen it recruited for the "secret war" against the communist Pathet Lao and North Vietnamese made their living growing the poppies from which the drug is manufactured. The CIA not only knew about it but, according to Victor Marchetti and John D. Marks, its proprietary airline, Air America, was sometimes used to ship the opium.

From 1980 on Americans became increasingly concerned about the "death squads" operating in El Salvador, who were said to have assassinated 40,000 people, including three American nuns and a religious co-worker, two U.S. unionists, and innumerable ordinary people whose only crime was that they were opposed to the rightists. In May 1984, however, Allan Nairn, a young journalist who spent a considerable time in El Salvador gathering his material, revealed in the *Progressive* that the murderous group traced its origins to "early in the 1960's" when:

> Agents of the U.S. Government in El Salvador set up two official security organizations that killed thousands of peasants and suspected leftists over the next fifteen years. These organizations, guided by American operatives, developed into the paramilitary apparatus that came to be known as the Salvadoran Death Squads. Today, even as the Reagan Administration publicly condemns the Death Squads, the CIA—in violation of U.S. law—continues to provide training, support, and intelligence to security forces directly involved in Death Squad activity.

General José Alberto Medrano, a CIA agent, is listed as the organizer of a rural paramilitary network that evolved into the present Death Squads.[34]

In pursuing its goals the CIA has little compunction about breaking the laws of the countries it is penetrating, or lying to Congress or the public to cover up its misdeeds. According to Fred Branfman, who spent four years interviewing participants, from the mid-1950s to 1972 the United States conducted a major war in Laos which involved 100,000 troops and resulted in tens of thousands of casualties. Yet when former Under Secretary of State U. Alexis Johnson was called to testify before the Senate Armed Services Committee in July 1971, he insisted that "the only U.S. forces involved in Laos are the air. We have no combat forces stationed there."[35] If one limits the meaning of "U.S. forces" to the army, navy, and the air force then technically this is true. But in fact, there were large numbers of CIA employees on the scene and it was they who were organizing, paying for, and directing the war operations, including that of the U.S. airmen who dropped 2 million tons of bombs on the hapless nation. Why didn't the United States openly admit its role and assign the job for the war in Laos to the Pentagon? Johnson explained that "under the Geneva Agreements [of 1964] we were prohibited from having American military personnel in Laos . . . [the] CIA is really the only other instrumentality that we have."[36] In its continuing quest for greater authority, the CIA was not unhappy to take on the job.

"Laos conclusively demonstrates that the CIA today has the *capacity* to wage full-scale war anywhere in the world," Branfman says.[37] (Indeed, it had other secret armies in Thailand, Burma, Cambodia, Vietnam, and perhaps elsewhere.) Yet American officials were denying that the United States was conducting a real war in Laos, costing at least a billion or a billion and a half a year. In order to cover up the CIA role in this war, whenever an American was killed in Laos his death was recorded as having taken place in Vietnam. And when the native tribespeople were decimated by the fruitless war, the CIA hired 17,000 mercenaries from Thailand to supplement the thinning ranks—another violation of American law.

The CIA, NSC, and the intelligence community generally live in a different world and by a different code from most people. Marchetti, who had direct personal experience with this way of life, describes it thus in his book written with John D. Marks, on *The CIA and the Cult of Intelligence:*

> Operating with secrecy and deception gradually becomes second nature to the clandestine operator. . . . As much as the operator believes in the rightness of his actions, he is forced to work in an atmosphere that is potentially demoralizing. He is quite often on the brink of the underworld, or even immersed in it, and he frequently turns to the least savory types to achieve his goals. Criminals are useful to him, and are often called upon by him, when he does not want to perform personally some particularly distasteful task or when he does not want to risk any direct Agency involvement in his dirty work. And if the clandestine operator wants to use attractive young women to seduce foreign officials, he does not call on female CIA employees. Instead he hires local prostitutes. . . . Other CIA men regularly deal with black-marketeers to purchase "laundered" currency. . . . "Sterile" weapons for CIA paramilitary activities are obtained in the same fashion from the munitions merchants who will provide arms to anyone able to pay the price.

And when the CIA needs "untraceable troops" for its counterrevolutions it hires them at "mercenary centers" in Brussels, Kinshasa, and

Saigon where "soldiers of fortune" can be recruited for "any cause for a price."[38]

The CIA has few qualms about utilizing the Mafia for its purposes. *Time* magazine (June 16, 1975) reported that "with the consent of the CIA, intelligence sources say, Detective [Richard] Cain [a former bagman for the crime syndicate inside the Chicago police] began recruiting Spanish-speaking toughs on the Windy City's West Side. Some of the hoodlums were sent to Miami and Central America for training in commando tactics." The syndicate, of course, was anxious to recover its Cuban gambling casinos, and the CIA wanted to overthrow the Castro government. They formed a united front. According to *Time*, "U.S. sources say that the CIA spent more than $100,000 on the operation, while [syndicate boss Sam] Giancana laid out $90,000 of the Mob's own funds for Cain's expenses."

Consorting with criminals and adopting the criminal code of ethics that "the end justifies the means," CIA agents do not find it repugnant to "shave" an American law or to take illegal action against an American. It is all for a "higher" cause, for a "just war." They do not accept the thesis that (at least formally) we are at peace; they are the practitioners of a permanent war, and they are ready to cut down anyone, foreign or American, who stands in the way.

So long as the number of people who operate on this ethic is relatively small and their influence meager, the effects are containable. But the size and influence of the CIA and its sisters in the National Security State are considerable. In addition to the Agency that operates directly under the NSC, there is the National Security Agency (NSA) which opens mail and reads telegrams, the Defense Intelligence Agency, Army Intelligence, Naval Intelligence, Air Force Intelligence, and others—a force of more than 150,000 people, spending upwards of $6 billion a year, and with influence within the American establishment far beyond these numbers. None are engaged in dirty tricks and dirty wars on the same scale as the CIA, most in fact limit themselves to intelligence. But the clandestine mentality is necessary for this work too, and inevitably it has spilled over to relations with the U.S. government, Congress, and the American people.[39]

In July 1983 the Center for National Security Studies, a watchdog organization that monitors such things, reported that a secret Army unit, called the Intelligence Support Activity, had been engaged in intelligence activities "without authorization and without reporting the actions to Congressional Committees, as required by law, between 1980 and 1982. . . . The Intelligence Support Activity provided assistance to former Special Forces Col. James (Bo) Gritz for an ostensibly private foray into Laos to search for American MIAs. The unit has also provided equipment to foreign governments."[40]

This failure to clear matters with congressional committees is a minor misdemeanor, but it is indicative of a frame of mind. The important thing about the intelligence community and the CIA is that they have carried their ethic into domestic byways, trampling on the civil liberties of American citizens and corrupting the very essence of the democratic process. It is in this way that the militarization of America leads us pellmell toward authoritarianism.

5

The Authoritarian Syndrome

In the Middle Ages wars were fought exclusively by the military class and the general population was virtually uninvolved. As technology has advanced, however, more and more civilians have become involved. Millions of workers and thousands of corporations today produce the ordnance that the military itself used to produce. Scientists and academics research and engineer a qualitatively new generation of weapons, and carry on a variety of psychological and social tasks such as propaganda and pacification. In addition, millions of people are inducted into the military or civil defense forces. Thus the civilian, like the soldier, has become a target for destruction by the enemy. Every worker that is killed and every factory that is immobilized reduces the supply of weaponry, food, and matèriel to the soldier on the battlefield. To be effective, then, the military must guarantee its "rear" as well as its "front." War today requires a total coordination between civilians in uniform and civilians in overalls—or, if you will, between "soldiers" in overalls and soldiers in uniform.

To fight a war in modern times a nation needs not only discipline at the front but "national unity"—discipline, conformity—behind the lines. The military has a definite stake in civilian morale. If a defeatist sentiment should develop, as it did during the Vietnam War, it can have a serious impact on the way the war is fought, or whether it can be fought at all. That is true not only of the traditional types of war, such as the Korea War, but for the secret wars conducted by the Central Intelligence Agency as well. If the public should become disenchanted with the National Security

State and demand that covert action be stopped, or if it should demand that the president accept checks on his power to make war, the military, the Central Intelligence Agency (CIA), the National Security Council (NSC), and all their sister organizations would be decisively hobbled.

It is well to recall that during both world wars the government took many steps to curb opposition, some of it clearly unconstitutional. On September 5, 1917, less than five months after the United States declared war on Germany, President Wilson's Department of Justice swooped down on the offices of the antiwar Industrial Workers of the World (IWW) in fifteen cities from Boston to Los Angeles, seized literature and records, and indicted 162 of its leading figures for violation of the Espionage Act. Needless to say, none of the Wobblies (as they were called) did any spying on behalf of the Kaiser or anyone else. Invoking the Act, therefore, was merely meant to silence their opposition to the war and the draft. A few days later a raid was conducted on the national headquarters of the Socialist Party, which also opposed the war. The raids, arrests, and convictions continued long into 1918. Two thousand Wobblies were rounded up in the first two months of that year and ninety-three were sentenced to terms ranging from ninety days to twenty years, plus fines totaling more than $2 million.

There were many other trials of antiwar leftists. Socialist Rose Pastor Stokes was given two years for writing a letter to the editor of the Kansas City *Star* in which she said "no government which is for the profiteers can also be for the people, and I am for the people while the government is for the profiteers."[1] The repression reached its peak with the June 1918 arrest of socialist leader and frequent presidential candidate, Eugene V. Debs, because of a speech in which he said: "the master class has always declared the war, the subject class has always fought the battles. The master class has had all to gain and nothing to lose, while the subject class has had nothing to gain and all to lose—especially their lives."[2]

Repression during World War II was more limited—primarily because Hitler and Nazism were universally hated—but the Roosevelt administration took a number of measures nonetheless to assure national unity, some that obviously skirted the law. Even before the war began Roosevelt secretly ordered the FBI—which since 1924 had lived under a policy set by Attorney General Harland Fiske Stone not to concern itself with "political or other opinions of individuals"—to begin investigation of fascists and communists. In 1940 Roosevelt authorized wiretapping "of persons suspected of subversive activities"—without warrants.[3] None of this was shared with the press, because the government, in the words of FBI Director J. Edgar Hoover, wanted "to avoid criticism or objections." In addition, pressure was put on the leadership of the trade union movement to give up the right to strike for the duration of the war—a fundamental and important right in times of peace. Byron Price, a former executive of the Associated Press, was put in charge of a censorship program which included self-censorship by the media under the guidance of Price and a staff of fifteen. The censorship of mail, cables, and communications was also conducted, but by a much larger staff of several thousand. Consequently, the mail of certain small leftist groups was held up. Further, a Custodial Detention Program was proclaimed with a "suspect list of individuals whose arrest might become necessary. . . ."[4] A month or two after the war began in Europe, Earl Browder, head of the Communist Party, was tried on the flimsy charge of passport irregularities and given the unusually harsh sentence of four years in prison. (He was released by Roosevelt a year later, after the Communist Party changed its position from antiwar to prowar.)

Of the greatest consequence, 110,000 Japanese-Americans, three-quarters of them born in the United States, were interned by the Army under President Roosevelt's Executive Order 9066. This policy, writes historian Howard Zinn, "came close to direct duplication of Fascism";[5] the majority of Americans now concede it was unjust. Other acts of the government include convicting eighteen leaders of the Trotskyist Socialist Workers Party on charges of conspiring to advocate the overthrow of the American government. They were sentenced to prison terms of twelve to sixteen months. Trotskyists—with barely a thousand members—were certainly not close to overthrowing the American government, but the government's real purpose in jailing their leaders was to warn others who might oppose the war effort.

In 1940 and 1941 Congress joined in imposing national unity on the United States. It passed two acts, the Smith Act, which made it a crime to advocate the violent overthrow of the government, and the Voorhis Act which required "subversive" organizations with "foreign" ties to register.

The objective of national unity was as demanding after World War II as it had been during the war. "The leaders of the postwar state," Robert Borosage observes, "viewed the public and Congress as objects to be manipulated in pursuit of their goals."[6] Their goals of course were to defend and expand an empire, and in pursuit of these goals they found it necessary to insulate the National Security State from criticism. Again, no one sat down to plan for a new national unity in minute detail, but like Topsy it just "grow'd" out of the circumstances. As the permanent war proceeded, the American establishment removed the American people from the decision-making process by applying to them the same methods it was using to create conformity overseas. While it did not go so far as to assassinate its opponents (it did, however, contemplate kidnappings) it conducted innumerable burglaries and break-ins; bribed people to spy on their neighbors; opened thousands of private letters; arranged for the blacklisting of many people from their jobs; made plans to place its critics in concentration camps; recruited thugs and criminals for its work; wiretapped the phones of critics with and without warrants; and knowingly violated the laws of the United States in the same way it violated the laws of Italy in 1947–48 or the laws of Guatemala in 1954.

Under the manipulation of the National Security State the American people have been effectively muzzled. Woodrow Wilson once stated that "so soon as you have a military class, it does not make any difference what your form of government is: if you are determined to be armed to the teeth, you must obey the orders and directions of the only men who can control the great machinery of war. Elections are of minor importance."[7] That is approximately what has happened to the United States since 1945–47. No matter who has been elected president or which party has been in control of Congress, military budgets have continued to rise, and restraints on the FBI, CIA, and other intelligence agencies have remained negligible.

Our government, for example, made no effort to reestablish formal or informal censorship of the press after World War II, but it achieved the same goal by withholding vital information and by outright deception and lying.

"Secrecy," notes a report prepared by the Library of Congress for the Senate Foreign Relations Committee in December 1971, "has been a factor in making foreign policy since the first days of the nation's history. . . . It is only in the period since the Second World War, however, that the problem of classified information has grown to its present dimensions."[8] The Atomic Energy Act, of course, cut off one big source of government activity from public purview. It was followed by the National Security Act of 1947, the Internal Security Act of 1950 (which made it a crime for a government official to turn over "classified" information to either a foreign agent or an adherent of a "communist organization") and a number of executive orders, culminating in Eisenhower's Executive Order 10501, which gave many federal departments and agencies the authority to "classify" government documents as secret, top secret, or confidential. Millions of documents were thereby kept from the public, not because they might feed valuable information to the Soviets, but because their divulgence would cause problems for the National Security State.

Among the bits of information withheld were items that had nothing to do with defense, but might reflect negatively on state officials. Ridiculous as it sounds, for instance, the menu for a dinner given for Queen Frederika of Greece at an American military base was stamped "classified" lest reporters comment on how lavish it was. A "secret" label was attached to newspaper clippings, already published, about a Navy communications project in Wisconsin. Some documents were classified out of bureaucratic constipation—when in doubt classify. Thus a weighty treatise on "The Shark Situation in the Waters About New York," published by the Brooklyn Museum before World War I, was designated secret. So too was a document by a physicist on bows and arrows.[9]

Many, probably most, of the documents were classified not because they might help the Russians if revealed but because they might cause difficulties with the American public. That is certainly true of the secrecy surrounding the establishment of the NSA in November 1952; its very existence was not acknowledged for five years. It is difficult to believe that the Russians didn't realize that the United States had facilities for intercepting telegrams and reading mail. The people who would have been most offended by this information were not the Russians, but the American people, some of whose mail was being opened by NSA. Even Congress was denied facts it needed to weigh pending legislation. A subcommittee of the Foreign Relations Committee looking into American commitments abroad, for instance, ruefully reported in December 1970 that the executive branch refused to enlighten it about tactical nuclear weapons because the "subject is of such high classification it could not be discussed before the Foreign Relations Committee under any circumstances."[10] Senator J. William Fulbright, then chairman of the Foreign Affairs Committee, correctly observed that "without information . . . Congress is scarcely able to oversee the execution of its laws, and if it cannot engage in these functions it is scarcely qualified to make the laws at all."[11]

There are provisions for declassifying documents after ten, twenty, or thirty years, but by that time the utility of the material is near zero. Even then, however, it is not automatically released to the press—but kept in government files which are open to zealous researchers only under an arduous Freedom of Information Act procedure. Even so the amount of material being "classified" must outstrip the amount being "declassified" by a wide margin. David Wise reports in his book *The Politics of Lying* that as of mid-1972, 43,586 people in the Departments of Defense, State, and Justice, and in the Atomic Energy Commission and the Executive Office had the right to classify documents. A Nixon executive order reduced the number to 16,238. A witness before the Moorhead subcommittee said that "hundreds of thousands of individuals at all echelons in the Department of Defense practice classification as a way of life."[12] Whatever the number of those authorized to classify, the amount of documents marked secret is monumental. A Pentagon witness before the Moorhead subcommittee estimated that a million cubic feet of the documents in the files of the Defense Department were "classified." According to the staff of the subcommittee, that would be equivalent to eighteen stacks each about the height of the Washington Monument—555 feet. "A legitimate system of restrictions," comments Arthur Schlesinger Jr., "grew after the Second World War into an extravagant and indefensible system of denial."[13]

It is inconceivable that Pentagon documents two miles high all contained secrets the Russians desperately sought, or that they had enough agents to procure them even under the best of circumstances. But secrecy became a mania in the United States during the permanent war. Richard M. Nixon, perhaps in an unguarded moment when the opposition party was in power, stated in 1951 that "the new test for classifying secret documents now seems to be not whether the publication of a document would affect the security of the nation but whether it would affect the political security of the Administration."[14]

President Kennedy, addressing the American Newspaper Publishers Association in 1961, urged them to use as a guideline for their news stories not whether it is news, but whether it is "in the interest of national security. . . . If the press is awaiting a declaration of war before it imposes the self-discipline of combat conditions, then I can only say that no war ever imposed a greater threat to our security. . . . The danger has never been more clear and its presence has never been more imminent."[15] A decade later General Maxwell Taylor, considered a liberal and intelligent officer, replied to the question as to whether the people had a right to know, that "I don't believe in that as a general principle." A citizen should only know, he said, "those things he needs to know to be a good citizen and discharge his functions."[16]

During the Reagan administration the government added an especially pernicious scheme to curb the public's right to know—it imposed censorship on its own employees. In March 1983 the president issued an executive order requiring employees with access to sensitive documents to clear in advance the full text of all speeches, articles, and books. In the past they had been merely required to sign a form stating they would not disclose the contents of classified material. Now they had to agree to submit their speeches and writings for approval, even after they had quit or retired, for the rest of their lives. According to the General Accounting Office, 156,000 officials and employees of the Defense Department were required to sign this secrecy agreement, plus many thousands in other departments. A study made by the *New York Times* indicated that in fact the censorship of present and past employees had begun two years before the Reagan executive order. The Defense Department had already reviewed 2,784 articles and books in 1981, 6,457 in 1982, and 10,088 in 1983.[17] President Reagan announced in 1984 that he had suspended the censorship provisions of his 1983 executive order, but the CIA continues an arrangement of this sort which long predated the Reagan order and there is little doubt that the matter will come up again. In December 1984 Undersecretary of Defense Fred C. Iklé announced that the administration would probably seek legislation to convict government officials who gave classified information to reporters. "We have decided to fight it on all fronts," he said of the growing number of news leaks.[18] Around the same time the Justice Department was seeking a court ruling that in effect would impose an official secrets act on the country. The frenzy to keep information hidden evidently does not yield to temporary setbacks.

As a corollary to withholding facts and opinions from within its own files, the government has set limits on access to ideas and information from abroad. The Reagan administration applied sections of the Foreign Agents Registration Act to inhibit contact with "dangerous" people, books, and films coming in from other countries. Nino Pasti, a former NATO general and former member of the Italian Senate, was denied a visa to the United States in 1983 to lecture here, presumably because of his opposition to the emplacement of cruise and Pershing II missiles in Europe. Hortensia Allende, widow of the assassinated president of Chile, was denied a visa to address California church groups on the grounds her speeches would be "prejudicial to the public interest." Tomas Borge, Nicaraguan Interior Minister was refused a visa because, in the words of a White House official, the government did not want to give him a "propaganda platform." In June 1982, 320 people from Australia, Africa, Canada, Europe, and Japan were refused permission to attend a United Nations Special Session on disarmament. Nobel prize winners Carlos Fuentes, Gabriel García Márquez, Csezlaw Milosz, French author Regis Debray, Italian playwright Dario Fo, and many others have also been excluded at various times because of their political beliefs, ones that Americans should have had an opportunity to hear and discuss. The same Foreign Agents Registration Act has been used to exclude books which the administration did not like, and to stamp as "propaganda" a number of films on such subjects as nuclear war and toxic waste.

How much secrecy and censorship has cost the American people is impossible to quantify. But there is no question that serious disasters would have been avoided if the American people had been given the true facts at critical moments. Had Americans known, for instance, that Washington was preparing an invasion of Cuba by an exile army in 1961, there is a good chance that the project would have had to be scrapped. The Kennedy administration evidently thought so because when it learned that the *New York Times* knew of the plans and might publish the story, it prevailed on the newspaper to withhold the item "in the national interest." After the fiasco President Kennedy told the *Times'* executive editor, Turner Catledge, that "if you had printed more about the invasion you would have saved us from a colossal mistake."

In his State of the Union address on January 20, 1961 Kennedy had assured Congress that "I shall withhold from neither the Congress nor the people any fact or report, past, present, or future, which is necessary for an informed judgment of our conduct or hazards." Certainly the American public was entitled to know of an act of war with such possible ramifications as the Bay of Pigs, but presidential rhetoric on the question of the public's right to know is seldom in tune with reality. For three years, for example, the Pentagon managed to keep secret from most members of Congress the fact that it had a MIRV program. MIRV—the multiwarhead missile that can be targeted so that each warhead hits an independent target—is not just another weapon. It changed the character of the nuclear arms race because with the same number of missiles it now became possible to mount three, four, ten times as many hydrogen bombs as previously. The "kill" capability of both sides grew astronomically, but the U.S. government evidently felt it was not necessary to share such knowledge with its constituency.

On January 17, 1966, a U.S. B-52 collided with a KC-135 refueling plane and exploded over the village of Palomares, Spain. In the process, it lost the four 25-megaton bombs it was carrying (each with a firepower 2,000 times as great as the bomb that fell on Hiroshima). Under some circumstances this might have become a major international crisis, for instance, if the bombs had fallen near the Czech border and large amounts of radiation had been released. The American people were clearly entitled to know what kind of risks their government was taking in their name. But for days thereafter Colonel Barnett "Skippy" Young, an Air Force information officer, insisted that the hundreds of men, planes, ships, and special equipment brought into the area on the double were searching only for "parts of the plane"—nothing was mentioned about the bombs or radiation. Finally two newsmen coaxed the story out of a garrulous sergeant that three of the four bombs had been recovered but "there's still a bomb missing." Colonel Young, however, continued to be mysteriously ambiguous. "Is there any risk of radiation," he was asked. "No comment." "Where can we get information, Colonel?" The reply: "From me. I have no comment to make about anything, and I cannot comment on why I have to say no comment."[19]

Here, as in so many instances, the information was not being withheld because it might give the Soviets gratuitous intelligence but because it is part of the military syndrome to be secretive, especially when an incident puts officials in a bad light. The Russians had an intelligence "trawler" in the waters nearby and undoubtedly could piece together what was happening. Every military reporter in the world knew that the Strategic Air Command was patrolling Europe with aircraft armed with nuclear weapons. The withholding of information was aimed only at the American people for fear they might learn that this was only one of at least thirteen similar accidents with nuclear weapons that had taken place in the previous eight years. Had they had such information, they might have questioned the policy of nuclear flights, and perhaps other aspects of the nuclear race.

The American people have spent trillions of dollars on the arms race since 1945, but how much of that was really necessary, how much was, instead, misspent because of a lack of information or because of misinformation? During the last decade the government has been telling the public that we desperately need a mobile, super-accurate missile because by the 1980s Soviet weapons would be so accurate they would be able to destroy all our 1,052 land-based missiles in a surprise attack. But an official "source . . . who had access to and had evaluated top-secret test data," told Reuters in March 1983 that Soviet rocket "accuracy isn't even within the ballpark of being able to launch a first strike against our Minutemen missile silos, not even with their large, powerful warheads." Other "sources" confirmed this estimate, and Professor Kosta Tsipis of MIT, a recognized nuclear authority, "also concludes," according to Reuters, "that the Pentagon has greatly exaggerated Soviet missile accuracy."[20] Who can tell where the truth lies? In the meantime, however, Americans are spoon-fed vague tales about how vulnerable we are to new Soviet missiles. Based on scant and unverified information, we are willing to spend billions of dollars on the MX, Trident, and other missiles to counter Soviet "accuracy."

Pulitzer prize winner, Thomas Powers, tells us in his book, *Thinking About the Next War*, that a secret national intelligence estimate by the CIA was suppressed by the Defense Secretary because it showed that "in the CIA's view Russia was not trying to achieve military superiority over the United States, was not planning a preemptive war against the United States, has a healthy respect for U.S. power and by implication understood that it could not bully the world but must reach an accommodation with the U.S."[21] Such a report obviously has great significance, for if it is true it indicates that our foreign and military policy is based on a wrong set of estimates. Yet the report Powers wrote about has never been made public. Instead, basing itself on the claim that the Russians are about to achieve or have already achieved military superiority, the Reagan administration in 1982 proposed a five-year $1.6 trillion military build-up.

On March 3, 1983, the story surfaced in the *New York Times* that the government was exaggerating Soviet military spending by 33 to 50 percent. Evidently leaked by a disaffected official in the CIA, the report claimed that "CIA specialists responsible for annual reviews of Soviet military spending now say that their previous estimates of increases of 3 to 4 percent each year, after inflation, may be wrong, and that the rate of growth may have been no more than 2 percent." The Defense Intelligence Agency disagrees with this estimate, but admits that while the Soviets have been spending more they have "been getting less" for their money because their industrial plant is inefficient. This internal debate in the Reagan administration has been studiously kept from popular review, though it obviously has earth-shaking significance for the nation. If we assume that the Soviet build-up is half what has been claimed, the American response might also be cut by half—say from $1.6 trillion to $800 billion. Or, the build-up might be eliminated entirely. The hundreds of billions made available thereby could be spent on health care, jobs, housing, schools, and other social improvements. The conflict between the United States and the Soviet Union might also thereby be mitigated. But by keeping the facts secret, the National Security State steers the nation in its own militarist direction.

The line between secrecy and lying—between withholding information and spreading misinformation—is a thin one and has been crossed by our leaders on numerous occasions. "Our government repeatedly resorts to lies in crises, where lies seem to serve its interests best," notes a former editor of the *Washington Post*, J. Russell Wiggins. "It will one day be unable to employ the truth effectively where truth would serve its interests best. The government that too readily rationalizes its right to lie in crises will never lack for either lies or crises."[22] Perhaps this is an overstatement but there have been far too many lies in far too many crises.

On April 19, 1960, in a letter to the Student Federation of Chile (which was publicized in the United States), President Eisenhower stated that "no official of this administration has ever made any public statements or committed any acts which may be reasonably construed as unfriendly toward the Cuban government and people." Just a month and two days earlier, as Eisenhower admitted a year later when he was out of office, the president had given the CIA instructions "to help these people [the Cuban exiles] organize and to help train them and equip them."[23] It's hard to imagine an act more unfriendly than training counterrevolutionaries to overthrow the Cuban government.

On April 28, 1965 President Lyndon Johnson went on television to announce he was sending the Marines into the Dominican Republic "in order to protect American lives." History has since proven that American lives had neither been lost nor were they in jeopardy. The real reason for the American invasion was to prevent a group of young officers, led by Colonel Francisco Caamano Deno, from restoring to office the legally elected president, Juan Bosch, who had been overthrown by an American-supported coup two years earlier. Later, on May 2, the president explained he had landed 22,000 troops because what began "as a popular democratic revolution" had been "placed into the hands of a band of communist conspirators." A list of fifty-three alleged communists, later enlarged to seventy-seven, was produced to justify the attack. None of these communists, it later turned out, had any position of command. "The Dominican people—not just a handful of communists—were fighting and dying for social justice and constitutionalism," said the *New York Times*. The Johnson claims were pure fiction. Among the more bizarre excuses used by the president was the statement made on June 17 that "some 1,500 innocent people were murdered and shot, and their heads cut off."[24] No one ever found those headless Dominicans but the deception had served its purpose.

A year or so earlier, on December 6, 1962, Pentagon information chief, Arthur Sylvester, made the startling statement that it's the government's basic right to lie in order to save itself when it's going up in a nuclear war. He was justifying the lies spread by the administration during the October Missile Crisis a month and a half before. After the storm of indignation that greeted this statement, Sylvester disowned it. In the process of disowning one statement, however, he made matters worse. Appearing before the Senate Permanent Investigations Subcommittee in March 1963, he declared that while the government does not have a right to lie to the people, it does have the right not to put out information that is going to help the enemy. If necessary, the government can mislead them. The "right to lie" seems to have become unalienable.

Spoon-fed "facts" placate the public rather than inform it. "Facts," for instance about casualties. "Once again," reads a dispatch in the *Chicago Daily News* (February 7, 1967), "the Pentagon has been caught in a credibility gap in connection with Vietnam. It has now acknowledged that U.S. aircraft losses there are three times as high as the officially announced figure." Previously DoD had confined its disclosures to the 622 combat planes lost from January 2, 1961 to January 31, 1967, but it now conceded that "planes lost in accidents, lost on the ground from enemy sabotage and mortar fire, or planes that ran out of fuel and had to ditch at sea" brought the figure up to 1,172—plus another 600 helicopters lost."

Another example: During his confirmation hearings as Secretary of State Henry Kissinger stated categorically that "the CIA had nothing to do with the coup [against Salvador Allende in Chile]."[25] But, as we have seen earlier, CIA director William Colby, testifying in April 1974, stated that the Forty Committee, which Kissinger directed, gave approval to such CIA activities. Richard Helms, a previous CIA director, made the same claim as Kissinger did in his May 1973 testimony. In January 1975, however, Helms admitted what everyone now knows, namely that the CIA had been heavily involved in undermining and ousting the Allende regime. (At the same hearing, incidentally, Helms conceded that he had been short of the truth two years earlier when he stated that the CIA had not engaged in domestic spying and wiretapping.)

Virtually every covert action brings in its wake a credibility gap. "We are not doing anything to try and overthrow the Nicaraguan government," said President Reagan in April 1983.[26] That same month he also made the claim that "Our purpose, in conformity with American and international law, is to prevent the flow of arms to El Salvador, Honduras, Guatemala and Costa Rica." This obviously made no sense, since the Reagan administration had been wheedling tens of millions of dollars from Congress for the contras who were certainly intent on overthrowing the Sandinista government. A manual prepared by the CIA for the contras, *Psychological Operations in Guerrilla Warfare*, gave them instructions on "neutralizing" adversaries and predicted that "when the infiltration and internal subjected control have been developed in a manner parallel to other guerrilla activities, a commander of ours will literally be able to shake up the Sandinista structure and replace it." Although both William Colby of the CIA and Ronald Reagan tried to dance around the meaning of the word *neutralization*, there was no doubt in the minds of responsible journalists that it was in fact a mandate for assassination. Among other things the tract called for kidnapping, blackmail, the recruitment of criminals, and "neutralizing." Congressman Norman Mineta asked the Reagan regime to explain "Why do you need this manual if you are there only for arms interdiction" to the Salvadoran guerrillas?[27]

Sometimes the government hides the very existence of an intelligence agency, as was the case with the NSA. Another, which came to light in 1983, concerned the Army's Intelligence Support Activity (ISA) which was quietly organized in 1980 to bypass congressional oversight procedures. From 1980 to 1983 "The Activity," as it was called, engaged in at least ten clandestine missions, including a foray into Laos, activities in Africa and Central America, and sundry others. Why the Pentagon, which already had a number of spy agencies under its roof, including the Defense Intelligence Agency, needed another one was not made clear.

Control of information gives the American government the ability to manufacture public opinion. For years various U.S. administrations have accused Muammar Khadafy, Libya's controversial leader, of being a terrorist bent on overthrowing numerous governments. It was not until 1980–82, however, that Americans learned from reports in *The Middle East* magazine, *Time*, the *New York Times*, the *Wall Street Journal*, and *Newsweek*, that in fact the United States itself had been involved in plots to overthrow Khadafy at least as far back as 1977.[28] That year the CIA prevailed on the French intelligence service (SDECE) to take covert action against Libya. With the support of the Egyptian government guerrilla bands were infiltrated into the North African state, but to no avail. According to reports in the *New York Times* two years later, another attempt was made in 1980, this time with American, Egyptian, and Saudi Arabian support. Again the raids were ill-fated, but the United States persevered. From leaks to leading U.S. journals, as reported by Jay Peterzell of the Center for National Security Studies, it is now evident that there was talk in February 1981 between American and French intelligence services of assassinating Khadafy. The plan aborted because French President Valéry Giscard d'Estaing was defeated at the polls that year.

Still the secret plotting continued. Peterzell notes that in May 1981 the *New York Daily News* "reported that U.S. officials (later identified as Secretary of State Alexander Haig) had begun describing Khadafy as a 'cancer that has to be cut out' and that a secret plan was drafted to use Egypt and other moderate Arab states to overthrow Khadafy either by fomenting a coup or a military invasion." In July of that year *Newsweek* carried a detailed story of how the Libyan government was to be overthrown, but a day later the Reagan administration passed the word that it was not Libya against whom covert action was planned but Mauritania, on Africa's west coast. Within a few hours the Mauritanian government was raising the roof with Washington. Whereupon the *Wall Street Journal* and the *Washington Post* were encouraged to write that the planned subversion was against Mauritius, an island on the Indian Ocean, not Mauritania. As other publications soon verified, of course, the target *was* Libya.

By keeping its own intention of secret intervention hidden the Reagan administration was able to paint the Libyan leader in the darkest terms. It pictured him as a prime source of political criminality around the world and let out the word that he had organized a "hit squad" to kill Reagan himself. Guards at the Mexican border were alerted to keep a wary eye out for the Libyan would-be assassins, and American oil companies were ultimately prevailed on to remove their employees from Libya. Whatever one may think of Khadafy and his government, however, it is indisputable that the United States—even before Reagan—had been plotting terrorist acts against the Libyan leader for some years before there was any hint of misdeeds on the other side.

Control of information may also give some government officials the power of political blackmail. For many years it was rumored that J. Edgar Hoover of the FBI had dossiers on the private lives of government officials and members of Congress which gave him power to make them dance to his tune. This was a power far beyond what we would expect for a subordinate in the Justice Department. The rumors were never substantiated and no one in Congress ever had the courage to ask for an investigation. After Hoover passed on, his successor Clarence Kelley was asked by Congressman Don Edwards's Civil Rights Subcommittee whether the FBI in fact did have such files. He denied it, but eleven months later confirmed that it did. By this time not much could be done about the matter; it was now grist to the mill of historians, not for day-to-day politicians.

Perhaps the most damaging deception of our times was the one that plunged us into a major war in Vietnam. The worst defeat in U.S. history might have been averted if Lyndon Johnson had told the American people the truth of what happened in the Tonkin Gulf immediately after the events of August 1964.[29]

In June 1971 the *New York Times* began publishing excerpts from the Pentagon Papers. This was a top-secret history of the war, consisting of 2.5 million words and commissioned by Defense Secretary Robert S. McNamara in 1967. Neil Sheehan of the *Times* reported that "for six months prior to the Tonkin Gulf incident in August 1964, the United States had been mounting clandestine military attacks against North Vietnam" and had actually drafted a congressional resolution giving it the power to intervene. It was merely waiting for a propitious incident to introduce it. A target list for bombing

North Vietnam had been drawn up in May 1964 and air strike forces had already been deployed for the opening phase of the bombing months before the alleged Tonkin Gulf incidents took place.[30]

The ensuing war was the longest in American history, and our defeat in it the most costly reverse we have ever suffered. It also took some 60,000 American and 2 million Vietnamese lives, and changed the world's perception of American power to the point where the oil countries were able to thumb their nose at the colossus of the Western Hemisphere and raise petroleum prices accordingly. America's position as a world power suffered immensely; the effects are still with us. It is not at all certain, however, that Congress or the public would have permitted the war to take place if it had known the true facts about Tonkin and the deceptions practiced by Johnson. Or, whether they would have allowed the war to continue as long as it did if they had been told of the mood of pessimism that prevailed in high places early on. The Pentagon Papers revealed, for instance, that as early as November 1965 McNamara was warning Johnson that the reinforcements he was approving could "not guarantee success," and in January 1966, the third-ranking official in the Defense Department, John T. McNaughton, expressed the fear that the United States was caught in "an escalating military stalemate." In October 1966 McNamara reported that "pacification" of the South Vietnamese population "has, if anything gone backward" and that the bombing of North Vietnam which Johnson felt would have great effect has neither "significantly affected the infiltration" of North Vietnamese forces into South Vietnam or "cracked the morale of Hanoi."[31]

The war in Vietnam could not have continued for seven long years if the Johnson and Nixon administrations had told the American people the truth and shared their doubts with them. And the permanent war, of which Vietnam was a segment, could not have been sustained for four decades if dissent had not been emasculated Denial of the right-to-know through secrecy and lying was one side of this campaign to prevent an effective opposition from forming. The other was to create a general atmosphere of fear, behind which the National Security State sought to silence nascent leaderships that challenged militarism and imperialism. To keep a whole nation at bay, it wasn't necessary for the government to muzzle everyone, only to take reprisals against the relatively few people who might offer guidance and direction. It was a strategy that did not succeed entirely, but it succeeded more than it failed, and it laid the groundwork for future campaigns against dissenters that may be more successful.

When President Truman decided to finance Greece's war against communist guerrillas in 1947, Arthur Vandenberg, Republican leader of the Senate, warned him that it would be necessary "to scare hell out of the country [i.e., the United States]," if he wanted to get congressional approval. The advice was most useful in promoting the permanent war. A few years before the Soviets tested their first atomic device and long before they had acquired long range bombers and missiles to deliver them, Lieutenant General Leslie R. Groves warned that in the first five hours of an atomic attack 40 million Americans would perish, and General Carl A. Spaatz insisted that it would be too late once the bombs started falling for any kind of defense. Both statements were wildly untrue at the time, especially since the Russians did not have as yet a single atom bomb. But by drawing an ominous picture of Russian strength the military was able to win approval of a $12 billion budget (a large sum at that time) for fiscal 1948. General Douglas MacArthur, no dove, warned in a speech to the Michigan State Legislature in 1952 that "our country is now geared to an arms economy which was bred in an artificially induced psychosis of war hysteria and nurtured upon an incessant propaganda of fear."[32]

As we noted earlier, 88 percent of the American people consider the Soviet Union hostile to us, and 71 percent believe it intends to make war on us. The propaganda of fear still obtains, and it is useful for wheedling ever larger sums out of Congress for the Pentagon. False images of the "Soviet threat" unfortunately have reinforced the American government's induced popular fear that the Russians can't be trusted, that if we don't spend more on weaponry they will soon be able to "take us over."[33]

Given this propaganda of fear the militarized state has destroyed or weakened most of the forces that might challenge it. This is particularly true for the Communist party during the first postwar years. At its peak the party could claim 80,000 to 100,000 members, 1 to 2 million sympathizers, and the support of eleven national CIO unions whose leaders were procommunist. One means of harassing the isolated left at that time was to use congressional committees, such as the House Committee on Un-American Activities (HUAC), Senator Joseph McCarthy's Internal Security Committee, or Senator James O. Eastland's Internal Security Subcommittee, for what amounted to nonjudicial prosecution. The hearings of these committees were not trials, but many communists or ex-communists who refused to name associates were eventually tried for contempt of Congress and imprisoned. Others found themselves blacklisted and lost their jobs.

In June 1947 leaders of the Joint Anti-Fascist Refugee Committee were sentenced to six months in jail and fined $500 for failing to turn over their records to HUAC. A few months later ten well-known Hollywood figures, the Hollywood Ten, were given sentences of up to a year and fines of $1,000 each for refusing to discuss their political beliefs or their former associates in the communist milieu. More important, they were blacklisted from their jobs. Eugene Dennis, a former seaman and teamster who was then general secretary of the Communist party, defied HUAC by claiming it was illegally constituted. He went to jail for a year and was fined $1,000.

Many similar cases caught the headlines, each one catering to latent fears and building a mood for continued reprisals. No one has ever tabulated the number of people discharged because they were named as communists, fellow travelers, or "Fifth-Amendment" communists (people who refused to answer on the ground that the Fifth Amendment to the Constitution protected them against self-incrimination). Many victims preferred to remain in obscurity in the hope of finding other work, but the figure is estimated by civil libertarians at many thousands. After the Soviet Union exploded the first atom bomb in 1949 and with the onset of the Korean War, the anticommunist crusade was picked up by Senator Joseph McCarthy of Wisconsin and "McCarthyism" became a synonym around the world for wild charges and flagrant transgressions of freedom.

The Communist party was not declared illegal—though a proposal to outlaw it was once considered by Secretary of Labor Lewis K. Schwellenbach—but it was so handicapped in its operations it could not function as a normal organization. There was almost no place in the country, for instance, where it could rent a hall. The Taft-Hartley law requiring unionists to sign affidavits that they did not belong to the Communist party or other "subversive" organizations was intended to force communists to disclose their identity to union members, whereupon, it was assumed, they would be made to resign. It was not as effective as expected because ways were found to get around it—by a pro forma resignation from the party for instance. Nevertheless a group of unionists in Cleveland were sent to jail for "conspiring" to evade the affidavit requirement, and leaders of the Mine, Mill, and Smelter Workers Union were put on trial at various times during the next decade and a half on similar, though not identical, charges.

A second law, the McCarran Act, passed during the Korean crisis, required communist, "Communist-front," and "Communist-infiltrated" organizations to turn over their membership lists to the government and to label their publications "communist." Members of such vaguely defined groups were prohibited from applying for passports or holding jobs in unions or the defense industry. If they were noncitizens they could be deported, and if recently naturalized, denaturalized. The penalty for nonregistration was a $10,000 fine and five years in prison for each day of noncompliance. While the cost of litigation drained communist energies and depleted communist coffers, the McCarran Act did not have its anticipated effect. More recently the McCarran Act has been used by the Reagan administration as a lever to deny hundreds of foreigners entry to this country to give speeches or attend United Nations disarmament sessions.

The one law that did do considerable injury to the communists was the Smith Act passed in 1940—the same one under which eighteen Trotskyists went to jail during the war. On July 20, 1948, twelve leaders of the Communist party were arrested on the charge of conspiring to "teach and advocate the overthrow and destruction of the Government of the United States by force and violence." Eleven were convicted in a prolonged nine-month trial (one was too sick to be prosecuted) and sent to jail for three to five years. One hundred and eighteen secondary leaders were also convicted, but all but one had their sentences reversed by the higher courts.

The worst blow of all to the Communist party was the loss of its base in the trade union movement, specifically in the CIO. In the growing anti-communist temper of the nation, the communists began to lose friends and allies at an accelerated pace. Joseph Curran, of the National Maritime Union, severed his links by 1947. In the process he cut to shreds a party faction in his union that at one time had numbered almost a thousand. Michaell Quill of the Transport Workers' Union similarly turned against the alliance with the communists he had maintained for fourteen years. Walter Reuther defeated a faction with a large communist segment in the United Auto Workers (UAW). By 1949 the CIO had expelled all twelve "communist-dominated" unions. All but a handful disintegrated; neither the communists nor any leftist political force has played a significant role in the House of Labor since then.

The Communist Party was driven into a twilight zone where it was not outlawed, yet could not function as an open party. It had to take elaborate precautions to guard its members from informers. Its sympathizers were loath to attend rallies for fear of being photographed and identified by FBI agents and police red squads. Landlords refused to rent halls or offices to the Party. Readers of its publications, and of other leftist sheets, canceled subscriptions to avoid being listed in FBI or HUAC files. Here and there factory workers were beaten up by fellow workers simply because they had been subpoenaed by HUAC or named by Senator McCarthy.

The Communist party was vulnerable because it slavishly followed the policies of Moscow at a time when public opinion here was so hostile to those policies. But it was a legal party under American law and neither it nor its members were charged with any overt crimes. There was no reason for congressional committees to harass it or for the government to prosecute its leaders. It was tormented only because it disagreed with the policies of the U.S. government, and it might have given leadership to many who similarly disagreed. Professors Bernard Karsh and Phillips L. Garman of the University of Illinois estimated that the communists controlled outright, unions with at least a quarter of the CIO membership (at that time a virile labor organization) and "wielded powerful influence" in unions with another quarter. Had the communists retained their position they might have organized militant strikes for economic demands and might have mobilized millions of people to oppose the anti-Soviet foreign policy of the Truman administration. The virtual destruction of the party and its labor base helped the National Security State enforce conformity and "national unity" to an extent that otherwise would have been impossible.

Under the shield of democratic expression and due process of law the Communist party might have suffered reverses, but it would not have been immobilized in the way it was after 1947. The National Security State deprived dissidents of their constitutional rights to free speech and privacy. It disrupted their meetings, operations, and personal lives. It hired provocateurs to initiate violence against them or to frame them for violent acts. Its aim, as with foreign adversaries, was to make it impossible for them to function effectively.

The U.S. government in the past had committed excesses in the name of "security." It is generally agreed today that the Alien and Sedition Acts of 1789 were a transgression on constitutional liberty (the former allowed for deportation of aliens who threatened "the peace and safety" of the nation, the latter punished those who published "false, scandalous and malicious writing" against the government). They were rescinded within a relatively short time. President Lincoln's suspension of habeas corpus during the Civil War falls into the same category. It too, however, was a temporary measure. The prosecution of opponents of World War I, the Palmer Raids and deportations that followed the war, and the incarceration of 120,000 Japanese-Americans and Japanese citizens during World War II were also blots on the escutcheon of democratic freedom, and most people today would admit they were grievous mistakes. But all these transgressions differed from those of the FBI, CIA, and similar agencies during the present permanent war. In the former instances the actions of government agencies were taken in the open by the authority of a specific (though ill-advised) law or an executive order by the president. The victim knew what was happening and could challenge the action in court—though he had little chance of reversing the injustice. During the permanent war since 1945–47 the action against dissidents has been, as described by the Senate Intelligence Committee, "generally covert. It is concealed from its victims and is seldom described in statutes or explained in executive orders. The victim may never suspect that his misfortunes are the intended result of activities undertaken by his government, and accordingly may have no opportunity to challenge the actions taken against him."[34]

The government in fact acts illegally against political opponents or would-be opponents because it knows that legal action, in the courts, would be unavailing. Department of Justice guidelines for the FBI in

1956 authorized "preventive action" where there is a possibility that violence may occur in the future and where "prosecution is impracticable." In other words the FBI was authorized to do harm to individuals and groups who had not violated any laws but who *might* do so in the future—a characterization that probably fits all of us, including the FBI. By the time the Senate Intelligence Committee wrote its report in 1976 this specific guideline had been dropped, but, notes the Committee, "the principle has not been rejected." The FBI still operates on a thesis of "preventive action," as does the CIA and other agencies. By way of example, an FBI field office in St. Louis sent a letter to the husband of an activist advising him that his wife was sexually unfaithful. The letter, said an FBI report, "contributed strongly" to the breakup of the marriage. Another anonymous letter by the Bureau in Mobile caused two instructors to be put on probation by their university. The mother of the well-known activist, Stokeley Carmichael, was "shocked" by a telephone call advising her that her son would be killed by members of the Black Panther Party. An FBI internal memorandum took credit for Carmichael's flight to Africa the next day.[35]

It is impossible to read the record of the intelligence community's activities since World War II without realizing that its central domestic purpose is to abolish dissent. All that stands in its way is the U.S. Constitution, but the FBI, CIA, and local police forces who have worked with them, repeatedly circumvent the Constitution, and commit acts for which ordinary citizens would go to jail for long periods. The people who do this do not consider themselves criminals; on the contrary they think of themselves as patriots. They believe they have the right to violate the law and to injure ordinary citizens with whom they disagree because they feel the nation is in a permanent emergency and that they are serving a higher purpose. The tension between the police state elements in our government and the American democratic tradition is constantly strained, but on the few occasions when the democratic process has stalled the illegality of the "second government," the second government has retreated temporarily only to find new methods and new institutional umbrellas in order to continue doing the same thing.

By way of example: In the early postwar years the main weapons used against the communists and other political nonconformists were the various congressional investigations, the loyalty and security programs, and the Smith Act. Taken together they not only punished or inhibited scores of thousands of activists but cast a conformist pall over the whole nation. As we mentioned earlier, in 1956 when it became apparent that the Smith Act might be declared unconstitutional or difficult to enforce because of stricter rules of evidence, the FBI instituted a new program called COINTELPRO (counterintelligence program) to spy on groups and people they considered opponents, burglarize their offices, tap their telephones, disrupt their meetings, spread false information about them, and in general reduce them to impotency. "The Supreme Court rulings had rendered the Smith Act technically unenforceable . . . made it impossible to prosecute Communist Party members at the time," lamented James B. Adams, the number three man in the FBI. COINTELPRO—defined by the Senate Intelligence Committee as "a sophisticated vigilante operation aimed squarely at preventing the exercise of First Amendment rights of free speech and association"—[36] was a means of doing the same thing in a somewhat different way. The victims were given no opportunity to defend themselves. Many, perhaps most, did not even know the FBI was engaged in a vendetta against them. The FBI, says the Senate Intelligence Committee report, "adopted extralegal methods to counter perceived threats to national security and public order because the ordinary legal processes were believed insufficient to do the job. In essence, the Bureau took the law into its own hands, conducting a sophisticated vigilante operation against domestic enemies."[37] Under the implicit guidelines of the various intelligence campaigns, an ordinary citizen was assumed to be guilty until proven innocent.

Originally there were seven counterintelligence programs. Five programs were against the Communist Party, the Socialist Party (followers of the former Soviet leader Leon Trotsky), White Hate Groups—such as the Ku Klux Klan—the New Left (especially Students for a Democratic Society), and black extremists (in particular the Black Panther Party). The remaining two programs were against "hostile foreign intelligence sources, foreign Communist organizations and individuals connected with them." Attorney General William B. Saxbe, who made these facts public in 1974, revealed the ambivalence of our two-tiered government when he stated that

COINTELPRO engaged in "practices that can only be considered abhorent in a free society." Six months later, Attorney General Edward H. Levi revealed that in fact there had been at least five other counterintelligence programs at various times. One was the Puerto Rican Bomber Program (1966) in which the FBI attempted on thirty-seven occasions to disrupt organizations favoring Puerto Rican independence. A second program was Operation Hoodwink, also started in 1966, in which the Bureau tried to initiate a little war between the national crime syndicate, the Mafia, and the Communist Party. "A dispute between the Communist Party, USA, and La Cosa Nostra," read a 1966 FBI memorandum, "would cause disruption of both groups." The other three programs, Levi said, were "classified."

All told, over a fifteen-year period, the FBI had planned 3,247 disruptive actions against American organizations, of which 2,370 were actually implemented. That the FBI was less interested in prosecution than in taking the law into its own hands is indicated by the statistics supplied by the General Accounting Office (GAO). Only 3 percent of the FBI's domestic intelligence campaigns resulted in any prosecutions (one out of thirty-three), and of these less than half led to convictions.

The Senate Intelligence Committee report of 1976 shed further light on COINTELPRO. Apparently before the program had been instituted in 1956, disruptive activities against the left, blacks, and others were conducted on an ad hoc basis. COINTELPRO, however, formalized and expanded such incidents. While it existed for fifteen years, COINTELPRO was officially interred only in 1971. Evidently the reason this happened was because of exposés such as Fred Cook's 1964 volume, *The FBI Nobody Knows*, critical books by a number of former FBI agents, and material released by a group of radicals who burglarized the offices of the FBI in the Pennsylvania town of Media, which showed that in the process of trying to discredit political opponents and prevent "security leaks" the FBI had conducted seventeen wiretaps against newsmen and former government officials. At the same time the Socialist Workers Party filed suit, revealing still more disruptive activities. And the Rockefeller Commission, which was investigating the CIA, found as a juicy byproduct of its study that the CIA and FBI had been engaged in a joint program to open the mail of American citizens.

In the light of all this, and pending congressional investigations, the FBI officially jettisoned COINTELPRO. But there was some doubt, at least in the mind of the Senate Intelligence Committee, that the program had really ended. "COINTELPRO-type activities may continue today," it observed, "under the rubric of 'investigations.' "[38] The Committee was able to trace at least three such operations after the program was supposed to have ended, and hinted that there might have been more.

The extralegal campaign against dissent began with the compilation of lists of communists, Trotskyists, antiwar activists, New Leftists, black leaders. Back in 1924 when Attorney General Harlan Fiske Stone reorganized the Bureau of Investigation (the predecessor of the FBI) and appointed J. Edgar Hoover as its chief, he set two guidelines: "The Bureau of Investigation is not concerned with political or other opinions of individuals. It is concerned only with their conduct and then only with such conduct as is forbidden by the laws of the United States."[39] But FBI programs beginning with the pre-World War II period, and accelerating after the war, concerned themselves with vast numbers of people whose opinions, not their acts, were the issue. Few, if any, had committed prosecutable crimes. The FBI, nevertheless, compiled a half-million files, each dealing with one or more individuals or organizations. The total number of "dangerous" or potentially dangerous people, by FBI standards, was approximately a million—not including files in field offices around the country. The CIA quickly followed suit by also entering the business of files and lists. Under Operation CHAOS it gathered information on 300,000 people and groups—no doubt duplicating many of those in FBI files. Started under President Johnson, in the 1960s, the CIA's rationale for CHAOS was that the Agency needed information about Americans who had links to foreign "enemies." Actually the purpose was to gather material on men and women who were active in the campaign to end the war in Vietnam, and this was a clear violation of the CIA mandate as prescribed by the 1947 National Security Act.

The Army, for its part, used 1,500 undercover agents (as of 1968) to infiltrate domestic organizations and gather information on 100,000 individuals and groups. Even the Internal Revenue Service (IRS) was enrolled to investigate 2,300 organizations listed as "Old Left," "New

Left," and "Right Wing" to see whether their tax-exempt status could be withdrawn, as well as 10,000 to 16,000 "officers, members and affiliates of activist, extremist and revolutionary organizations," whose personal taxes were reviewed to see if they could be financially punished for their dissent.

From amongst the various lists, the FBI compiled, a special "Security List" varying from 11,000 to 20,000 people who were to be placed in concentration camps in case of a "crisis." In 1950 Congress had passed an Emergency Detention Act which established standards for those who would be incarcerated (there had to be "reasonable ground to believe" they would probably "engage in acts of espionage and sabotage") and provided for hearings after arrest. But to punctuate the police state frame of mind of the "second government," Attorney J. Howard McGrath instructed the FBI to disregard Congress and "proceed with the program as previously outlined," because the law was "undoubtedly in conflict with the Department's [own] proposed detention program."[40]

Compiling such lists is not as innocent an endeavor as the intelligence agencies make out. To begin with, the material is assembled by agents and paid informants whose proclivity is to see the dark side of the people they are investigating. Morton Halperin, a former aide to Henry Kissinger, and three associates who wrote *The Lawless State*, estimate that in the 1950s one-third of the FBI staff, about 1,600 agents, and 5,000 paid "subversive informants" were infiltrating organizations to gather names and data. Since the informers were sometimes paid on an incentive basis their zeal for identifying "communists," "communist supporters," and "radicals" often went far beyond the bounds of objectivity; so too the program itself. The FBI was not satisfied to probe the Communist Party; under the COMINFIL (communist-infiltration) program, initiated in the early postwar period, the Bureau went far afield to ferret out "communist infiltration." It investigated moderate and innocent organizations such as the National Association for the Advancement of Colored People (NAACP), the Committee for a Sane Nuclear Policy (SANE), the American Friends Service Committee (a Quaker organization), Women Strike for Peace, Martin Luther King, Jr.'s Southern Christian Leadership Conference, and similar groups, on the theory that they might be harboring communists. The U.S. Attorney General stated in his 1955 annual report that FBI investigations under this program covered "the entire spectrum of the social and labor movement in this country"—political groups, black groups, veterans groups, religious groups, labor unions, farm groups, youth organizations, the women's movement.[41] The penetration was necessary, it avowed, to "fortify" the government against "subversive pressures," not to enforce any laws necessarily, but to strengthen the government's hand against political opponents.

To get the facts on their quarries the agents and informants often broke the law themselves by turning the Bureau, the CIA, and all other agencies who participated in the intelligence crusade, into extralegal institutions with a double standard in legal and moral matters. One standard obtained to themselves—the right to act lawlessly in the interests of a "higher" purpose. The second standard applied to groups and institutions which disagreed with the official viewpoint. Spying for political purposes has been anathema to the American tradition from the beginning of the Republic because it chills political discussion. Many people, for example, are loath to come to meetings or speak up at them for fear the FBI will be reporting their words and associations. The spies themselves participate in the proceedings in order to gain acceptance, and sometimes even become officers of the organizations they spy on to subvert them. Thus Mary Jo Cook was recruited by the FBI in 1973 to infiltrate the Vietnam Veterans Against the War (VVAW) in Buffalo. The FBI, she later said, wanted her to report on meetings, identify everyone she could, their relationships with each other (including "who they were sleeping with") and other data. To get that kind of information she accepted a leading role in VVAW, went to regional and national meetings, stole VVAW mailing lists which she turned over to the FBI, and stole position papers and legal documents the VVAW had developed for use in pending trials against them in Florida and New Jersey. She also reported on groups outside the VVAW—"I ended up reporting on groups like the United Church of Christ, American Civil Liberties Union, the National Lawyers Guild, liberal church organizations [which] quite often went into coalition with the [VVAW]." In November 1974 Cook quit as an FBI informant because she felt the VVAW was a lawful organization, but in the meantime she had furnished information on 1,000 people.[42]

To gather information, then, the FBI, as well as local police red squads and other intelligence agencies, often violate the law themselves. Incomplete estimates offered by the FBI to the Senate Select Committee on Intelligence indicated that FBI agents had committed 239 burglaries ("surreptitious entries") against "at least fifteen domestic subversive targets" from 1942 through April 1968, plus another 509 secret entries without warrants to install microphones against 420 separate targets, all between 1960 and 1975. "We do not obtain authorization for 'black bag' jobs from outside the Bureau," reads a 1966 FBI memo. "Such a technique involves trespass and is clearly illegal; therefore, it would be impossible to obtain any legal sanction for it." Nonetheless, says the memo, "black bag" jobs "represent an invaluable technique" in "combatting subversives," and presumably must be continued. Mailing lists, files, and records were also stolen in less harrowing ways; by picking them off a desk while the receptionist was occupied, for example, or by pilfering from filing cabinets while volunteering for clerical work. But these too were crimes which the "law enforcement" authorities blithely overlooked.

The information gathered on dissidents was the first step toward disrupting nonconformist groups—especially on the leftist side of the spectrum—and, if possible, driving them out of business. An FBI memorandum of July 1968 lists a dozen types of activities for agents and informants, including the publication of "leaflets designed to discredit student demonstrators"; spreading the false words that New Left leaders are "informants" for the FBI; instigating "personal conflicts or animosities" between New Left leaders; using "friendly news media" and law enforcement officials to disrupt New Left coffee houses near military bases; using cartoons, photographs, and anonymous letters to "ridicule" the New Left; and using "misinformation" to "confuse and disrupt" New Left activities such as notifying members that events have been canceled.[44]

Information and dirty tricks complemented each other. The information was rarely used for a legal prosecution but, rather, to compromise and create difficulties for groups and individuals who disagreed with the National Security State on such issues as the arms race or civil rights. A few examples will suffice: In 1968 the National Mobilization Committee to End the War in Vietnam was preparing for demonstrations at the Democratic Party convention in Chicago and soliciting sites from sympathizers to house out-of-towners. Agents of the Chicago FBI filled out 217 forms with fictitious names and addresses so that demonstrators would make long and useless journeys to non-existent houses and, consequently, become angry with their leaders. The same thing happened prior to a much larger demonstration in Washington a year later. The Washington Field Office, noting the citizen band employed by the National Mobilization to coordinate activities of the demonstration, used the same citizen band to supply misinformation and countermand orders. The result, of course, was considerable chaos. Spies and agents were generally instructed to create dissension wherever possible. An FBI informant, for instance, spread the word that the leader of one faction of SDS was buying drugs with movement money, that a second leader had embezzled funds. The Field Office reported that "as a result of actions taken by this informant there have been fist fights and acts of name calling at several of the recent SDS meetings." In another instance a San Diego informant spread the rumor that a 30-year-old group leader was "either a bisexual or homosexual" in the hopes the rumor would cause disarray in the ranks. Here and there the Bureau set up chapters of the Communist Party made up exclusively of FBI agents, in the hopes of initiating a national faction fight in communist ranks.[45]

The gamut of dirty tricks against American citizens was only limited by human imagination. Dr. Morris Starsky was dismissed by Arizona State University after the FBI mailed anonymous letters to faculty members considering renewal of his teaching contract, informing them he was a member of the Socialist Workers Party.

The Bureau used a host of devices, under its "snitch jacket" technique to neutralize targets by spreading false rumors that someone was an FBI informant. Legitimate communists were driven from their party and legitimate peace activists from their movements by such hoaxes. Employers were informed of the political affiliation of leftists, causing not a few to be fired. Here and there the Bureau also interfered with the judicial process. An anonymous letter was sent by the FBI to a county prosecutor, for instance, advising him that a student leader who had participated in a demonstration had "subversive connections"—the faceless accuser claimed that the woman's adoptive father was a Communist Party member. Even the electoral process was not immune to dirty tricks—the FBI secretly mailed a letter to a list of conservative people underscoring the fact that a Midwest lawyer, running for a city council post, had represented "subversives." The Bureau also contacted a "confidential source" within the Mellon Foundation to deny a $150,000 grant to Unity Corporation, a black group; the organization subsequently went bankrupt. Local police were encouraged by the FBI to arrest as many leaders as possible of the Student Nonviolent Coordinating Committee (SNCC) in 1967 "on every possible charge until they could no longer make bail." As a result, the SNCC leaders spent a good part of the summer in jail. Even worse, the FBI exacerbated the hostility between two black groups, the Black Panther Party and an organization called US, until it led to serious violence. A series of cartoons were produced to intensify the bad feelings. An FBI memo, headed "Tangible Results," notes that though "no specific counterintelligence action can be credited with contribution to the overall situation" of shootings, beatings, and "a high degree of unrest in the ghetto area of Southeast San Diego," it "is felt that a substantial amount of the unrest is directly attributable to this [FBI] program."[46]

The FBI not infrequently acted as agent provocateur. In a 1970 lawsuit the Alabama branch of the American Civil Liberties Union (ACLU) charged that an FBI agent "committed arson and other violence that police used as a reason for declaring that university students were unlawfully assembled." One hundred and fifty students were arrested.[47] An FBI agent, who infiltrated the ranks of the Black Panther Party in Chicago, drew a floor plan of the apartment of Black Panther Party leader Fred Hampton and it was then transmitted to Chicago police who used it to raid the apartment and kill Hampton. In another instance the FBI revived a defunct right-wing paramilitary group which it renamed the Secret Army Organization (SAO). One of its informants, Howard Godfrey, was paid $250 a week plus expenses between 1967 and 1972 to insinuate himself into the group and become one of its leaders. Godfrey told a California court that he was also given $10,000 to $20,000 worth of weapons for the terrorists. The organization engaged in "repeated acts of violence and terrorism against the left," including destruction of property and firebombing of cars, and pumping two bullets into the home of an antiwar activist, named Peter Hohmer, which wounded a young woman. In the latter incident an FBI agent hid the gun used in the crime for six months and the Bureau arranged for Godfrey to avoid prosecution.[48]

The fanatic one-sidedness with which the National Security State views its mission was illustrated by the FBI's campaign to destroy the leader of the civil rights movement, Dr. Martin Luther King, Jr. Federal Bureau of Investigation chief J. Edgar Hoover never had a shred of evidence that King had violated a single federal law or planned to do so, yet he conducted a vendetta to destroy him both politically and physically, including the use of warrantless wiretaps and the placement of microphones. At one point, just thirty-four days before King was to receive the Nobel Peace Prize, the FBI surreptitiously mailed a composite tape based on microphone surveillance of King's hotel rooms in Washington, San Francisco, and Los Angeles (evidently of a personal and compromising nature) to the King headquarters in Atlanta suggesting King commit suicide or suffer exposure. The letter read in part: "King, there is only one thing left for you to do. You know what it is. You have just 34 days . . . You are done. There is but one way out for you. You better take it before your filthy fraudulent self is bared to the nation."[49] The FBI chief contemplated mailing the tape to King's wife, Coretta, in the hopes it would break up their marriage. After calling the civil rights leader a "notorious liar," the FBI subsequently offered the material to a number of prominent newspeople in the hopes they would publish its details, but the offer was spurned.

Another distressing feature of the vendetta against King was the partial, if sometimes grudging, support it received from two supposedly liberal presidents and two attorneys general. Both Robert F. Kennedy and Nicholas Katzenbach, who claimed to be sympathetic to the civil rights crusade, approved warrantless surveillance of King and some of his supporters, and neither Kennedy nor Lyndon Johnson ever ordered Hoover to stop his illegal efforts. Part of the reason no doubt was that Hoover flaunted the communist issue at the two presidents and their attorneys general. He claimed that two of King's associates were communists or sympathizers, and neither the Kennedy nor the Johnson team dared interfere with the FBI chief's effort to confirm that fact. Hoover never succeeded, but the campaign continued.

One of the weapons Hoover could wave over President Johnson's head was that the chief executive had illegally used the FBI for partisan political purposes. On the pretext that the FBI was needed to protect him at the Democratic Party Convention in Atlantic City in August 1964, and to prevent civil disturbances (functions the Secret Service and local police were adequately equipped to do), Johnson had thirty FBI agents assigned to the site. The agents were used to spy on the activities of Democratic Party black dissidents. Microphone surveillance was placed not only on King, but on SNCC and CORE leaders, and through them Johnson was able to discover the strategy of the Mississippi Freedom Democratic Party which was threatening to cause a rumpus at the convention unless it was seated in place of the all-white delegation from that state. Hoover evidently had similar tidbits, some of it personal, some political, on other officials, including the Kennedys, and cashed in his chips when the occasion demanded. His power was so great that Robert Kennedy was said to have authorized the first wiretap on King, because, in the words of Kennedy's press secretary "if he did not do it, Mr. Hoover would move to impede or block the passage of the civil rights bill. . . . "[50] That a second-line public official, subordinate to the Attorney General, should have such power, especially a second line official in the police machinery of the nation, is a worrisome phenomenon.

The campaign to destroy King started slowly. It clearly had nothing to do with law enforcement, but rather with Hoover's intense personal dislike of King (whether for racial or personal reasons, it is not quite clear). Initially, after King had led the sensational Montgomery Bus boycott in the mid-1950s and formed the Southern Christian Leadership Conference (SCLC) "to organize a register-and-vote campaign among Negroes in the South," Hoover ordered that King and his organization be immediately placed under "racial matters" surveillance.

The surveillance was upgraded, however, to a COMINFIL (communist infiltration) covert action after King gained national and international attention for his nonviolent demonstration in Albany, Georgia in 1962 (which led to 700 arrests), and after open criticism by King that the FBI frequently stood by while local police and thugs beat up civil rights demonstrators. Hoover's fury (all of it purely personal) was now unrestrained. The FBI was ordered to review its files to uncover "subversive" material on King, and the black leader himself was placed on the "Reserve Index," to be put in a concentration camp in case of "national emergency." A full COMINFIL investigation was begun, and though nothing was ever found to prove significant communist penetration of the civil rights movement, the campaign against King continued until his assassination in 1968—and beyond. In his reports to the Attorney General, his supposed "boss," Hoover tried to emphasize "communist connections." He did not dwell on the fact that King was a long-time Gandhian pacifist, close to the former head of the Fellowship of Reconciliation, A.J. Muste, who sent two of his people, Bayard Rustin and the Rev. Glenn Smiley to Montgomery to train King's forces in nonviolent resistance. When Congress considered making King's birthday a national holiday, an FBI official briefed congresspeople on King's private affairs in order to influence them to vote against it.

The FBI did more. It spread rumors that King had a secret Swiss bank account. It prevailed on the Internal Revenue Service (IRS) to audit SCLC finances. It pressured the Ford Foundation and the National Science Foundation, unsuccessfully, to withhold grants from SCLC. It prodded magazines and publishers not to publish articles and books by the civil rights leader. Hoover and one of his top assistants even considered finding another black leader to elevate as King's "successor" in the black movement.

The FBI's extralegal campaign against domestic dissidents has been supplemented by that of the CIA, the NSA, the IRS, the military intelligence agencies, and local police red squads, each of whom used whatever pretext was at hand to expand its scope. Though the National Security Act of 1947 specifically forbade domestic activity by the CIA, the agency spread its network amongst emigrés living in the United States on the excuse that they had valuable information about their home countries, or leads to spies and informants abroad. The Cuban community in Miami was infiltrated by the CIA for the same reasons, as well as to ferret out possible counteragents of Fidel Castro. For a decade or more, starting in 1960, Cuban refugees were paid by the Agency to spy on other Cubans.

The CIA issued its own secret executive orders, wrote its own charter, but always expanded its prerogatives to include spying on

Americans—and disrupting their lives. In the course of its daily functions the Agency came into contact with businesspeople who gave cover to CIA agents abroad, changed CIA money, and if they were multinational corporations they also provided facts about the nations where they had branch operations. In 1963 the CIA established a Domestic Operations Division to direct and coordinate "clandestine operational activities of the Clandestine Services conducted within the United States against foreign targets." One of its functions was to burglarize foreign embassies, another was to target Americans who might be foreign agents.[51] In 1956 the Agency put entertainer Eartha Kitt under surveillance and "confidential" sources reported on her behavior in Paris, New York, and points between. In 1952, on the pretext that subversive Americans might be communicating with foreign agents by mail, or vice versa, the CIA intercepted selected mail at the LaGuardia and Kennedy airports in New York. "This thing is as illegal as hell," said the CIA's director of security, Howard Osborn, in 1969, but it continued.[52] A memorandum written seven years previously had called on law enforcement agencies to cover up for the CIA by denying any such activity was under way. The memo also proposed that the Agency "find a scapegoat to blame for the unauthorized tampering with the mails." When the FBI discovered that the CIA was engaged in this illegal activity (because it approached the postal authorities to do the same thing), the Bureau didn't take steps to have CIA functionaries prosecuted for illegal actions. Instead, the FBI made a deal with the CIA to share the illegally procured information, and it provided the Agency with a "watch list" of mail to look for.

Among those whose mail was opened and copied were people sympathetic to the Soviet Union, North Korea, North Vietnam, and China. Among those on the CIA's own watch list were the American Friends Service Committee, authors John Steinbeck and Edward Albee, a number of congresspeople and senators, the Federation of American Scientists, and many American peace organizations. Most of the mail opened, however, was opened at random. By the time the program was terminated in 1973 (primarily because the postal authorities were becoming uneasy about their involvement in illegal acts) the CIA had looked over 28 million pieces of mail, taken pictures of 2 million, and opened 215,000 letters.

Another pretext used by the CIA for domestic activities was to provide security for its own operations. Thus an employee suspected of being a communist was kept under surveillance for eight years on the theory he might leak something to the Soviets. The Office of Security, given this mandate, went further: it investigated reporters (like Jack Anderson, Michael Gelter, Les Whitten) who were publishing unfavorable or unauthorized information about the Agency. In 1967, on the thin excuse that demonstrators were threatening its recruiting program on the campuses, the CIA set up Project RESISTANCE to check on students who defied it. Before long the Agency was gathering information on literally thousands of campus radicals and antiwar activists. Project MERRIMAC was originated by the CIA Office of Security on the pretense the Agency needed protection from demonstrators who might threaten CIA personnel. MERRIMAC's activities included infiltrating agents into Women Strike for Peace, the War Resisters League, the Black Panthers, CORE, and the Washington Ethical Society. They did the usual things: copied license plate numbers, took pictures of demonstrators, and gathered tidbits of information, such ás the sources of members' income. Flowing from this operation, the CIA offered surveillance training to local police red squads from coast to coast. In a Chicago case, brought by antiwar activists who were spied on by the local police red squad, the CIA's role was so patent the judge ordered it to make available to the plaintiffs its files on them. State and local police shared their data with the CIA, perhaps because the CIA made its own, larger files available to them, perhaps because it supplied some of them with spy equipment. In one case the local police accompanied the CIA on a burglary mission.

In August 1967 the CIA initiated Operation CHAOS. The operation was predicated on the gratuitous assumption that antiwar and other activists might have connections with foreign intelligence agencies. Earlier that year the nation's leading antiwar publication, *Ramparts*, had carried a sensational exposé revealing that the CIA had for many years funded the National Student Association (NSA) through dummy and sometimes legitimate foundations. This was enough of an excuse for CIA to start beating the bushes to prove that there was a foreign intelligence angle to antiwar activities in the United States. The investigation was extensive, including surveillance of antiwar activists while they were traveling abroad, burglarizing homes and hotel rooms, wiretaps, buggings, and similar niceties. Oddly enough an Agency report issued in 1971 concluded that "there is no evidence . . . that foreign governments, organizations or intelligence services control U.S. new left movements." Operation CHAOS, nevertheless, continued to expand. It exchanged reports with the FBI at the rate of a thousand a month. By the time it came to an end in 1974 it had cross-indexed the names of 300,000 U.S. citizens, done personality studies on 7,000 Americans (and 6,000 foreigners), and completed a file on 1,000 domestic organizations.[53]

The web of domestic spying and covert activities at home by FBI, CIA, local police, and other agencies, all working in concert, all exchanging information, has spanned the nation and cut deep into its structural fabric. "An American police state has evolved," writes David Wise. "It has emerged in spite of the Bill of Rights and the protections of the law and the Constitution. We have created a uniquely *American* police state. . . . "[54]

The intelligence campaign against Americans reached a climax of sorts under the Nixon administrations. In June 1970 a frustrated Richard Nixon called together CIA chief Helms, FBI chief Hoover, the director of the Defense Intelligence Agency, Lieutenant General Donald V. Bennett, the director of NSA, Vice Admiral Noel Gayler, his two top aides H.R. Haldeman and John Ehrlichman, and a young member of his staff, Tom Charles Huston, to discuss the "inadequate" information he was getting about the antiwar movement. Opening the meeting at the Oval Office Nixon read a statement prepared by Huston: "We are now confronted with a new and grave crisis in this country. . . . Certainly hundreds, perhaps thousands, of Americans—mostly under 30—are determined to destroy our society. . . . They are searching out for the support—ideological and otherwise—of foreign powers and they are developing their own brand of indigenous revolutionary activism which is as dangerous as anything which they could import from Cuba, China, or the Soviet Union."[55] He ordered the group to cooperate with Huston to prepare a tighter intelligence plan. What emerged was a formula for totally uncontrolled police activity, formalizing what was already being done—wiretaps, break-ins, mail openings, surveillance—and expanding it. The agencies were to collaborate in their efforts and the president was to remove previous restrictions on their activities, such as those limiting electronic surveillance. Summing it up a few years later, the Senate Select Committee on Intelligence commented that "Henceforth, *with presidential authority*, the intelligence community could at will intercept and transcribe the communications of Americans using international communications facilities; eavesdrop . . . on anyone deemed to be a 'threat to the internal security'; read the mail of American citizens; break into the homes of anyone tagged as a security threat; and monitor in various ways the activities of suspicious student groups." A permanent interagency committee on intelligence evaluation was to be established, with J. Edgar Hoover as chairman, and Huston as "personal representative of the President" to coordinate matters.

The Huston plan was approved by Nixon but it was undercut by J. Edgar Hoover who felt he already had such powers and wanted no other bureaucratic agencies to seize the same prerogatives. Though Nixon's approval was rescinded, to appease Hoover, the same practices continued. What curtailed them, finally, was not a bureaucratic commitment to end lawbreaking by intelligence agencies, but the Watergate scandal. Nixon was forced out of office in August 1974 to avoid impeachment for the cover-up of a burglary by members of his Committee to Re-Elect the President, and it was obvious the Senate would convict him. (As we have already seen, Nixon was not brought to book for much worse crimes, such as conducting a war in Cambodia without congressional approval.)

Watergate for a time slowed the momentum toward a police state. The Ford and Carter administrations did not eliminate the practices of their predecessors, but they moved warily. The impulse toward authoritarianism brought about by the militarization of America, however, remained strong, churning under the surface, and when Ronald Reagan took office in 1981 it forcefully reasserted itself. Many of the activities which former administrations, when confronted, admitted were illegal, were now flaunted as government policy. In December 1981, for instance, Reagan issued Executive Order 12333 which authorized the CIA to spy on Americans within the United States when the "interests of U.S. foreign policy are at stake." That kind of wording is a license for conducting covert activity against anyone—the CIA can always claim that a vigil of seven people in front of a local post office calling for the United States to stop funding the El Salvador government is an affront to "U.S. foreign policy." An earlier draft, signifying the administration's bent of mind, went much further: it authorized the CIA to legally open mail, burglarize homes and offices, place individuals and groups under wiretap and electronic surveillance—all without court orders, all simply on the CIA's own motion. These provisions were removed from the final draft, but the newer version was bad enough: "a wide-ranging assault on civil liberties," according to the American Civil Liberties Union. That we are rapidly returning to earlier abuses is made evident by newspaper reports early in 1984 that twenty-one domestic political organizations were being jointly monitored by the FBI and CIA. Congressman Don Edwards's Subcommittee on Civil and Constitutional Rights revealed in April 1984 that the number of sanctioned FBI covert operations had risen from 176 to 1978 to more than 300 in 1983 under Reagan, and that the FBI's covert operations budget had skyrocketed from a million a year in 1977 to $12 million in 1984.

That the government was still intent on carrying out COINTELPRO-type operations was made clear when the Justice Department defended its agents in a lawsuit filed by a black activist, Muhammad Kenyatta, for COINTELPRO actions against him in the 1960s. These actions included threats on his life, repeated arrests by the police, emplacement of a large dead bird on his couch while he and his wife were out of the house, and similar acts. The Justice Department claimed in its brief on behalf of the government that all the activities against Kenyatta, including forgery, "were part of the FBI's law enforcement responsibilities to protect the citizenry." The brief insisted that FBI agents were entitled to immunity from prosecution because they functioned "under the authority of higher officials at FBI headquarters who assured them that their actions did not violate the law." As Anthony Lewis of the *New York Times* noted, the Justice Department's position reinforced the old COINTELPRO mentality and the notion of federal agents that they were "perfectly free to use those methods against whomever they feel like it."[56]

In 1982 Reagan pushed through the Agent Identities Act which made it a crime to reveal the names of covert intelligence agents, even if the source of the information was already public. As of this writing the Act has not been enforced too strictly, but it caters to the growing restrictive mood. The penchant for keeping information from the public was also punctuated by Reagan's National Security Decision Directive 84 (NSDD 84) which called for prepublication censorship of speeches, articles, and books by government employees with access to classified information,. even after they have quit the government. The Directive was stymied by congressional roadblocks, but in June 1984 the General Accounting Office reported that even without implementation of NSDD 84 there had been a sizable increase of the number of government employees outside the intelligence community who were required to sign lifetime prepublication review agreements. Thus, while there is no formal censorship of material written by journalists there is effective partial censorship—by withholding information at the source.

The tendency to withhold information from the public was augmented by complex "reforms" of the Freedom of Information Act, which would have the effect of closing more doors to government information. New orders gave government bureaucrats greater authority in classifying government documents and even *reclassifying* documents that had previously been released to the public; visas were denied to hundreds of foreigners whose views the Reagan administration disagreed with; effective banning of travel to Cuba continued; and the Foreign Agents Registration Act was utilized to brand an antinuclear film from Canada as "propaganda."

Perhaps the greatest threat for the future was a Reagan administration bill introduced in 1984 which would make it a crime, punishable by as much as ten years in prison and a $100,000 fine, for providing "support services" or acting "in concert" with groups or countries designated by the Secretary of State as "terrorist." Under the Prohibition Against Training or Support of Terrorist Organizations Act of 1984, the Secretary would have exclusive right to determine which groups or countries were "terrorist," without judicial review. Innocent as all this may sound, its practical effect would be that the Secretary could designate the Sandinistas in Nicaragua, the guerrillas in El Salvador, perhaps the PLO in the Middle East, the Kampuchean government in Southeast Asia, the Castro regime in Cuba, as "terrorist." Members of any group in the United States that gave them support—such as the Committee in Solidarity with the

People of El Salvador (CISPES)—would be subject to imprisonment and a fine. Thus any person or group which spoke out in favor of the Irish Republican Army, the African National Congress in South Africa, or the guerrillas in the Philippines would be violating the proposed Reagan law and be subject to dire consequences—at the very least a stern FBI investigation.

The *Philadelphia Inquirer* of October 25, 1984 reported that "The FBI has quietly been investigating protest groups that oppose the Reagan administration's Central America policies, according to congressional and administration sources." Eleanor Stein, Michael Ratner, and Sara Rios of the Center for Constitutional Rights, in testifying before a House Judiciary Subcommittee in August 1984, documented a "pattern of current FBI harassment and surveillance of individuals and groups engaged in solidarity work with Central America, the Mideast, Cuba, Northern Ireland and Vietnam." The pattern is reminiscent of the harassment under the former counterintelligence program (COINTELPRO). They include forged letters canceling an activist's travel plans to Nicaragua; a forged letter from a telephone company falsely advising a young woman that the FBI was subpoenaing her phone records in a drug investigation; numerous visits to neighbors and friends of various people; informing a member of CISPES in Tampa that there were terrorists in his organization; and infiltrating CISPES just as the communists and Trotskyists had been infiltrated years before.

Michael Ratner of the Center for Constitutional Rights predicts that the term *terrorism* may be used as justification for bypassing the Constitution in the same way that the term *communism* was used thirty years ago. It may be the shield under which the administration will try to regain the untrammeled right to intervene militarily overseas, to limit domestic opposition to foreign intervention, restrict further access to information about government activities, and lift restraints on intelligence agencies, raise their budgets, and mute criticism against them. These would be steps of an incremental nature, none of which by itself would have the impact of a Watergate or a Joe McCarthy assault, but would make serious inroads on whatever civil liberties still stand intact. "The new tactic of suppression," comments Ira Glasser, Executive Director of the ACLU, "is much quieter, almost stealthy, more difficult to see and therefore harder to resist. But it is nothing less than a covert action against the First Amendment and, ultimately, democracy itself."[57] Slowly but insidiously the nation has learned to accept inroads on liberty it has not accepted in the past. Glasser, summarizing our values in the nuclear age, states that "secrecy is the norm. The right to information struggles vainly to establish itself. The classified state is now accepted, and all we fight about are the exceptions. Spying, furthermore, is routine. Everybody spies. It is nearly unthinkable to oppose peacetime spying."[58]

Back in 1863 Sir Thomas May noted that "men may be without restraints upon their liberty; they may pass to and fro at pleasure; but if their steps are tracked by spies and informers, their words noted down for crimination, their associates watched as conspirators—who shall say they are free?"[59] That is an apt description of the current state of affairs.

The campaign by the National Security State to establish an iron-tight national unity without effective dissent has not been an unmitigated success. A number of movements have slipped through the crevices, most notably the civil rights movement that reasserted itself in the 1950s and the antiwar movement that challenged U.S. policy in Vietnam beginning in the 1960s. In both instances dissenters won partial victories. The feminist movement also recorded a number of major successes in the 1960s and 1970s. But the National Security State could absorb some of these setbacks—for instance the civil rights victories—without too much pain. The establishment's defeat in Vietnam was of more consequence, inspiring greater opposition to policies in the mideast and Central America. But the National Security State was far from dismantled by these setbacks. Its basic structure in fact remained intact; steeped in secrecy, operating in illegality, it continued unchecked, fostering a continuing rightist mood in the nation. Popular support for militarism was unabated as indicated by the ever increasing military budgets of recent years. The Reagan administration was able to flaunt illegality with impunity. The "covert" war against Nicaragua, for instance, was openly admitted and financed for three years by funds openly voted in Congress. The resistance to the war in Vietnam and the campaign for civil rights from the mid-1950s to the early 1970s were aberrations against the tide. Despite the enormous energies that were expended in these campaigns, it is noteworthy that no movement emerged to defy the National Security State itself. There was no real challenge to the system per se, even on the relatively small scale as that offered by the socialists of 1912, the Progressive Party of 1924, or the communists of 1937. Short of an economic cataclysm, both the National Security State and its twin policies of imperialism and militarism evidently were in no immediate jeopardy.

6

The Rearrangement of Power

The lawless acts committed by the CIA, FBI, and the other members of the National Security State do not occur in a vacuum. They are sustained by a power grid of immense size, without which the syndrome of illegality would have vanished long ago. At the apex of this power grid is the presidency, what in recent years has been called the imperial presidency. With prerogatives that would have made King George III envious, the imperial presidency does not hang in midair, however. Fanning out from it, like an octopus with multiplying tentacles, is a vast agglomerate of institutions and constituencies dedicated to militarism. This agglomerate has not only abused power on a grand scale, but absorbed and co-opted many forces to perpetuate that power and immunize itself from serious challenge. C. Wright Mills' term *the power elite* does not really capture the flavor of this new phenomenon in American life. Dwight Eisenhower's *military–industrial complex* comes closer—though it leaves the impression of an alien growth on the surface of the body rather than a metastasized lesion gnawing at vital organs inside. The zest for expansion, for gaining new pockets of power and influence, has been the distinguishing factor both of the imperial presidency and the military–industrial complex. It is the obverse side of the loss of power by the Congress and the public.

The term *imperial presidency* implies one which functions like a monarchy, disregarding the principle of separation of powers, subverting the principle of government by consent of the governed. Since the Republic was founded presidents have often flouted those basic principles—but never for long and they have never been able to make it a way of life. They have always had to retreat, back to the confines of an imperfect democracy leaving scars but not a permanent disfigurement of the presidency. In the last half-century, however, we have faced three grave emergencies and, under the stress of those emergencies, America has allowed its presidency to make a 180-degree turn away from what was originally intended. Under the cloak of "emergency" the presidency has become a rogue elephant, taking unto itself not only the unilateral right to make war, including covert war, but to pass laws (euphemistically called "executive orders"), and sign binding treaties (euphemistically called "executive agreements") without oversight by Congress, sometimes without even informing Congress.

As with so much else in the saga of American militarization the roots of the problem go back to the 1930s and Franklin Roosevelt. During the Great Depression Roosevelt asked for and received from Congress "emergency" powers to deal directly with the economic and other crises, without waiting for the legislature to act. The trouble was that after the crises were over, the emergency laws remained on the books. From 1933 to 1976, 470 laws or sections of laws delegated emergency powers to the president. He was given the authority on his own, according to a report of the Senate Special Committee on the Termination of the National Emergency, to "seize property, mobilize production, seize commodities, institute martial law, seize control of all transportation and communications, regulate private capital, restrict travel, and—in a host of particular and peculiar ways—control the activities of all American citizens."[1] When Roosevelt placed American citizens of Japanese descent in concentration camps during World War II it was on the far-fetched theory that he had such a "right" under the commander-in-chief clause of Article 2 of the Constitution. Subsequently, he established the Office of Price Administration and the Office of Economic Stabilization to regulate prices, wages, and profits, by executive order. Matters so weighty as the operation of the economy are clearly within the province of the legislature, but the president held that under his own provisional proclamation of "unlimited emergency," all this was also within his domain. At one point, in a Labor Day address to Congress, Roosevelt made the startling threat that "in the event that Congress should fail to act, and act adequately, I shall accept the responsibility, and I will act."[2] Thirty years later, in peacetime, President Nixon created an equally elaborate bureaucracy to manage wages and prices, again without consulting Congress, merely by his own Executive Order 11615.

The emergency powers laws have since been repealed, but chief executives argue that they have a right to issue executive orders (which in effect are laws) by virtue of "residual powers" not specifically spelled out in the Constitution but, rather, implied or "inherent." According to John Ehrlichman, counsellor to President Nixon, the president has a "residuum of power . . . which authorized him . . . to take such actions as he may deem necessary."[3] By that definition the president becomes an absolute monarch. Nixon in fact spoke of the president as a "sovereign" with special rights. In response to an interrogatory by the Church Committee as to whether he believed "that actions, otherwise 'illegal' may be legally undertaken pursuant to Presidential, or other high-level authorization," he compared the power of the president to that of a king. "It is quite obvious," he wrote, "that there are certain inherently governmental actions which if undertaken by the sovereign [sic] in protection of the interest of the nation's security are lawful but which if undertaken by private persons are not. . . . In 1969, during my Administration, warrantless wiretapping, even by the government, was unlawful, but if undertaken because of a presidential determination that it was in the interest of national security was lawful."[4] No better evidence of the drift toward a police state in militarized America has been forthcoming: the president, Nixon was saying, can determine on his own that someone endangers national security and then act against him even if the method is patently illegal. Clearly, if the "sovereign" (president) has the *inherent right* to do something illegal, the courts have no right to review it or the Congress to legislate on it. We reach the stage James Madison warned about when the Republic was in its infancy: "The accumulation of all powers, legislative, executive, and judiciary, in the same hands, whether of one, a few, or many, and whether heredity, self-appointed, or elective, may justly be pronounced the very definition of tyranny."[5]

From Eisenhower to Reagan presidents have issued about 3,000 executive orders. Some of them instruct government departments on specific means of carrying out a law and are obviously without tarnish; but hundreds are "presidential laws": substitutes for laws that only Congress has a right to pass. In 1952 President Truman secretly established a whole new institution of government, the National Security Agency, by executive order. The CIA covert actions program was put into effect by executive order, though there is no specific authority for such action in the National Security Act of 1947. The loyalty oath program was introduced by an executive order, number 9835. The FBI's enlarged powers are the result of presidential not congressional law. More recently President Reagan, who like his predecessors wields power like an emperor, ordered U.S. oil companies to leave Libya and the subsidiaries of American companies in Europe (though covered by European laws) to stop selling pipeline equipment to the Soviet Union. American firms were told they could not engage in certain trade with Poland, American citizens were told they could not spend U.S. dollars in Cuba (effectively prohibiting travel there)—all on Reagan's personal authority. President Carter before him cut off grain shipments to the Soviet Union and ordered American athletes not to participate in the Olympics, again solely on his own authority.

"Presidents have come to rely on executive orders in order to make up for their inability to mobilize Congress. . . ," assert two legal experts, Joel L. Fleishman and Arthur H. Aufses. "Thus when they seek a particular policy, but doubt their ability to move it through Congress, they can simply attempt to achieve their aim through an executive order."[6]

Getting around Congress is also the reason that recent presidents and their subordinates have been signing "executive agreements" with foreign nations. In this way, they avoid formal treaties that require a two-thirds vote of the Senate—a vote that may not be possible to muster or one which might provoke too much controversy. How many such agreements have been made is not known; *U.S. News and World Report* (July 21, 1969) once reported that there were "at least 24," with nations such as Spain, Iran, Jordan, Ethiopia, Tunisia, and so on. In 1962 Secretary of State Dean Rusk signed an agreement with the foreign minister of Thailand, Thanat Khoman, pledging that the United States would defend Siam not only from outside aggression but from civil war. "Under the secret agreement," reported Flora Lewis of the *New York Times*, "the United States has been providing Thailand with something between $175 million and $250 million a year for Thai forces. The aid has been hidden in the defense budget under other programs so that Congress never knew what the money was going for."[7] After the Vietnam War heated up in 1965 Washington constructed large air bases in Thailand and eventually dispatched 48,000 soldiers to the country. It was at this point that Richard G. Stillwell signed a secret military agreement with the Thais (called a "contingency agreement") which in every respect was a treaty, but was not submitted to the Senate. It spelled out the number of American soldiers to be sent in and the theaters of operation they were to be responsible for in case of combat. Yet, not only was this agreement not put to the Senate, the Senate Foreign Relations Committee was refused a copy. In the past, executive agreements generally have been entered into with foreign nations on matters of minor consequence (such as the opening of consular offices) but not on matters of war. More and more, however, what used to be the subject of a treaty requiring Senate approval has become the subject of an executive fact, often buried under a top secret classification.

Apologists for the executive grab of power have come up with all sorts of ingenious justifications in addition to the theses of "inherent power." One is the so-called principle of "adaptation by usage," which means that if the president has done something for a long time without being called to task by Congress or the courts, he automatically acquires the right to continue doing it. That is like arguing that if a pickpocket practices his craft for ten years without being caught he can never be imprisoned. Mitchell Rogovin, special counsel to the CIA, explains in a widely circulated memorandum that the president's authority to order covert activity abroad stems from his "broad powers with respect to the conduct of foreign affairs." There is no doubt the president has such powers, but how does that justify an illegal application of them? That's like saying that a policeman, who has the right to apprehend shoplifters, also has the right to shoot them without trial. Other justifications are equally circuitous. The Rogovin memorandum claims that when Congress authorizes funds for a certain activity—the CIA's covert activities for instance—that automatically ratifies what is being done. But Congress only knows generally, as the Rogovin memorandum itself concedes, what the CIA (or FBI or NSA) are doing. It is not apprised of "specific activities." The appropriations are contained in comprehensive bills including hundreds, if not thousand of items. Debate on individual items is either infrequent or curtailed, especially after they leave committee.

Apologists for the imperial presidency sometimes argue that attempts to limit certain actions, actually authorize them. Thus it is said that the War Powers Act, which limited the president's power to make war, in fact was a general approval of presidential war-making, the theory being that the president may make war in all instances other than those proscribed. The Freedom of Information Act, which gives citizens access to government documents, is said to certify the government's right to classification of millions of documents. The Omnibus Crime Control and Safe Streets Act is said to be a recognition of the executive right for national security wiretapping. But the tendency has been more and more for the president and his aides to do what they want without worrying about legal niceties. "I find it inconceivable," the director of the CIA Counterintelligence Staff told a Senate committee, "that a secret intelligence agency of the government has to comply with all the overt orders of the government."[8] When CIA director Richard Helms supplied Henry Kissinger with a CIA study of the domestic student movement he admitted in his cover letter that the right to make this study "was not within the charter of this agency. . . . Should anyone learn of its existence it would prove most embarrassing for all concerned."[9] Needless to say Kissinger did not report Helms to the FBI for violating a law, or himself for the cover-up—the kind of crime for which Richard Nixon was forced to resign.

If the imperial presidency is something unique in the American saga, the military–industrial complex on which it rests and without which it could not exist is even more so. This agglomeration of power helps to immunize the imperial presidency and the National Security State from popular rebuke and possible dissolution. It constantly arranges and rearranges power in its own direction and toward its own philosophy. And it has a zest for expansion that adds to its authority and keeps opponents off balance.

The anchor of the military–industrial complex, of course, is the military. This is a fundamental reversal of the American past, because, as we have shown earlier, for most of U.S. history the military has been small in size and has played a negligible role in political affairs. It is true that some generals later became presidents of the country, but while in the armed forces they played little or no role in politics. Andrew J. Goodpaster and Samuel P. Huntington observe that "Each successive group that rose to a preeminent role in American society had its own reasons for being suspicious of the military: to the eighteenth-century Whigs and Jeffersonians large military forces were a threat to liberty; the Jacksonians saw them as a threat to democracy; the dominant industrial and business groups after the Civil War saw them as a threat to economic productivity and prosperity; and the progressives and liberals saw them as a threat to reform. Almost everyone thought large standing military forces were a threat to peace."[10]

The refashioned power elite in America which emerged after 1945 was more formidable than any ever known before. At the base of the power pyramid was the Pentagon, the fountainhead, though not the brainpower of the complex. Above the base, not necessarily in the order of importance, was:

1. A civilian–militarist faction in Congress. Beyond the many congresspeople and senators who were militaristically inclined because of the military installations and factories with defense orders in their districts (all but 20 or 30 of the 435 congressional districts fit this category), many members of Congress were directly associated with the Pentagon. According to a tally made by William McGaffin and Robert Gruenberg of the *Chicago Daily News* some years ago, 100 of the 435 representatives and 30 of the 100 senators carried officer rank (active, inactive, and retired) in the military forces, including such influential stalwarts as Republican senators Strom Thurmond of South Carolina and Barry Goldwater of Arizona.[11] Not all the legislators wearing military hats are hawks but a vast majority are, and some not accidentally so. One congressperson told McGaffin and Gruenberg than when he was appointed a member of the Armed Services Committee the Army "offered to make me a colonel" in the reserves, even though he had never risen above corporal in the regular services.

2. The large contractors who do business with the Pentagon, a sort of Who's Who of American industry. Two-thirds of the procurement dollars spent by the Pentagon go to the 100 largest companies

in the country, but there are in addition 20,000 companies which receive primary contracts and 100,000 who flourish on subcontracts.

3. A select group of organizations that act as a liaison between industry and the military, such as the American Defense Preparedness Association or the National Security Industrial Association.

4. More than a dozen research organizations subsidized by the Defense Department, popularly called think tanks, such as the Rand Corporation, headed for the most part by former defense officials. For example, former Rand president H.S. Rowen was once Deputy Assistant Secretary of Defense, General Maxwell D. Taylor, onetime chairman of the Joint Chiefs of Staff, later became president of the Institute for Defense Analysis. The purpose of the think tanks has been to research knotty problems in many areas, including the social sciences, and to formulate strategic plans for the Pentagon. Much of their hard-line conclusions are translated into popular articles in the news media. For example, Albert Wohlstetter, who served as associate director of projects at RAND, was a master at "proving" that "the thermonuclear balance . . . [is] in fact precarious." Such themes are picked up by other researchers and by not a few journalists. They have the voice of authority behind them.

5. A considerable number of private research and educational organizations, such as the Hoover Institution for the Study of War, Revolution and Peace, the American Security Council, the Heritage Foundation, the Center for Strategic Studies, the American Enterprise Institute.

6. The leadership of the AFL-CIO, especially the international affairs department now headed by Irving Brown; as well as a number of satellite organizations under its control such as the American Institute for Free Labor Development (AIFLD).

7. A significant section of the academic community whose fate is tied to the Pentagon including such prominent professors as Edward Teller and Edward N. Luttwak, such major universities as the Massachusetts Institute of Technology (MIT), Johns Hopkins, Georgetown, and the "contract centers" run by elite universities.

Another militarist ally is that complex of trade associations and chambers of commerce in every locality, buttressed by the local mayors and the mass media, seeking defense contracts to bolster the economy of their communities. There are almost 9 million people who depend on the military for part or all of their paychecks: 2 million troops on active duty, 1 million in the reserves, 1 million civilian employees, 1.2 million retirees who receive pensions, 3 million in the defense industry. There are also another couple of million workers employed by the subcontractors who produce for the Pentagon. "This is a cohesive group," says Admiral Gene LaRocque (Ret.), "which wraps itself in military values."[12]

Beyond that are the 30 million living veterans—about a third of the adult male population. Not all of these people uncritically accept the militarist line, but millions are members of veterans groups such as the American Legion and the Veterans of Foreign Wars which in general support militarism. In 1982 Marine Corps Colonel James A. Donovan (Ret.) counted about 6 million members in twenty-seven veterans organizations—exclusive of ladies' auxiliaries and other satellite groups. The American Legion alone boasted 2.6 million members in 16,000 posts, and it had four paid lobbyists carrying its message to Congress. The Veterans of Foreign Wars (VFW) had 2 million members, plus 650,000 in the Ladies Auxiliary, and a Political Action Committee which endorsed promilitarist candidates for office.

The veterans organizations are not heavy handed with their political propaganda. Instead, they win friends by performing services—getting medical care for individual veterans, participating in funerals and parades. But their leaders are deeply involved with the military and they usually reflect its views. A VFW spokesperson boasted that his new commander was "at the Pentagon Monday, State Department Tuesday, White House Wednesday morning, Veterans Administration Wednesday afternoon for briefings." He also noted that "the 14,000 delegates to our convention are conservative. We are liberal on benefits for veterans, but conservative in politics. When the nation turned against the Vietnam War it had no effect on us; we took the position that there must be no more 'no-win' wars, the Pentagon's position."

Though there is no central office for the military–industrial machine, and no full-time functionaries running it, there is a certain camaraderie between its elements. The Pentagon often gives legislators friendly to the "cause" free plane rides (sometimes just to a football game) and they are wined and dined like Mideastern potentates, all at the taxpayers' expense. When the late Senator Richard B. Russell (Dem.-Ga.), chairman of the Appropriations Committee, wanted to go to a convention the Air Force generously flew him there in a VIP jet. While at the event he received an urgent message from the Senate majority leader than an important vote was coming up. The Air Force flew him back 2,000 miles to Washington, with a colonel acting as host, a chef broiling steaks, and a bartender serving drinks. Interestingly, when Russell held hearings on the antiballistic missile (ABM) which the Pentagon was supporting, no one opposed to the ABM was called to testify. The senator and his counterpart in the House at the time, George D. Mahon (Dem.-Tex.), acknowledged that they hadn't called a single witness to their budget hearings except those from the administration.

Those who link their fate to the Pentagon are rewarded by the Pentagon. Melvin Price of the 21st Congressional District of Illinois and chairman of the House Armed Services Committee until he was removed early in 1985, was rewarded with a 2,500-acre air force base for his congressional district. The base directly employs 11,000 military and civilian personnel and it provides another 4,000 jobs through spin-off activities. This lush testimonial to Price's clout was in addition to another boon in 1977 which brought the largest military air traffic control system in the Western world to Price's district. The late Congressman L. Mendel Rivers, chairman of the Armed Services Committee, once boasted that he had brought to his South Carolina district 90 percent of its lush defense activity, including a Marine Corps air station, an Army depot, a shipyard, a Navy training center, two Polaris missile facilities, a Navy supply center, two Navy Hospitals, a Marine corps recruiting depot, and a payroll of $200 million a year. When another Air Force base was proposed for Senator Russell's state of Georgia, a general wryly remarked that "one more base would sink the state." Only a few members of Congress benefit so handsomely but almost all get some Pentagon money to bolster the economy of their districts, and each dollar makes a friend.

How this system works can be gauged by the way the B-1 bomber was promoted. The idea for such a swing-wing strategic plane was first sketched out in 1962. Eight years later Rockwell won the contract to produce it and Senator George Murphy of California boasted that its production would provide 43,000 jobs for his state. By 1973, however, there were some doubts about the utility of the plane; a Brookings Institution study indicated it was only a "marginal" improvement over the existing fleet of B-52 bombers. The cruise missile, moreover, made the plane obsolete, and the pending "stealth" bomber even more so. "The B-1," said former defense official, Ivan Selin, "is three times nuttier than the MX."[13] Many others had similar doubts and in 1977 President Jimmy Carter canceled production.

Nonetheless Rockwell and the Pentagon refused to be sidetracked. The big corporation spent considerable sums on entertainment and lobbying trying to convince all and sundry that B-1 was an excellent program because it would provide jobs. Air Force officers enlisted the United Auto Workers (UAW), which expected to get a good share of the jobs, to join the campaign. "We called to the UAW lobbyist's attention the number of jobs here, and he did a good job with Congress," Air Force lobbyist Grant Miller told David Wood of the *Los Angeles Times*. In addition, other groups were enrolled in the effort. "I had a list of every B-1 contract over $10,000, the location of the contract by state, congressional district and town, and a map showing the number of dollars and employees," Miller recounted. "We'd sit down, make assignments, decide who we needed to work on. We'd find out who had the most influence with that guy, and we'd get the Air Force Association or somebody to work. It was really an orchestrated effort." The lobbyists included Air Force officers and industrial engineers who had a stake in having the plane built. The 5,200 subcontractors for the $30 billion program were spread out over forty-eight of the fifty states, where each, according to Wood, "can generate powerful coalitions of workers, union leaders, local businessmen and government officials to bring pressure on Congress." There was also an "old boy" network of subcontractors and others who had been aligned for many years, through common membership in the Defense Science Board, the Air Force Scientific Advisory Board and similar bodies. "It's a closed club," a congressional aide told the *Los Angeles Times*. "A few years after a program like this gets started there comes to be a consensus that the airplane absolutely must be built. . . . The program picks up forward momentum, and probably no one can stop it for whatever reason."[14]

"With its enormous size and spending power," concludes Rone Tempest of the same newspaper, "the military-industrial complex creates constituencies that make 'captives' of congressmen, state officials, labor unions and even presidents, who often support questionable military spending out of fear for their political lives. Under such pressure the built-in 'checks and balances' of American government repeatedly break down." What keeps the ball rolling says Paul H. Nisbet, a defense securities analyst for Prudential-Bache, is "jobs." Even liberals who speak of containing the arms budget, like Senator Alan Cranston of California or Howard Metzenbaum of Ohio or Edward M. Kennedy of Massachusetts, almost never vote against military appropriations that might deprive their constituency of jobs. "The nation's unemployment rate could be as much as double without defense as a prop," Nisbet claims.[15] That statement is open to question, as Professor Seymour Melman has pointed out on many occasions, since the nation could convert to peacetime production and provide far more jobs per billion dollars spent than militarism does. But the defense jobs are here and definite; the conversion jobs Melman speaks of are for the future and in some minds questionable.

The Pentagon, as the anchor of the military–industrial complex, woos Congress and the public as ardently as Romeo wooed Juliet. Senator William Proxmire stated some years ago that the Defense Department employed 339 lobbyists to maintain contact with Congress, inform congresspeople about contracts in their districts, process inquiries about young people in the services, and perform other duties. A *St. Louis Post-Dispatch* series in April 1983 puts the figure a little lower, "200-plus," but still substantial. At the end of World War II there were only five such legislative agents. Beyond the lobbyists are the 6,000 public affairs officers who woo the public at a cost of hundreds of millions. The cost of the propaganda machine is so great that when Defense Secretary Weinberger in 1981 ordered a 10 percent cut in the budget for Defense Department films and publications, the *Washington Post* commented that "the Pentagon can't tell you what that means in dollars. It knows its films will cost $458.2 million this year, and that there were 647 publications in 1979, the last time anyone counted. Nobody knows how much they cost."[16] As of that date the Pentagon was spending $112 million on recruitment advertising. It arranged trips to military installations for prominent businesspeople, helped Hollywood produce scores of promilitary films (like *The Green Berets*), provided Army and Navy bands for all kinds of occasions, assigned speakers for any number of meetings, and in general worked assiduously to inculcate its brand of "Americanism" in the body politic—synthetic patriotism, obedience to authority, conformity.

Adjacent to the militarist establishment itself and running parallel to it are a number of constituencies which have either monetary or ideological interests in the militarization of America. One of the largest is the Christian fundamentalist movement which takes seriously such right-wing notions as that of a Heritage Foundation report that "individual liberties are secondary to the requirement of national security and internal civil order."[17] The fundamentalists, led by such men as the Reverend Jerry Falwell, are numbered in the tens of millions (one estimate, in the *Washington Spectator*, perhaps inflated, is 45 million), and their views seem to penetrate many mainstream milieus, including the 1984 Republican Party convention. "The single strongest impression I take away from the Republicans in Dallas [where the Party held its 1984 convention] concerns the degree to which the true believers of the religious right have penetrated and influenced the party of Lincoln," Haynes Johnson wrote in the *Washington Post*.[18] Falwell went on the air during the 1984 presidential campaign to praise Ronald Reagan as "a President who wants to build up our military strength" and to denounce "the freeze-niks, ultra-libs and unilateral disarmers [who] are after him."[19] Along with such fervid defense of militarism, the fundamentalists conduct campaigns against unorthodoxy, including campaigns to remove "dangerous" books from library bookshelves and schoolrooms. According to People for the American Way, this network "with the narrowest religious and political views" is operating in forty-eight states. Under its prodding "libraries are removing books. Teachers are diluting lessons. Publishers are even watering down textbooks." The Moral Majority in North Carolina provided an "Index Prohibitorum" of books "unfit for young leaders." One of the books the fundamentalists claim "would make a nice bonfire" is Aldous Huxley's *Brave New World*, because "it failed to express adequately the merits of capitalism."[20]

What makes the military–industrial complex so formidable is its concentration in certain fields and the high level of collaboration between its components. Almost a third of the nation's mathematicians are employed somewhere in the complex, a quarter of the physicists, almost a third of the engineers, a tenth of computer programmers. These men and women are not necessarily puppets, but if they have doubts about the military program they usually keep it to themselves. Many of them, like Dr. Edward Teller, are prime salespeople for the arms race generally and certain weapons specifically. There exists, says Dr. Gordon Adams, a specialist in military matters, "an 'Iron Triangle' " of "defense contractors, the Pentagon, and Congress. . . . It's a closed circuit, a network of access and influence and information. It grows like Topsy and reinforces itself—almost independent of the will of any one player."[21] The one thousand defense industry representatives trying to influence Congress to buy their wares, collaborate with 200 or more Pentagon "legislative liaison" people, all seeking the same ends. The lobbying is intense with each of the ten largest contractors, fielding staffs of twenty-four to eighty people in their Washington offices, hoping to add to awards that already range between $2 to $6 billion.

The lobbying is supplemented by contributions to the political chests of military-minded congresspeople. In the 1982 elections the political action committees (PACs) of the ten largest defense contractors contributed heavily to members of the House and Senate Armed Services, Appropriations, and Science and Technology Committees. McDonnell Douglas and Lockheed rewarded thirty-six of the thirty-nine members of the House Armed Services Committee up for election in 1982. Rockwell, Raytheon, and Hughes Aircraft PACs gave generously to all ten members of the House Appropriations subcommittee on defense. Nine of the ten largest defense contractor PACs made substantial donations to the chairman, Representative Joseph P. Addabbo. The head of McDonnell Douglas's office in Washington admits candidly that "we actively support the candidacy of members who would further the interests of the McDonnell Douglas Corp. We're not going to give to a candidate who consistently recommends that the defense budget be slashed in half."[22]

Until the Internal Revenue Service (IRS) decided on stricter standards, defense companies charged off their lobbying and public relations expenses against their taxes, so that the government was paying a good part of it. Sperry Corporation which does about a quarter of its business with the government making electronic equipment, charged off as an expense a portion of its costs on the "The Changing Environment for International Enterprise" symposiums and a two-volume set of the proceedings it sent to 10,000 business, congressional, and media contacts. Boeing charged the government for some of the expenses for its fiftieth anniversary celebration and some of the costs for producing, copying, and distributing 110 prints of a movie of Boeing's history. The IRS has become a bit tougher in the last few years, but cynics believe that lobbying and public relations costs are still being hidden as expenses passed on to the government for payment. Fred Wertheimer, president of Common Cause until a few years ago, summarizes the effect of lobbying and campaign grants thus: "The defense industry has tremendous political influence in the first place. It has the economic clout from jobs in people's districts. It has the national security appeal. When you combine all that with the PAC money, it makes it very difficult to get the best defense judgements out of Congress."[23]

The individuals who guide the destinies of this complex are a select group who know each other well and who tend to shuttle back and forth from one milieu to the next. Arms specialist Gordon Adams estimates that as of January 1985 there were 1,900 former Defense Department officers working for defense corporations (often in procurement and frequently dealing with Pentagon officials who once were their subordinates or associates), and about 750 business leaders (usually in defense industries) who have transferred to government from business. W. Paul Thayer, formerly chairman of LTV and of the U.S. Chamber of Commerce, became Deputy Secretary of Defense in 1983. Richard D. DeLauer, vice president of TRW, metamorphosed in 1981 into Under Secretary of Defense for Research and Engineering. Jerome Ambrose, an Army undersecretary who helps make acquisition policy, was formerly a vice president at Ford Aerospace which had a lush contract to produce the Sergeant York DIVAD antiaircraft gun. (The *Chicago Tribune* of January 11, 1985, called this weapon on which $4.5 billion was to be spent, "woefully inadequate" and reported that the Defense Department "is now investigating the fact that four generals connected with this costly lemon retired and took well-paid jobs with Ford Aerospace." Later in the year the program was scrapped.)

Symptomatic of the tendency to shift back and forth from industry to government and vice versa, General Lauris Norstad, former Supreme Allied Commander in Europe, accepted the job as president of Owens-Corning Fiberglas; Admiral William M. Fechteler, after retiring as chief of naval operations, became a consultant to a division of General Electric; Admiral Arleigh Burke, another chief of naval operations, became a director of many corporations and head of a think tank at Georgetown University. On the other hand many an industrial, legal, and academic figure has shifted from private industry to key posts at the Pentagon. The first Secretary of Defense, James V. Forrestal, was a former president of the Dillon Read investment firm; Secretary Charles E. Wilson made the changeover from General Motors (he is not to be confused with the Charles E. Wilson of General Electric); Neil H. McElroy came to the Pentagon from Procter and Gamble, Robert S. McNamara from Ford, Clark Clifford from a law firm which included among its clients Du Pont, RCA, General Electric, and Phillips Petroleum. David Packard, the richest man who ever served as Deputy Secretary of Defense, was co-founder of Hewlett-Packard, a Palo Alto electronics and computer firm which in 1968 did more than a hundred million dollars business with the government. Willis Hawkins, vice president of Lockheed, later turned his talents to the Army as assistant secretary for research and development. Scientists and engineers by the thousand find themselves moving from the payrolls of industry to government and back again, often working on the same weapons system.

Two dozen private organizations function as liaison between defense corporations and the Defense Department, and between members of the armed forces and the Pentagon. Typical perhaps is the evolution of the American Defense Preparedness Association. Prior to World War I, all ordnance was produced in government arsenals; the Great War, however, taxed facilities so much that the military had to turn to private industry for some of its hardware. Unfortunately, neither industry nor the military had any experience in dealing with each other. There was no mechanism by which each could inform itself rapidly what the other was doing or planning; and industry knew very little about how to get around in the bureaucratic maze of government.

To remedy this situation for the future, Bernard Baruch, wartime production czar, helped form the Army Ordnance Association (AOA) in 1919. Its results during World War II were heartening enough so that AOA's functions were extended beyond the Army and its contractors to all the services. In time it changed its name to American Ordnance Association and later American Defense Preparedness Asssociation. Today it boasts 40,773 members, 730 of them corporations (including the eighteen companies that did a billion or more dollars a year of business with the Pentagon in 1982) who pay $100 to $1,500 a year dues, and individuals who pay $20.[24] The president in 1984 appropriately enough was a retired four-star general, Henry A. Miley. As its prospectus points out, ADPA is a "liason between sciences, industry and the armed forces in the research; development, and production of superior weapons." Its twenty-seven technical divisions arrange briefings for corporations and engineers that they could not arrange for themselves, and its fifty-one regional chapters sustain pride in the military establishment by arranging for speakers to various functions, and by sending delegations to visit defense plants, installations, and naval ships.

On the other hand, when the Pentagon needs help, ADPA draws on industry for reciprocal service. For instance, some years ago when General Frank Besson was beset by explosions in several Army ammunition plants under his command, ADPA sent out a rush call for seven top experts in private business to visit the factories and suggest remedies. "I called DuPont," says an ADPA spokesperson, "and asked them for the best man they had, and they gave him to me immediately, free of charge for as long as I needed him." During the Vietnam buildup the Army found itself lacking sufficient suppliers for fire control equipment. "Within a week," says the same spokesperson, "we provided them with a list of 85 qualified companies that had the know-how and equipment to convert to that kind of production."

Other defense and service organizations include the National Security Industrial Association, comprised of 313 defense contractors, a staff of twenty-five, and an annual budget of a million; Aerospace Industries Association, which has forty-seven corporate members, a staff of sixty-five and a budget of about $5 million; the Air Force Association, 181,000 individual members and 200 corporate members, with a full-time staff of seventy-two as of 1983; the Navy League, with 45,000 members, plus 175 corporations, and a staff of thirty; the Association of the U.S. Army with 165,000 members (three-fifths of them on active duty in the Army), and others in various industries such as electronics and shipbuilding. "We exchange information about the needs and requirements of the Army and the capabilities of industry," says a public relations officer of the Association of the U.S. Army. The Association also provides services for active duty soldiers such as prevailing on a utility in Clarkesville, Tenn. to waive deposits for members of the armed forces, or testifying before appropriate congressional committees on soldier-related problems such as the G.I. Bill or medical care for families of retired Army people. Always in the forefront of its concerns, however, is "education"—education to "inform the public and Congress of the need for a strong national defense." A weekly column is sent to 900 weekly newspapers around the country and to some small town dailies.

There is nothing particularly sinister in mechanisms of this sort—if one accepts the assumptions of the permanent war. But "necessary teamwork" often ranges beyond the manufacture of weapons to the manufacture of public opinion. It could hardly be otherwise, for it would be difficult to win approval for a new weapons system or the military stance generally if the nation were not conditioned to believe that it faces an intractable enemy ready to destroy it. Cynics call this molding of public opinion the "software" end of the business, just as necessary, evidently, as the "hardware." One often reads in the publications of these organizations dire warnings that U.S. missile superiority "is about to disappear," or about the "rapid increase in offensive and defensive Soviet missile capability," which puts the lie to Russian pretensions at "limitation of the arms race."

During the Nixon administration Charles Colson formed an ad hoc committee of twenty-five to twenty-eight veterans groups, liaison organizations, and similar forces. They met once a month, listened to military briefings, and coordinated their activities. They lobbied for such issues as the draft, more funds for the Pentagon, retention of the Panama Canal under U.S. ownership, and other hard line programs. Though their contact is now on an informal rather than formal basis, they remain a formidable force with large sums of money at their disposal (much of it filtering in from arms manufacturers) and a network of publications to spread the word.

The alliance of militarists and "civilian militarists" as Professor Irving Louis Horowitz calls the Pentagon's allies, sometimes trails off independently on its own, revealing a worrisome independence from civilian control. By way of example, when the antiballistic missile (ABM) became a major issue in 1969, the promilitarist American Security Control "underwrote a study by 31 leading experts from the Council's Subcommittee on National Strategy to investigate the problem." Its findings were published in a 72-page study: *USSR vs USA—The ABM and the Changed Strategic Military Balance*. Around the same time the Foreign Policy Research Institute of the University of Pennsylvania, also strongly oriented toward the Pentagon and a recipient of many of its research contracts, rushed into print with a volume: *Safeguard: Why the ABM Makes Sense*. Along with fifteen articles *for* the ABM it carried a single piece by Dr. Jerome Wiesner against it, in order, as the publishers said, "to make the volume as complete as possible." The Hudson Institute, headed by Herman Kahn, also prepared a book on the subject—while it held a $70,253 contract for a secret study of the strategic implications of ABM. Kahn denied there was a "conflict of interest," but Senator Edward Kennedy insisted that the work "appears to be financed in part by the Department of Defense."[25]

Simultaneously the Pentagon itself developed a plan to "sell" ABM. Appropriately the plan was marked "classified"—for "national security" reasons. Drafted by Lieutenant General Alfred E. Starbird and approved by Army Secretary Stanley R. Resor, it outlined a variety of activities: feeding information to technical publications to help them write favorable articles; conducting orientation tours for the press, congresspeople, military personnel, scientific, fraternal, and civil groups; and generally encouraging a favorable public attitude toward the placing of ABM sites near major cities. Reporters were offered a trip by Resor to Kwajalein and New Mexico to witness test firings of ABM missiles at first hand. Building trades labor leaders were given a special briefing on the subject, in return for which at least two large national unions—the carpenters and the electrical workers—carried pro-ABM pieces in their magazines.

The secret plan was brought to light by a Washington newspaper and had to be canceled because of the resulting public outcry, in and out of Congress. But private groups took up the cause where the Pentagon left off. One such "spontaneous grassroots" organization was the Citizens' Committee for Peace and Security, which published newspaper advertisements throughout the country claiming that "84 percent of all Americans say that the United States should have an ABM system." This was surprising in view of the Gallup poll which showed 25 percent in favor of ABM, 15 percent opposed, and a majority with no opinion. Subsequently the Senate Foreign Relations Committee revealed that among the signers of the ad were eleven key officials of eight companies which held more than $150 million in ABM contracts, including IBM, Motorola, Sperry-Rand, General Electric, Martin-Marietta, Lockheed, Brunswick, and American Machine and Foundry. It was also learned that Colonel Charles West, the committee's chief staffman, was mobilizing support for the program not from any private office but from an office in the White House where he was serving as a "consultant" to presidential aide Colonel Bruce Jacobs.

Contrary to the image it cultivates of not participating in civilian politics, the Pentagon, on its own and through its allies, is heavily involved in shaping public opinion. If it agrees with the content of a movie, for instance, it will help a producer film it, and on very generous terms. The military also produces its own films, such as *The Army and Vietnam*, and *Strategy for Peace*. It solicits and receives a considerable amount of free time on television and radio and it places many articles with friendly media. Thousands of Pentagon public relations people insinuate its message everywhere. As early as 1951 Senator Harry F. Byrd could report that the Defense Department (DoD) "this year is using 3,022 civilians and uniformed persons in advertising, publicity, and public relations jobs at a payroll cost of $10,109,109."[26] And what the Pentagon does not do to "sell" militarism is done by other segments of the military–civilian alliance, much of it, directly or indirectly, with government funds.

The deviltry that is caused by this purposive effort at opinion molding is illustrated by the three "missile gap" scares of the 1960s. The first one in 1960 was promoted by DoD and its allies, says former Budget Director Charles L. Schultze, "at a time when there was not a single Soviet ICBM (intercontinental ballistic missile) deployed." The nation "was led to near hysteria over the prospect that the Russians might have large numbers of missiles within a very few years. Later we learned that they actually built only three percent of the missiles predicted by 1963. . . . "

The second gap was an "antimissile gap," the carefully cultivated impression that the Soviets were placing an ABM system throughout their country. This resulted in a demand to target more warheads on the Soviet Union and to develop the multiple independently targeted reentry vehicle (MIRV) so that the total of U.S. warheads might be increased from 2,400 to 8,000 or 10,000. Later it was revealed that the Russians had only a small ABM system around Moscow, which by 1970 was obsolete.

In 1969 a third missile gap was manufactured. The Russian SS-9, we were told, was a "first strike weapon against our Minuteman force." According to the militarists, the nation needed to go ahead with the Safeguard ABM in order to respond to this challenge. As might be expected, the Russians had no first strike weapons at the time.[27]

What begins as an article in one of the promilitarist journals or as a document in a public or private think tank becomes, what John Kenneth Galbraith calls, "conventional wisdom." It is repeated by top Pentagon and government officials who command headlines, by friendly columnists and newspaper editors, until a majority of the nation begins to believe it. Thus there evolves such firm "wisdom" as:

> "We have to fight fire with fire—guns with guns."
>
> "If we don't fight them in Vietnam we'll have to fight them in California."
>
> "You can't trust the Russians."

Obviously any private person or group has a right to its opinion. But there is a *public* quality to this opinion-shaping campaign by the military–industrial complex: first, because much of it is paid for directly or indirectly by the government, and second, because it is a self-serving effort to gain dollars or power from public institutions. Worse still, the manufactured theorems continuously fan out from the militarist opinion makers so that if the effect is subtle it is, nonetheless, overwhelming. Dr. Ralph McDonald of the National Education Association (NEA) said many years ago that there are two ways of destroying freedom—through concentration camps and through "influencing public opinion."[28] There are no concentration camps in the United States—though the FBI has a secret list of American citizens it intends to put in them when it gets the word—but there is no doubt that public opinion has been influenced by the military–industrial complex into an authoritarian and promilitarist mold. And to compound the problem, the very operations of the military–industrial complex rearranges the power structure in the United States so that the militarist faction becomes more impregnable.

7

The Co-optation of Dissenters

By a process of political osmosis the militarist élan has seeped into important milieus which normally would be antiestablishment. Like so much else in the saga of the permanent war this too was neither premeditated nor venal. In fact, many establishment figures themselves have been much concerned about this development. In his famous farewell address to the nation on January 17, 1961, President Eisenhower referred to the effects of this process on academia: "The prospect of domination of the nation's scholars by Federal employment, project allocations, and the power of money is ever present—and is gravely to be regarded."[1] Despite such misgivings, however, the necessities imposed by a permanent war have prodded the militarist state to co-opt allies not only in academia, but the labor movement, the student movement, book publishing, foundations, even the churches. And to the extent that these elements have aligned themselves with the National Security State they have weakened countervailing power, and to that extent democracy itself.

The co-optation of union and academic forces have been particularly significant. The former because it made it possible for the CIA to penetrate foreign labor movements without which its work might have been sterile in many places; the latter for the reasons alluded to by Eisenhower. Their stories are worth recounting to illustrate the insidiousness of the process.

For decades the AFL-CIO leadership, and before that the AFL, has condemned unions in communist countries for being agencies of their governments. But in recent years, as Bernard Nossiter observed in the *Washington Post*, "to some extent at least, American unions have acquired the same image through their relationships with the foreign policy bureaucracies of Washington."[2] The American labor hierarchy became a segment of the military–industrial complex partly to protect millions of jobs dependent on armaments, partly because of its conservative philosophy. (The CIO, though more liberal and less inclined to act as a government agent, lost its independent role when it merged with the larger AFL in 1955.)

Prior to the Second World War, the interest of the AFL in international affairs had been minimal. In 1937 the menace of fascism in Europe and the competition of the CIO at home, drove the AFL temporarily into the ranks of the International Federation of Trade Unions. But on the whole its participation in international affairs had been remote and of minor importance. World War II, however, changed matters. With victory in the offing it was obvious that something had to be done to help unionists in Europe who had been living underground during the years of Nazi and fascist domination. Their aid would be pivotal in rebuilding the continent when the fighting ended.

Two union officials of uniquely opposite backgrounds teamed up to provide help for noncommunist labor leaders in Europe: David Dubinsky, president of the Ladies' Garment Workers' Union and a former dress cutter who had once been a socialist, and Matthew Woll, an arch conservative and bitterly anticommunist head of the photoengravers union. Together they established the Labor League for Human Rights "for war relief purposes and for support of labor causes everywhere." The League offered humanitarian aid for European unionists still in the underground or coming out of it. Dubinsky's New York locals raised $300,000 to rescue many such people and keep them in food and shelter.

In 1944 the two American union officials, now joined by AFL president William Green and George Meany, who would soon succeed him, got down to more serious business. They established the Free Trade Union Committee (FTUC) to revive unions in Europe and Japan and "to help such unions . . . to resist the new drives of totalitarian [i.e. communist] forces." Ironically they chose the former head of the Communist Party, Jay Lovestone, for executive secretary.

A vigorous and intelligent man in his midforties, Lovestone had been one of the founders of the Communist Party after World War I and its general secretary in 1929 when Moscow ordered him expelled. He had made the mistake of picking the wrong horse in the three-way fight between Stalin, Trotsky, and Bukharin—he had aligned himself with Bukharin. Once separated from the official Communist Party, he formed the Communist Party (Opposition) and for a decade tried to regain admission to the Communist International. Lovestone continued to defend the Soviet Union as the "citadel of labor, showing the workers the real way out of the awful hell of capitalism." Then early in the 1940s he dissolved his organization and began the turn toward an anticommunism which soon became as fierce as his anticapitalism. Former comrades brought him together with Dubinsky.

He was an ideal choice for the FTUC. He spoke the language of European Marxists—a language alien to most U.S. labor leaders and to the State Department—and he had contacts with other former communists in the old world who, like himself, had been expelled from their parties by Stalin. He also commanded a small bank of associates, most notably Irving Brown, son of an active teamster, who had worked his way through college, participated in various union and unemployed movements, and joined with Lovestone in the mid-1930s. In addition, the group included men and women of similar hue, equally conversant with left-wing and Marxist rhetoric, equally committed to saving the world labor movement from communism. This was in fact the first contingent of cold warriors, embarked on an anticommunist crusade at a time (1944–47) when the American government still nursed residual hopes of coexisting with the Soviets and when the communists themselves were in a remarkably moderate mood.

The transformation of the Lovestone–Brown team is instructive. Whatever else may be said of them they were not crude. Their strategy rested, as Brown explains it, on two prongs. First and foremost, they sought "safe" leaders in Europe, Japan, and what is now known as the Third World, to build effective mass movements. Thus they worked for a while with genuine nationalist revolutionaries, including Ahmed Ben Bella in Algeria and, up to his death, with Patrice Lumumba in the Congo (Zaire). They denounced fascist Spain, apartheidist South Africa, and the dictatorships of Paraguay and Haiti, on the theory that such forces offered communism its strongest rationale.

The trouble was that when it proved impossible to find allies like Ben Bella and Lumumba, the Lovestone team was prepared to support almost any force or measure that might defeat communism, including military coups and interventions. The bottom line was whether the person or plan helped or hindered the communists. Brown often explained to visitors when he was in Paris that collaboration with the American government was on the same order as Lenin's willingness in 1917 to travel in a sealed train through Germany to get back to Russia. If it were all right for Lenin to accept help from the Kaiser to fight the Czar, it was all right for Brown and Lovestone to accept help from Washington to defeat Moscow. In the Brown–Lovestone scheme of things, the world was bipolar and you had to choose one side or the other: being neutral was as bad as being communist. Neutralism was a "conscious or unwitting ally of Soviet imperialism" because it didn't align itself with the United States, the only nation capable of defeating the Soviets. Neutralists like Jawaharlal Nehru of India were referred to as "aides-de-camp" of communism.

The communists, having played so decisive a role in the European underground, inevitably assumed leadership of many unions when Nazi troops were expelled. They predominated in Italy and France, were influential in Greece, and had sizable forces elsewhere. Brown and Lovestone were unwilling to accept this state of affairs. Their first order of business was to prevent the communists from entrenching themselves in Germany, and to split off noncommunist union leaders in Italy and France. Initially their method of operation was prosaically simple. Europe was digging out from the shambles of war; everyone was hungry. Union leaders lacked food for their families, typewriters, mimeograph machines, newsprint, and offices for their unions. A man who could produce such items was months, perhaps a year or two, ahead of his rivals. The Soviets were providing for communists and procommunist laborites in their zones of occupation. The AFL, under Operation Food, sent 5,000 packages to Germany, 15,000 to France, 2,000 to Austria, and 5,000 to Greece, all to unionists of their choice. It also provided equipment, supplies, and cash. By such methods Brown built a cadre of union leaders in Germany who, with the aid of the American military government, emerged at the head of the reestablished trade unions. Dubinsky was probably right when he wrote in January 1949 that had it not been for AFL aid "the Communists . . . might by now have seized control of the reviving German trade unions."[3]

It is considered unethical for unionists of one country to interfere in the internal affairs of unions of other countries, just as it is for nations to interfere in the internal affairs of other nations; but Brown and Lovestone did so constantly, with few pangs of conscience. The AFL team desperately needed money—millions—which was only available from the U.S. government; the CIA needed an entrée into the labor movements of Europe and the Third World which it could not acquire easily on its own. A marriage with the State Department and the CIA was inevitable.

In France and Italy, where unified labor federations were communist controlled, Brown's work consisted of artificially splitting the movement. In France Brown prodded his friends to break from the unified General Confederation of Labor (CGT) as quickly as possible, and to refuse any collaboration with the communists in strikes. Beginning in May 1947 a wave of walkouts took place for wage increases. A few business unionists and moderate socialists, arguing that the strikes were both unnecessary and politically inspired, used them as a pretext to withdraw from the CGT and regroup around a publication called *Force Ouvrière.* The aging Leon Jouhaux, leader of French labor for decades, opposed the split as premature. He argued that it would be better to remain within CGT and win over a larger constituency. But he was overruled and carried along. The resulting Force Ouvrière was a minor force at birth and remained so for decades. The only thing it didn't lack was cash, which was secretly supplied by Brown in part, at least, from the treasury of the newly established CIA.

On May 20, 1967, a former CIA official who directed the program of anticommunist fronts in Europe for a few years, Thomas W. Braden, recorded in an article for the *Saturday Evening Post:*

> In 1947 the Communist CGT led a strike in Paris which came near to paralyzing the French economy. A takeover of the government was feared. Into this crisis stepped Lovestone and his

> assistant Irving Brown. With funds from Dubinsky's union, they organized Force Ouvrière, a non-Communist union. When they ran out of money they appealed to the CIA. Thus began the secret subsidy of free trade unions. . . . Without that subsidy postwar history might have gone very differently.

The split engineered by the AFL in the Italian labor movement took a different form from that of France. Here Brown and Harry Goldberg, another Lovestone aide, made common cause with the Catholics in the labor movement because the socialists, both right and left wing, refused to accept their blandishments and decided to remain with the Italian General Confederation of Labor (CGIL). The Lovestone team, bent on breaking away any unionists they could from the communist-controlled federation, therefore financed a split from CGIL by a small group of Catholics. In Greece, Brown built a little empire around Fotis Makris, a right-wing politician who took over the unions after the government had purged them of the communists.

The most interesting drama of this period was Brown's support for a strikebreaking effort in Marseilles, France. In 1949–50 communist dock workers refused to unload American arms in Marseilles or any other ports. Whether they were right or wrong is beside the point; it was something for French labor and the French government to decide. But Brown injected himself into the situation foursquare. He subsidized (with CIA funds, according to Thomas Braden) a man named Pierre Ferri-Pisani to form a "Mediterranean committee" for the purpose of getting the weapons unloaded. Ferri-Pisani's thugs beat up and hospitalized dock workers, tossed them into the river, and killed a few until the waterfront was finally cleared. According to the British magazine, *Private Eye*, Brown paid out $225,000 for this and similar strikebreaking in Italy and North Africa.[4]

The AFL was a sizable organization in the postwar period, with 9 or 10 million members, but it had nowhere near the money to play its self-assigned role in international affairs—until, that is, it formed a partnership, and allowed itself to be co-opted by the CIA. The agency was giving Lovestone and his team $2 million a year in those days, says Thomas Braden.

The AFL-CIO became an integrated part of the National Security

State. Part of its international affairs machine functioned sub rosa, not only secretly splitting labor movements on all continents or forming new ones with its own anticommunist philosophy but, also, by gathering intelligence. On October 5, 1947, the *New York Times* reported the formation of the Free Trade Union Center in Exile, made up of emigrés from Central Europe and Russia, with headquarters in the offices of Force Ouvrière in Paris. According to the *Times*, it also "appears to have at its disposal a working intelligence division." Edwin Lahey, Washington correspondent of the *Chicago Daily News*, noted that "Lovestone insists rather sheepishly that there is no formal connection between him and the Central Intelligence Agency, nor between him and the Department of State, [but] it can be stated without qualification that the CIA . . . has in recent years obtained much of its primary information about international communism from Lovestone." A *Chicago Tribune* dispatch of December 17, 1954, stated that "Lovestone readily agreed that his AFL Free Trade Union Committee is engaged in intelligence work." A laudatory *Reader's Digest* article on Irving Brown by a former AFL staffer, Donald Jahn, reported that Hans Jahn, head of the German rail union, "told me about an undercover organization he has set up. . . . Irving Brown helped us. . . . Much of what he [Brown] has done in the cloak-and-dagger realm cannot be recounted. It would endanger the lives of his associates and jeopardize their missions."

Another segment of the AFL-CIO team functioned in the open, as U.S. government officials. George P. (Phil) Delaney was appointed a special assistant in the State Department to serve as the AFL-CIO's liaison. In addition there were sixty-five labor attachés in American embassies abroad, who, according to Dan Kurzman of the *Washington Post*, "must always get Lovestone's stamp of approval." There were also 150 labor personnel either attached to the Agency for International Development (AID) missions abroad or working for AID and the State Department at home. If the numbers were not large, the machine nevertheless was formidable. What the U.S. government could not do directly itself because it would be flagrant meddling in the internal affairs of other nations, and what the CIA could not do openly because it was suspect, the AFL-CIO machine did on their behalf. The AFL-CIO was able to provide information for the CIA that it could not get on its own, or could only get with greater difficulty. By way of example, the Oil, Chemical and Atomic Workers (OCAW), headed by O.A. "Jack" Knight, helped establish a worldwide International Federation of Petroleum and Chemical Workers (IFPCW) early in the 1960s. It was, in the parlance of the left, a "paper organization." Victor Reuther, former head of the international affairs department of the UAW, writes that the affiliates, except for OCAW and the Venezuelan unions, were "weak, poorly organized, and almost without funds." But Knight contributed generously to the Federation, four or five times what the OCAW was required to pay. The money, it turned out, came from CIA dummy foundations, such as the Hamilton Fund and the Midland Foundation. According to Reuther, what the CIA got for its money was "information it wanted from Venezuela, Argentina, Brazil, India, Indonesia, Italy, Japan, Lebanon, Malaya, the Netherlands, Nigeria, Turkey, Iran, Saudi Arabia—wherever petroleum refining was done."[5] In ostensibly innocent relationships between unions of one country and another, the AFL-CIO foreign affairs machine threw its weight toward the making and unmaking of governments, with the purpose of aligning them into the American empire.

An extreme example of this sort of behavior was the attempt to overthrow the government of British Guiana in 1962. Guiana, a small nation with only 600,000 people at the time, was still under British rule, and Cheddi Jagan—an independent Marxist and spokesperson for the Indian majority—was its prime minister.[6] Since the colony was awaiting independence there was much anxiety in Washington and London about a "second Cuba." What seemed like a golden opportunity to dispose of Jagan came when the prime minister introduced a new labor relations law (modeled on the American Wagner Act) which caused concern among Guianese union leaders who believed that if elections were held they might lose control of the sugar union, which was the largest union in the country. They decided to call a national strike rather than allow this to happen, and in this situation, Neil Sheehan of the *New York Times* reported, "the Central Intelligence Agency, working under cover of an American labor union" stepped in to give the strike support and direction.

The influx of American union officials to this tiny land in 1963 was remarkable. It included Andrew McClellan, a Latin American specialist for AFL-CIO's international affairs department; Ernest S.

Lee, George Meany's son-in-law; and William C. Doherty, the head of the American Institute for Free Labor Development (AIFLD). Controlled by the AFL-CIO were William Howard McCabe and Arnold Zander of the State, County, and Municipal Workers union, Gene Meakins of the Newspaper Guild, Gerard P. O'Keefe, acting director of the Asian-American Free Labor Institute (AAFLI), and four or five others. According to a secret report by the British police superintendent on the scene—quoted by Susanne Bodenheimer in the November 1967 issue of *The Progressive*—O'Keefe was financing "the activities of the 'security force' (organized gangs) . . . including assassinations and destruction of public buildings with 'explosives and arson.'" Others concentrated on training, giving advice, and passing out money for strike relief. A Guianese union official named Pollidor said that the strike benefits for the 25,000 workers came entirely from American sources. What emerges is a strange picture of an American labor hierarchy, using CIA funds to subsidize a foreign union strike, for the purpose of overthrowing a legitimate government. The strike failed in this objective, but it was an important factor in Jagan's subsequent electoral loss to Forbes Burnham.

Four years later some of the people and organizations involved in this incident admitted receiving CIA money regularly. The Newspaper Guild conceded it had taken $1 million from CIA foundations. Zander put the sum he obtained from the CIA at $12,000 to $15,000 a year, but *New Politics* magazine put it at $100,000, and "considerably greater sums" for McCabe.

As the AFL-CIO activities fanned out, it established the American Institute for Free Labor Development (AIFLD) in 1962, and in the following years the African-American Labor Center (AALC) and the Asian-American Free Labor Institute (AAFLI). The function of these bodies was to train unionists around the world in the CIA brand of anticommunism, and to use them in critical moments to carry out the policies of the U.S. National Security State. Money for education, housing, and other social projects, came from the exchequer of the U.S. government—at first from the CIA but after 1967 when the CIA connection became public knowledge, from the Agency for International Development (AID) whose image was less tarnished. William C. Doherty, Jr., Executive Director of AIFLD, once boasted that 92 percent of his budget came from government funds, the rest from the AFL-CIO and "some 95 business establishments with interests in Latin America."[7] The American Institute for Free Labor Development helped build 18,048 housing units in the hemisphere at a cost of $77 million (mostly from AID funds), but its primary overt activity has been education.

In the twenty-one years after AIFLD was formed (with the participation, incidentally, of such notorious antilabor employers as J. Peter Grace), some 440,758 workers were given labor courses by AIFLD instructors, including almost 4,000 who had gone through advanced training at the Front Royal Institute in Virginia and the George Meany Center for Labor Studies in Washington. The courses include standard items such as labor history, grievance machinery, union administration, and the like. But they also stress, in such courses as "Political Systems: Democracy and Totalitarianism," the overriding need to combat communism and neutralism.[8]

A disillusioned former AID official in Bolivia recalled: "By the definition of AIFLD anyone who wanted a raise was a communist. Its whole purpose was to make the 120 or so men it trained into government supporters. It was willing to do something for union men only if they would kick the communists out of their union."[9] In more critical moments, the unionists trained by the three AFL-CIO bodies were enlisted either to help the CIA overthrow governments it didn't like (in the Dominican Republic, Brazil, Chile) or buttress conservative regimes it did like (in Vietnam).

In 1963 the regime of Juan Bosch in the Dominican Republic was under severe pressure by business because it refused to outlaw the Communist Party and it refused to denationalize, and sell to private entrepreneurs, hundreds of millions of dollars of property seized from the deposed dictator Rafael Trujillo. The chorus against Bosch's "softness" on communism was joined openly by the American military attachés and by Fred Somerford, the U.S. labor attaché. They were joined by CONATRAL, the union federation linked to AIFLD, which ran a newspaper ad calling on the workers to put their faith in the "armed forces" to restrain communism; it was jubilant when the armed forces overthrew Bosch; and it was the only labor federation in 1965 which supported intervention by American marines.[10]

The role of AIFLD and its trainees in Brazil during the military coup of 1964 against president Joao Goulart was perhaps more consequential. In March 1964 Goulart threatened to nationalize petroleum refineries and institute a land reform that would deprive large landholders of some of their holdings. In the wake of this "crisis," General Humberto Castelo Branco executed a coup on April 1, with CIA aid and encouragement. William Doherty, chief of AIFLD, boasted on a radio program three months later that AIFLD labor students who were trained in the United States, were "so active they became intimately involved in some of the clandestine operations of the revolution before it took place on April 1. What happened in Brazil was planned—and planned months in advance. Many of the trade union leaders—some of whom were actually trained in our institute—were involved in the revolution and in the overthrow of the Goulart regime."[11] Later, hundreds of AIFLD students were assigned by Castelo to "reorganize" militant unions whose leaders were ousted by the dictatorship.

The activity of the American labor hierarchy has paralleled that of the American establishment to a distressing extent. For example, while Richard Nixon, Henry Kissinger, and the ITT corporation were trying to rid Chile of President Salvador Allende—a socialist who was democratically elected—AIFLD, in May 1971, assisted in the formation of an anti-Allende Confederation of Chilean Professionals (CUPROCH) which joined in the truck owners' and merchants' strike of October 1972 to destabilize the Allende regime.[12] The following year Allende was overthrown by General Augusto Pinochet Ugarte, Latin America's most brutal dictator in recent years.

During the Vietnam War the AFL transmitted CIA and other U.S. funds to a labor movement in that country which was little more than a shadow but, nonetheless, served to flesh out an image of democracy for the Thieu regime. Early in August 1969, Senator J. William Fulbright charged that the Kennedy and Johnson administrations had given the AFL-CIO a $33 million "payoff" to its three institutes for support of the Vietnam War. The federation's president, George Meany, called the charge a "gratuitous insult," but admitted that the three groups had received such money "to carry out the foreign policy of the United States government." Fulbright insisted it was improper for the U.S. "to provide money to any private organization to go out and influence foreign governments and their parliaments."[13] Victor Reuther, former head of the UAW international affairs department emphasized the other side of the problem in September 1982 when he said during an interview: "How can you work hand in glove with the CIA and the multinationals in overthrowing Goulart or Allende and still stand up to them in the United States?"[14] The answer of course is that you can't, and the labor movement has, no doubt, paid a price for the misguided activities of its hierarchy. In recent years the movement has been losing more than half of the elections it has participated in for union recognition, as well as millions of its members. Its bargaining power has been weaker than at any time since the 1930s; millions of its members, even in the period of economic upswing, 1983–85, were forced to give back benefits they had gained in previous years. Not all of this can be attributed to collaboration with the government, but there is no doubt that the collaboration caused a decline in militancy and effectiveness.

The effect of the partnership with government (and to an extent, industry) in international affairs was to make the union leadership more secure for a time, the rank and file relatively more impotent, and the unions themselves more institutionalized. In critical moments, such as a major national strike or a breakdown in national bargaining, union leaders sometimes applied to government leaders to effect a compromise behind the scenes. But in the end, that did not slow the decline of unions in the smokestack industries, construction, and trucking, nor did it help in unionizing such pockets of antiunionism as the South. Nor did labor win any significant social benefits, such as national health insurance, in return for its co-optation by the National Security State.

As the saga of the AFL-CIO indicates, the National Security State cannot be effective without allies in the world outside of itself. While some of those allies are traditionally pro-establishment—for instance, big business and almost all veterans organizations—others are not. The extent which nonconformist allies can be co-opted to the militarist machine deprives the nation of the countervailing power which is the backbone of democracy. Next to the labor hierarchy, for instance, the most important milieu drawn into the military–industrial complex has been academia.

Before World War II academia stood on the sidelines of the military game. The War Department had no need to call on the campus for help because weapons were pretty simple. Electronics were rudimentary and nuclear physics was still a preoccupation of the ivory towers, seemingly with no practical value. The rudiments of atomic energy were still not developed. World War II, however, witnessed a qualitative change in weaponry, and with it a qualitative change in the relationship between the military and the professors. The Manhattan Project to produce the atom bomb was the prototype of this relationship. At its height, it enlisted thousands of scientists and engineers, most of whom were working on specialized subtasks without knowing what the final product would be.

As nuclear energy development and electronics were harnessed to the war machine, considerable segments of academia were harnassed to what was then the War Department. The University of Chicago became the site for the first controlled nuclear chain reaction. Massachusetts Institute of Technology (MIT) performed miracles in developing radar at its radiation laboratory. Johns Hopkins became the specialist in the self-deteriorating proximity fuse. The University of California worked on the atom bomb, and later the hydrogen bomb. Sonar, snorkels, guided missiles, walkie-talkies, jet planes, and many other weapons of war were the end result of basic and applied research on the campus. Equally important, the universities turned out the tens of thousands of scientists, engineers, and mathematicians to man the ramparts in factories, the War Department, and the new contract centers placed on many campuses.

When the war was over, academia had a choice of remaining conscripted to war research or breaking the umbilical cord. Some nationally known scientists, like Leo Szilard, had second thoughts about the miracles they had wrought—especially the atom bomb—and refused to be further involved. The wartime Office of Scientific Research and Development (OSRD) had been deactivated because of a dispute in professional ranks as to whether to go ahead with work on the hydrogen bomb. The only military agency still making money available to the universities on a sizable scale was the Office of Naval Research.

Before long, however, the Pentagon realized the significance of research and development (R&D) for its future and eager academics were again ready to accept its money. The Department of Defense's R&D budget rose from a half-billion at the end of the war to $8 billion in the 1960s; that of the Atomic Energy Commission (AEC) jumped from $37 million in 1947 to $1.7 billion in 1969; and that of the National Aeronautics and Space Administration (NASA) from $35 million to $4.6 billion. At that time, more than two-thirds of the $18 billion spent by the government for R&D went to those three agencies, and of these sums something like $450 million annually was given to universities, plus $700 million to university-related contract centers on which the universities were paid a management fee. If these sums seem small compared to what was allocated to industry for R&D, it should be noted that at the time the 2,200 colleges and universities themselves spent only $10 billion for education. Key universities like MIT, Johns Hopkins, and Stanford would have been greatly reduced in size and prestige if it were not for military R&D money. The Massachusetts Institute of Technology R&D budget for 1967–68 was $174 million, 95 percent of which came from government coffers and $120 million from defense sources alone. By fiscal 1985 military-related research and development was costing the government $39 billion ($34 billion from the Department of Defense alone), and the share of the universities had grown apace.

Much of the money filtering to academia from the Pentagon was for basic and, to some extent, applied research rather than development, which was left to industry. They were therefore more important in the scale of military procurement than the sums tended to indicate. It can cost hundreds of millions to develop a new weapons system whose utility was discovered in a university laboratory for a few hundred thousand dollars of basic research. The fact is, as former University of California president Clark Kerr has noted in his book, *The Uses of the University*, that "intellect has also become an instrument of national purpose, a component part of the 'military-industrial complex.' "[15] Former Air Force Secretary Robert C. Seamans, Jr. proclaimed that "we cannot provide the necessary weapons for defense without the help of university research laboratories."[16] The United States, he said, would suffer a severe technological setback if government-supported research were halted on the campuses.

Not all professors and researchers were without pangs of conscience over their new activities. Their rationale was sometimes ingenious. University officials, queried about work on chemical and biological weapons (CBW) for the most part denied they were conducting such research, despite the fact that the Pentagon itself listed them as doing so. When award-winning journalist Seymour Hersh pressed them, he received three explanations:

1. The research was basic work and had no connection with CBW.
2. The research was unclassified work that was available to all.
3. The research was strictly defensive in nature.[17]

This had the familiar ring of George Meany's argument before Senator Fulbright's committee that moneys used to buy satellite unions abroad were being spent only in the interests of "fraternal solidarity, humanitarianism in the best sense of the word." Many academics justified their work on behalf of the war machine on the grounds that "if I don't do it, someone else will."

Moreover, money for new laboratories, for high professional salaries, for paying the school's overhead, eased the conscience of academia. Except in a minority of instances the university's conscience became immune to what it was doing. The Army Chemical Center listed eleven universities which collaborated in its poison gas program, including such prestigious schools as UCLA Medical School, Baylor, Texas, Stanford Research Institute, and Cornell Aeronautical Lab. The Army biological labs listed eight universities which experimented with death-dealing germs, including Johns Hopkins, Maryland, Minnesota, Yale, and the Illinois Institute of Technology (IIT). The Army Dugway Proving Ground, where a plane spraying nerve gas in 1968 missed its target and killed 6,000 sheep, enlisted talent from IIT, Utah, Utah State, and the ever-present Stanford Research Institute. The Air Force recruited brains for CBW from Cornell, IIT, and Florida; the Navy from the University of California at Berkeley. As of 1967 the Pentagon's list of contractors in this field included fifty-two colleges and universities, or one of every forty schools of higher learning in the country.[18]

Not all professors and colleges enrolled in the military–industrial complex. But enough sectors were involved so that it affected the whole character of academia, and its morality. The universities did for the National Security State what it could not do for itself, or could not do without serious damage to its image. For instance, in 1955, a year after the United States grudgingly approved the accords signed by France and the Vietminh at Geneva ending their war, fifty-four professors from Michigan State University acted as cover for the U.S. to violate the Geneva accords. Their main job was to train the palace guard (a virtual army) and the police, as well as to supply them with guns, ammunition, tear gas, trucks, grenades, and other weapons. According to Robert Scheer they also controlled the secret police. As a whole, this project was the most brazen interference by a university in the internal affairs of another nation, and undoubtedly contributed to the full-scale war that later ensued under President Johnson.[19] Individual professors allayed their consciences by arguing they were not involved in the "dirty work" part of the project. And some did excellent work—for instance Professor Frank C. Child who did a survey of the economy. The same division of labor, however, exists in the army itself: the master sergeant who runs the office is not killing people like the machine gunner who shoots down enemy troops, but they are both part of the same process.

Among the items academia made possible for the Pentagon was secret research by the Pennsylvania Institute for Cooperative Research on herbicides and defoliants (soon to be used in Vietnam), aerial systems to disseminate arsenic compounds by the same university, and incendiary weapons such as flamethrowers and napalm by Cornell, Tulane, and Oklahoma universities. Oklahoma's assignment was to look into the "susceptibility of potential target components to defeat by thermal action"—acadamese for how to kill guerrillas with incendiary bombs. The process sometimes became tangled. The University of Maryland medical school grudgingly accepted money from the Pentagon to study a certain type of disease on the rationale it was research that fitted into a *pattern* of nonmilitary studies it was doing. That was true, but the military gave funds because it had hopes that the virus involved might make a good biological warfare agent.

The same can be said of the space program. As of now, landing on the moon has no military significance and scientists engaged in the moon–space project feel no pangs of conscience about furthering the goals of militarism. But an integral part of the space program is the development of space stations and the shuttle, which definitely have a military objective. In the world of military research it is difficult to delineate where "peace" work ends and "war" work begins. Project Agile, for instance, was once the Pentagon's major program for research in counterinsurgency, but one of its jobs was to develop a new plastic container for the rice and "numcom" sauce eaten by South Vietnamese soldiers. The scientists working on this project may have felt they were performing a nonwar service, but as *Newsweek* commented, they were contributing "to raising the fighting potential of the Vietnamese G.I."

Money corrupts, and big money corrupts grandiosely. Just as the 100 top defense contractors receive the bulk of Pentagon contracts, so the largest and most prestigious universities get the major share of DoD, AEC, and NASA money. The California Institute of Technology (Caltech)—formerly headed by President Nixon's science advisor, Lee A. DuBridge and then by former Air Force Secretary Harold Brown—was given $3.5 million by the Pentagon for research in 1968, and $5 million by NASA and AEC. This was more money than it received from the whole student body for tuition that year. Grand new buildings that might otherwise not be built on such prestigious campuses rise up only because of military funds. The Stanford Space Engineering and Science Building was erected with $2 million from NASA and $1 million from the Air Force. The materials science program underwrote new facilities at Brown and Cornell, among others. And more important than the buildings are the computers and technical equipment which might also be out of the university's reach without Pentagon largesse.

Government money draws many of the best professors and the best students to the top universities specializing in war work. A survey published by Brookings some years ago revealed that one quarter of the scientists at twelve top universities received part of their regular salaries from federal funds, and that at one of these schools there were 151 professors whose full pay came from the federal treasury. To expect such men and women to be neutral on the issue of militarism, or to be antimilitarist, is stretching human nature a bit too far. With rare exceptions few of them preach pacifism to their students, or do picket duty against a nuclear facility.

A professor working at one of the federally funded research and development centers (contract centers) administered by such schools as Johns Hopkins, Columbia, MIT, or University of California is assured a salary much higher than he might get either as a teacher or working directly for the Pentagon. Thousands do consulting work for industry or think tanks on the side, augmenting or even doubling what they earn at the university or contract center. Many academics become rich in spin-off operations from research they first did for the military. Along Route 128 in Massachusetts there are a few hundred such spin-off firms from MIT and Harvard, where professors continue to do what they were doing at contract centers and continue to receive DoD money, but now pocket the profits as private entrepreneurs. A similar complex of 200 aerospace and electronics firms exists around Stanford on the West Coast.

Profits and higher earnings, of course, are not the only factors that drive the academic community into the military–industrial complex. There is also the matter of equipment and grants. It takes hundreds of thousands of dollars, sometimes millions, to equip a modern physics or biological laboratory. For those who toe the militarist line, that money is available from the three militarist sources. A professor or graduate student who wants the best facilities to work with is virtually forced toward these institutions. That is where he or she can do the most advanced work, and that is where the prestige is.

This is not only true in the physical sciences, but also in the behavioral sciences which are so dependent these days on expensive computers. Years ago Professor Kenneth Boulding of Michigan tried to get a quarter of a million dollars for his Center for Research and Conflict Resolution to study unilateral initiatives that might slow or end the arms race. He was turned down. On the other hand, the Center for Research in Social Sciences (CRESS) and the Human Resources Research Office (HumRRO) which did work for the Army received many millions for social science studies. For example, CRESS, part of the American University complex in Washington, DC handled, under a different name, Project Camelot which studied counterinsurgency problems in Chile, Brazil, and other places. At George Washington University, HumRRO trained soldiers in firing anything from an M-1 rifle to a Nike Zeus missile and gave them crash language courses and other skills needed for counterinsurgency. Protests led such schools to reduce or sever ties with the military, but the Pentagon no doubt found other academic allies for social research.

Far too many professors and schools let themselves be drawn to "where the money is." When asked to comment on the military–industrial complex, a high official of an eastern university told two newspaper reporters, "I must be careful of what I say. I have millions in research I'm in charge of. Now that's off the record."[20] That is hardly the spirit of a free academia. Such professors outline projects for DoD, the Department of Energy (which is in charge of producing nuclear bombs), and NASA, not necessarily because that is their main scholarly interest but because that is where money is available. Their research becomes *mission* research for a government agency, rather than the quest for knowledge based on their own proclivities. In the course of time, therefore, there has emerged a solid complex of civilian militarists on campuses who foster and promote mission research. These are the professors who serve on a host of government advisory boards, such as the Defense Science Board (DSB), the President's Science Advisory Committee (PSAC), and the like. In 1969 there were eighteen such professors from the University of California alone, including the rabidly militaristic Edward Teller. Some of these professors and university chancellors have served on the boards of Ford, General Electric, McDonnell Douglas, and the like.

During the Vietnam War student protests forced many academic institutions to curtail research for the Pentagon. In 1972, under campus pressure, the University of Michigan Regents passed a resolution that the "University will not enter into or renew any agreement or contract, or accept any grant, the clearly foreseeable and probable result of which . . . is to destroy human life or to incapacitate human beings."[21] The trend, however, has now been reversed. As of 1981 some 250 colleges and universities were receiving a billion dollars annually in military-related contracts—more than they received from corporations that year.[22] The funds, of course, are not equally divided: two institutions, MIT and Johns Hopkins, usually got a larger portion than any of the others. But even small amounts of a million or two, sometimes a few hundred thousand, can be a boon to colleges strapped for money.

The tendency therefore is to overdevelop those departments

which have a good chance of garnering funds from the Pentagon, NASA, and the Department of Energy, while neglecting those that don't. The humanities are neglected in favor of science, engineering, mathematics, and business, because those are the areas more eligible for military-oriented grants and future jobs for graduates. Teaching is neglected in favor of research—for the same reason. To get the military money, the universities must also bend age-old academic principles of free inquiry and openness—agreeing, for instance, to seek security clearance for some professors and administrators, and to keep the results of research classified. The National Security Agency has been trying for years to prohibit publication of any material that might help in codebreaking.[23] Pentagon research funding guidelines in 1981 made it a crime to discuss research results dealing with U.S. military technology with foreign scholars and students. Steve Burkholder, a former research fellow of the Congressional Research Service, reported in June 1981, that at Princeton, "which has long proclaimed itself a center for the free exchange of knowledge and ideas, the volume of research has reached such proportions that more than 160 of its employees—including the president and the provost—now hold security clearances. . . ."[24]

George Gamota, director of the University of Michigan Institute of Science and Technology, expressed a widely held view among university administrators when he said that a school's value must be judged by its research and "product-orientation." He told a school dissident that there was "a glut of people in less critical areas" such as the humanities, and he suggested that the universities could do with "half the current number of professors . . . in those fields."[25]

Military grants do not always pay for projects with "obvious military utility" says the Committee on the University and the Military at the State University of New York (Stony Brook), "but the funding source does make a difference. Of all the possibly interesting questions that could be investigated, scientists tend to study those problems for which funds have been made available. Thus the new DoD policy is creating a narrowed pattern of research interests by encouraging the training of scientific investigators in some specialties to the neglect of others." The tendency is to influence not only the ratio of teaching to research and the humanities to science, but the very direction of science technology. "Who then," asks the Committee, "will underwrite ecology research, medical studies [such as aging], investigations of pressing social problems, experiments in the arts? Can we expect many DoD-funded investigations of the structure of Aristophanes's antiwar play Lysistrata? Or indeed, an unbiased history of the antiwar movement?"[26]

Ira Glasser in a 1968 speech on the Bill of Rights at the University of Michigan, best sums up the story of academe's co-optation by militarism:

> Whatever universities once were and are still supposed by some of us to be, they now must be considered a new kind of institution, defined more by their obligation to serve the state than by any obligation to either teach or discover new knowledge. The transformation of the university is a direct result of the extension of military values into the lair of freedom. Course offerings, curricula, faculties, and libraries have to a growing extent been shaped and limited by national purposes as defined by military and paramilitary agencies.[27]

The co-optation of educational systems into the military–industrial complex reaches a notch or two below the university level. It begins with the glorification of militarism in the high schools and elementary schools. An analysis of eleven "widely used junior high and high school history texts" by researchers for the *Bulletin* of the Council on Interracial Books for Children illustrates the subtlety of militarist indoctrination. None of the books "raised philosophical questions about the acceptability of war," or made any effort "to show the extent of human suffering." While the texts did not glamorize war per se, they nonetheless were embellished by "the detail given to military strategy, in the adjectives used to describe particular wars, and in the ways U.S. war leaders are extolled. . . . " War leaders and wars are referred to in value-laden terms such as *heroic*, *courageous*, and *terrific*. Ten of the eleven history books "dismiss the effects of the bombings [of Hiroshima and Nagasaki] in two sentences or less." Five do have pictorial illustrations of one of the two bombed cities, but only one shows people. None of the eleven books disputes the standard Truman argument that the atom bombs "saved" many American lives. None questions the validity of Eisenhower's and Kennedy's nuclear threats. The antiwar movement of the 1960s gets mixed treatment, some realistic, some ridiculous, but the antinuclear movement of the 1970s and 1980s "is dismissed in a sentence or two about critics who question the safety of nuclear power plants."[28] Glorification of war in our educational system is nothing new, of course, but it has an added significance in a period like the present when the establishment is trying so hard to promote militarist values. It supplements and reinforces everything else.

These same cultural values are instilled in pre-high school children in schools, books, TV, movies, toys, and lately videogames, making them prey, in the words of Patrice Wagner, assistant editor of the *Village Voice*, "for recruitment efforts, a fact the Pentagon has not overlooked."[29] Television programs like "Private Benjamin" or "At Ease" make it appear that service in the armed forces is a lark; movies like *An Officer and a Gentleman* salute its values. Though some school systems demur, the military usually has access to high schools: it is sometimes offered a recruitment office on school premises. The services, like veterans' organizations, appeal first of all to self-interest—the military will prepare you for a better career, take you to exotic places, make you a leader, "all while serving your country." "Be all that you can be, keep on growing," states an Army television jingle. "Be all that you can be, 'cause we need you in the Army." Ron Alridge of the *Chicago Tribune* points out that "none of the commercials shows soldiers, sailors, airmen and marines doing what they are trained to do, which is to fight."[30]

The Pentagon spends about $600 million a year for recruitment, including an advertising budget as large as that of some soap manufacturers. Between 32,000 and 35,000 recruiters each contact more than 300 high school seniors to enroll them in the armed forces. To get leads for the recruiters, the military has a program of nine tests, called Armed Services Vocational Aptitude Battery (ASVAB) which are administered by recruiters in uniform to more than a million and a half students in 16,000 high schools. "Students are told that ASVAB is designed to "give you a good idea about your talents" and "help you find the right career," but in fact it is, as one newspaper columnist put it, "part of a larger effort to use the schools as adjuncts of the enlistment program."[31] By and large school administrators help the recruiters by making space and names available to them.

The propaganda is soft-sell, to begin with, but it is persistent. Military bands, with a budget larger than the federal government allocates for civilian arts, are used "to increase recruiter visibility." The 6,000 musicians in these bands, according to the DoD, "impart the professional image of the military to the potential recruit through radio and television appearances, concerts, shows, and performances at local schools." In addition, as Robert K. Musil reported in the *Nation*, the military used sports clinics which in 1974 alone "reached more than 12,000,000 Americans through radio, TV and newspapers, and were performed before more than 550,000 high school students." Tens of thousands of showings of films produced by the armed forces similarly serve to build respect for the military and its values.

A Junior ROTC program, taught by retired military officers, provides military training in 1,600 high schools. Here, as quoted by Musil, is part of the text used by the Army in such programs: "You may want to take silent weapons in killing, stunning, or capturing individuals. The trench knife and bayonet are excellent weapons. . . . Clubs, blackjacks, sticks, and pistol butts are used chiefly to stun; however a hard blow on the temple or base of the neck may kill. . . . " History, as taught in Junior ROTC classes, refers to Indians as "savages" who must be "pacified"; the Mexican War, we are told, started "when Mexican forces ventured north to the Rio Grande"; and World War I when "news of the Zimmerman note gave evidence of German meddling with American affairs." The two chapters on World War II, writes Irwin Stark in an op-ed column for the *New York Times*, "never mentions the atomic bomb, Nazism, Fascism or the holocaust." As for Vietnam, it "illustrates graphically the dangers and sacrifices the U.S. is willing to suffer on behalf of the policy of military assistance in opposition to aggressive communism." Soviet and Chinese communists are dismissed as having "imperialistic designs" on the United States and other free nations.

Students who want to assure themselves a place in specialized military classes, say computer programming, may enter the Delayed Entry Program in their junior year of high school or earlier, continuing their high school education until induction after graduation. Students are also allowed to enroll in any of 500 colleges, simultaneously enlisting in the Army and taking courses in their spare time from

Army duty. The Army pays the major share of the tuition. The Pentagon's relationship with the Chicago school system may be typical of its nationwide relationship. Of 115,000 high school students, as of November 1982 5,500 were enrolled in Junior ROTC, each taking forty minutes of military training courses every day given by forty-six retired officers. Of the graduates, 1 in 12 (8 percent) is recruited into the armed forces and approximately 100 receive scholarships for military colleges. Though the Board of Education does not have a citywide policy for recruiters to visit classes, the general practice, with some exceptions, is for each principal to set up meetings where recruiters can make their pitch.

How much our society has paid or will pay for this militarization of high schools is impossible to determine. But innumerable young minds, capable of innovative and socially useful endeavors, no doubt have been sidetracked into conformist modes of thinking; young people who might have dedicated themselves to changing the status quo for the better have instead been taught to accommodate themselves to it.

The co-optation of high school youth, the universities, and the labor movement to the National Security State has neutralized a good part of potential opposition to the permanent war. But it is only symptomatic of an ongoing proclivity to do the same throughout our society. In a 1964 hearing of the House Subcommittee on Foundations, Congressman Wright Patman uncovered the names of eight foundations that had been acting as conduits for the CIA—the so-called Patman Eight. Three years later a popular antiwar journal, *Ramparts*, opened a Pandora's box by disclosing that from 1952 to 1967 the CIA had been funding the National Student Association (NSA), the nation's leading organization of students. In both instances, opportunity knocked and the National Security State stepped in.[32]

After World War II student groups from the communist world took the lead in organizing a world student movement and visiting Western student groups to carry their message. Since they had access to government funds in their countries their task was easier than that of American student organizations which had to fund themselves in such endeavors. Thereupon the CIA stepped into the breach, with its usual armloads of money. Two hundred and fifty

U.S. students, for instance, were sponsored to attend youth festivals in Moscow, Vienna, Helsinki, and, as the Church Committee reports, "were used for missions such as reporting on Soviet and Third World personalities or observing Soviet security practices." Here and there the CIA enrolled a student as an "asset" to do intelligence work. The arrangement, of course, was kept secret from rank and file NSA members. "Only the NSA president and the international affairs vice president would be witting of the CIA connection," reports the Senate Select Committee on Intelligence.[33] The CIA also injected itself into the election of NSA officers every year, to make sure of continued control, providing money and advice to the contenders of its choice. "Although the CIA's involvement with the National Student Association was limited to the organization's international activities," concluded the Church Committee, "CIA influence was felt to some extent in its domestic programs as well. The most direct way in which such influence may have been felt was in the selection process for NSA officers. The Summer International Seminars conducted for NSA leaders and potential leaders in the United States during the 1950's and 1960's were a vehicle for the Agency to identify new leaders and to promote their candidacy for elective positions in the National Student Association." The CIA's support of "friends," the investigating committee concluded, "turns into control of their actions and ultimately to creation of new friends."[34]

The Patman revelations helped unravel the "cover" of numerous foundations in addition to the "Patman eight." So extensive was this practice that of the 700 grants of $10,000 or more made by 164 foundations—other than the Rockefeller, Ford, and Carnegie foundations—from 1963 to 1966, CIA funded in part or in whole 108 of them, including almost half of those for international activities. A prestigious institution such as the Center for International Studies at MIT was secretly funded by the CIA. The CIA's in-house study of the matter justified the use of foundations on the ground that it was the most efficient way to conceal the CIA's hand. Some foundations were out and out CIA conduits. Throughout the late 1960s and 1970s new revelations indicated how far the intelligence community had penetrated American domestic life and how it had misused thousands of people whose normal functions should have been open and objective. The Domestic Collection Division of the CIA and the Foreign Resource Division were in contact, according to the Church Committee, "with many thousands of United States academics at hundreds of U.S. academic institutions" for information "ranging from a debriefing to a continuing operational relationship." Several hundreds academics at more than a hundred colleges and universities were enlisted by the CIA to introduce the Agency to other academics "for intelligence purposes." The Agency subsidized the publication of more than 1,250 books, none of which were identified as U.S. government propaganda. It utilized fifty accredited American journalists and media employees to gather intelligence, and when the practice was exposed, the CIA announced in 1976 that it was now using twenty-five "unaccredited" journalists, such as freelancers, stringers, and news executives. Even a few missionaries and church personnel were enrolled as spies.[35]

The Church Select Committee on Intelligence reported that the CIA admitted using twenty-one religious personnel for covert projects or clandestine spying. A U.S. priest informed the CIA about the activities of student and religious dissidents. Some missionaries were said to have done work for the Agency on a grand scale; Jesuit Father James Vizzard charged that a Belgian Jesuit, Father Roger Vekemans, had been given $5 million by the CIA in the early 1960s to finance an educational program in Chile. Vekemans denied the charge, but Vizzard repeated the claim.[36] In December 1975 Senator Mark Hatfield of Oregon introduced a bill that would make CIA use of missionaries for intelligence operations illegal. William Colby, Director of the CIA refused voluntarily to disassociate the CIA from the religious community, on the ground that "in many countries of the world representatives of the clergy, foreign and local, play a significant role and can be of assistance to the U.S. through CIA. . . . "; and President Ford's counsel, Philip Buchen, wrote the Senator that: "the president does not feel it would be wise at present to prohibit the CIA from having any connection with the clergy."[37]

To put the matter in perspective: the co-optation of thousands of people in such areas as labor, academia, and the media for the intelligence and covert activities of the National Security State deprives the United States of a significant bastion of freedom. It is precisely in these milieus that the inspiration often comes for dissent and new ideas, without which democracy is impossible. The intrusion by the

National Security State into their daily affairs cuts off or reduces another source of countervailing power.

The founders of the United States did not believe that governments were inherently trustworthy. They were not anarchists, opposed to government in principle, but they believed government had to be reined in, watched, balanced, constantly reminded it was the servant not the master of the people. The system of separation of powers between executive, legislative, and judicial branches was meant to check tendencies to dictatorship and abuse of power, to prevent, as James Madison put it, a monopoly of power in one branch. That safeguard is now in serious disarray, undermined by the imperial presidency and the National Security State.

A second check on illegitimate authority was expected to come from the people themselves. Armed with the various rights of free speech and free assembly in the first ten amendments to the Constitution, the Bill of Rights, the people would have an incentive to form all kinds of dissenting organizations, write all kinds of innovative articles, and take all kinds of measures of protest to see to it that government officials did not abuse their prerogatives; that the government truly expressed the will of the governed. This countervailing power of the people was to be as important in guarding democracy as the institutional safeguards, or more so.

The tragedy today is that this dike too is in danger of being overwhelmed by the National Security State. With the checks and balances of government already seriously breached, the imposition of conformity on individuals and groups outside government can bring an end to countervailing power, and lead to full control of our lives by the imperial presidency and the military–industrial complex.

8

The Other Costs of Militarism

The purpose of global imperialism was to make America richer, more comfortable, more secure. How close has it come to these objectives?

While it may be immoral for strong nations to dominate weak ones, it has always proved profitable. Imperialism paid immense dividends to Britain, France, and the other imperial powers of the nineteenth and early twentieth centuries, not only to their upper classes but to some extent to their lower classes. Workers in the mother countries were better off than they otherwise might have been because employers at home could "bribe" them with the extraordinary profits earned by exploiting colonial people. In these respects America too has followed the pattern. Its gross national product, in real dollars, adjusted for inflation, more than doubled from 1950 to 1970, and real earnings of working people and corporations followed apace or better. True, there remained large pockets of poverty in the country, particularly among blacks and other minorities—involving about 35 million people by the most recent figures—but they were appreciably smaller than the "one-third who are ill-fed, ill-clothed, ill-housed" that Franklin Roosevelt talked about in the 1930s. Unlike other times in American history, poverty was no longer "majority poverty," and the nation's people, for the most part, enjoyed material amenities they never dreamed possible a half-century ago: automobiles, private homes, the wherewithal to send children to college.

But the benefits of imperialism have been offset by political and social deficits in a way that older imperialisms did not have to contend with, and there is now grave doubt that the material benefits can be sustained much longer as well.

The primary cost that the United States has paid for its imperial policy has been the permanent war, with all its associated surcharges. That includes more than 100,000 battlefield deaths in Korea and Vietnam (not to mention a couple of million Koreans and Vietnamese), $3 trillion in arms expenditures, and a sextupling of the national debt. But most of all, it includes the establishment of a National Security State and the unyielding trend toward totalitarianism.

These were developments that the first postwar leaders did not expect. Though Truman and his aides did not practice the kind of "benign" imperialism Roosevelt prescribed, they did not anticipate much opposition to their global plan either. At Potsdam, after Truman had been advised of the successful test of the first atomic bomb, Winston Churchill noticed that he became cockier: "When he got to the meeting after having read this report he was a changed man. He told the Russians where they got on and off and generally bossed the whole meeting."[1] That cockiness remained in evidence for some time. Bernard Baruch, presidential advisor and financier, expressed the mood of near omnipotence that pervaded Washington forthrightly: "America can get what she wants if she insists on it. After all we've got it—The Bomb—and they haven't and won't have it for a long time to come."[2] Even after it became evident that the Soviets were not going to subordinate themselves to American wishes, the United States fully expected that the policy of "containment" would bring about "the breakup . . . of Soviet power," or at least its "mellowing" within ten or fifteen years at most.

Apart from these costs, imperialism and the permanent war it spawned have exacted other tribute from the American people. Consider some of the side effects of the militarization of America. Though it cannot be measured with arithmetic exactitude, the diversion of $3 trillion to military preparedness that might have been used for improving the infrastructure, providing more social and health benefits, prison reform, building new mental institutions, and other social amenities have had an indisputable impact on the nation's physical and mental well-being. The slowdown in rebuilding the nation's infrastructure, for instance, primarily because the needed funds are going for arms, certainly poses a problem for the future. The Transportation Department asserts that 45 percent of the nation's bridges are "deficient or obsolete," requiring $47.6 billion in repairs. The Joint Economic Committee, as reported by the *New Republic* in August 1982, claims that New York City alone "will soon have to replace or repair 1,000 bridges, two aqueducts, one large water tunnel, several reservoirs, 6,200 miles of streets, 6,000 miles of sewers, 6,000 miles of water lines, 6,700 subway cars, 4,500 buses, 25,000 acres of parks, and hundreds of police and fire stations"—all because funding for the infrastructure fell by 30 percent from 1965 to 1980.[3] The cost to the nation in lost production and lower productivity must be substantial.

The effect of militarization on health is more difficult to measure, but it too is not insignificant. Tens of thousands of waste dumps, many containing deadly dioxin, are festering because the government does not feel it can spend the $40 billion it admits are needed to clean them up—or the $200 billion that Samuel Epstein of the University of Illinois claims are needed. Sometime in the next decade or two, however, we will pay a price for the delay.

We are already paying a price for the radiation that has entered our biosphere. The exact amount of radiation from nuclear testing and nuclear power, as well as the problems we will incur from nuclear waste when the reactors are put in storage, may be a matter of controversy, but there can be no dispute that they have already caused a certain amount of cancer and other diseases, and that they will cause more in the future. An inordinate incidence of cancer and heart problems were later noted, for instance, in the American troops that had entered Nagasaki for clean-up duty forty-five days after the atomic bomb was dropped in August 1945.[4] The same was true of Utah residents who lived not far from test sites in Nevada, and soldiers who were brought close to testing areas such as Yucca Flats to gauge their reaction to radiation. As noted earlier, Nobel laureate Linus Pauling estimated in 1958 that the carbon 14 emitted in atmospheric tests of nuclear devices "would cause an enormous number of deaths and widespread genetic damage."[5]

Mutations induced by radiation may not become apparent for generations. The Committee of the National Academy of Sciences noted in 1972 that

> the spectrum of radiation-caused genetic disease is almost as wide as the spectrum from all causes. . . . A genetic death may be the death of an embryo that no one ever knows about, or it

> may be the failure to reproduce . . . [or] it may be a lingering and painful death in early adult life that causes great distress.

Basing themselves on the BEIR "assumptions of genetic risks from ionizing radiation," Harvey Wasserman and three associates concluded in their book, *Killing Our Own*, that "if a single exposed radiation worker produces two children, who in turn have two children each, and so on through the generations, to the twentieth generation, there may be as many as 2,097,152 human beings put at risk from the single exposed worker."[6] Twenty generations of course means at least 400 years, and the Wasserman assumptions may be too high, but there is no disputing that radiation constitutes a major and invisible health problem that never existed before, and now threatens the well-being of millions of people.

The psychological effects of militarization in a nuclear age are also relatively invisible and easy to overlook, but they are substantial. To begin with, the potential for killing hundreds of millions of people is so gruesome that it requires of us that we either end the arms race forthwith or, if we continue, that we devalue and dehumanize the enemy. "War in and of itself," write psychiatrists William Beardslee and John Mack, "is so fearsome that psychically we have 'turned it off.' " The same Americans who were outraged to learn that the Nazis had killed 6 million Jews, now contemplate with equanimity—because they have "turned it off"—the potential death of dozens of times that number of Russians. Dehumanization is needed, say the two psychiatrists "as a coping mechanism in the face of the magnitude of the new reality which surrounds us."[7] We don't dare think of the Russians as human beings who love, cry, hate, feel, think; otherwise our guilt feelings would be overpowering. This psychic repression exacerbates what Jerome Frank calls "the impulse to violence," and weakens "the countervailing drives towards fellowship and community" that are indispensable for human survival.

The qualitatively greater scope for violence in this era of permanent war and nuclear bombs has compounded the psychological problem. Robert Jay Lifton of Yale, winner of the National Book Award for his study of Hiroshima survivors, speaks of the "psychic numbing" of young people who took part in the air raid drills of the 1950s, and to an extent the rest of us. "It came out," Lifton says, "in dreams, in fantasies, and then the suppression of that terror . . . in which one tried to put it aside." In adult life these same people, according to Lifton, manifested "a kind of moving back and forth between numbing and a certain amount of anxiety. . . . "[8] A second symptom, which he noted in children but which applies to adults as well, "is the sense that nothing can be depended on to last, that the threat of extinction renders life unmanageable. This 'new ephemeralism' includes doubts about the lasting nature of anything and similar doubts about the authenticity of virtually all claims to achievement."[9]

The "new ephemeralism" may explain the beatniks of the 1950s—young people who "resigned" from their parents' world because they had lost faith in their parents' social values. They devoted themselves therefore to escapism, to wine, sex, and fantasy. The "new ephemeralism" may also explain some features of punk rock that also seem to imply resignation from "a hopeless world." "The new values" of the postwar world, writes social historian Marty Jezer, "were fragile. What was the meaning of life when it could be snuffed out on a moment's notice? What did affluence mean in the face of nuclear death? What good was postponed gratification when there might not be a tomorrow?"[10] There are other facets of postwar life which presumably are affected by the "new ephemeralism" and "psychic numbing." Lifton talks of a radical new situation between parent and child. The fundamental parental responsibility of seeing the child safely into some form of functional adulthood has been undermined. Marriage itself, he says, may also be threatened in another way. This long-term commitment becomes much harder to make in the face of uncertain biological continuity.

Psychological judgments, even by "authorities," are difficult to confirm, but there is no question that in the period of militarization since World War II there has been a substantial growth in violence, juvenile delinquency, and the number of youthful runaways. "The positive correlation between the rate of delinquency and war and cold war cannot be ignored," noted Bertram Beck, director of the Special Juvenile Delinquency Project of the Children's Bureau, as early as 1954. The emergence of gangs and gang warfare have similar causes, which Jezer says "mirror international affairs. Young people carved up their cities into little neighborhoods for security and self-defense. Within each neighborhood a kind of patriotism was strong."[11] The new ephemeralism has similarly contributed to the vast increase in the use of drugs such as marijuana and cocaine.

Not all social problems are due to the militarization of America. Lifton, for instance, is careful to point out that such ills as juvenile delinquency existed long before the present era. But "the imagery of extinction adds to existing effects and intensifies them. Every existing relationship is under a shadow. The tendency to violate law is intensified, because of the feeling that everything is temporary." The feeling of transience increases alienation, breaks down old symbols—of belief in government, for instance—and adds to selfishness and narcissistic tendencies.[12] "This is a world," says literary critic Morris Dickstein, "which drives people to entirely personal concerns. This is a world in which they see no mode of fulfillment in large communal or public concerns."[13]

In a microcosm what Dickstein describes is the narrow self-centeredness that militarism expresses on the terrain of world affairs.

There are of course strong social tendencies in our culture that have not been snuffed out: folk music and rock music that express resistance to the present order, books that challenge war and imperialism, art that speaks of humanity and warmth. And, of course, since the mid-1950s many young people have expressed the spirit of rebellion by picketing, demonstrating, committing civil disobedience to win civil rights for minorities and women, to end the war in Vietnam, and the nuclear arms race. Even in a period of permanent war America has not been a solid mass of conformity. But the *trend* is in the opposite direction, toward acceptance of the status quo and the National Security State. For the vast majority of Americans, those under fifty-five or sixty, there has never been any other way of life. Simple patriotism guides them to accept that which is; to place their faith in their presidents, and above all to justify the costs and abuses of the permanent war on the theory that the game is worth the candle. That is especially true in economic matters.

There was a general feeling for many years after World War II that military spending, whatever its liabilities, provided millions of jobs and kept us prosperous. In fact it did: The hundreds of billions we spent on arms and armies from 1940 on finally pulled us out of the Great Depression. Unemployment, once 25 percent of the work force and still 17 percent in 1939, fell to an insignificant 1.2 percent by 1944. In the twenty-one years from 1947 through 1968 it ranged from 2.9 percent to a high of 6.8 percent. So intoxicating was the improvement that the nation's leaders concluded we could indefinitely afford both guns and butter without hurting our economy or reducing our standard of living. The position paper prepared for the National Security Council in 1950, NSC-68, states emphatically that "the United States could devote upward of 50 percent of its gross national product to military expenditures, foreign assistance, and investment,"[14] (more than twice the percentage then being spent for these purposes) and not only retain its high standard of living, but increase its gross national product as well.

For a time these optimistic words seemed infallible, particularly as American programs stimulated markets overseas. The domestic market was assured. There was a pent-up demand for automobiles, homes, the new gadget, television; and there were many billions of dollars around to buy them. Between 1940 and 1945 the national income had doubled, bank deposits had gone up apace from $41 billion to $83 billion, and in what amounted to forced savings, workers had plowed tens of billions into government bonds that could now be converted into cash and consumer goods. Moreover, while the rest of the world, including allies such as Britain, had been bled white, their physical plant and financial reserves dissipated, the American economy was intact and its financial reserves had skyrocketed. American exports during the war had more than tripled, and its balance of payments were so favorable that by war's end the United States had accumulated a stockpile of $29 billion in gold (gold was then $35 an ounce), or 77 percent of the world's resources.

Summarizing the American position early in the postwar era, James McMillan and Bernard Harris in *The American Take-Over of Britain* record that "on the production side the U.S., with six and a half percent of the world's population, harvested one-third of the world's grain; half its cotton; smelted 55 percent of its steel and other basic metals; pumped 70 percent of the world's oil; used 50 percent of its rubber; generated 45 percent of its mechanical energy; produced 60 percent of its manufactured goods and enjoyed 45 percent of the entire annual income of humanity."[15] By contrast, Britain's wealth had declined by 30 percent, her exports, on which she depended for survival, had fallen by half, and her gold reserve was down to a mere $12 *million*. There was an enormous market out there and the United States was the only nation capable of accommodating it, so American exports and investments skyrocketed. Corporate profits in the major industries were so large, management could grant annual wage increases, even during recessions, with little pain, passing the costs on to the consumer.

American problems became more evident, however, as the permanent war continued and our allies recovered. Competition for the world's markets became keener. The military budget, it became evident, was turning into more of a burden and less of a boon—exactly as the intellectual father of capitalism, Adam Smith, had warned two centuries ago. "The whole army and navy," he wrote in *The Wealth of Nations*, "are unproductive laborers." They produce "nothing for which an equal quantity of services can afterwards be procured."[16] The *Wall Street Journal* echoed these sentiments centuries later. Military spending, it conceded, "is the worst kind of government outlay, since it eats up materials and other resources that otherwise would be used to produce consumer goods."[17]

The arms race imposed a number of burdens on the economy. Military spending, unlike spending for new steel-mill machinery, produced no goods of value. But it had to be paid for, either in the form of higher taxes or inflation. In effect, then, it imposed a tax on every item produced, making the United States less competitive on the world market than it might otherwise have been, especially against nations like Japan which were spending proportionately much less on their military machine. This, plus the fact that the economies of other industrial nations inevitably revived, caused the United States to lose much of its competitive edge. Our share of world exports fell from 40 percent of the total in 1962 to 25 percent in 1979. In metal-working machinery the United States and Germany had been on a par in the early 1960s, each commanding a third of the world market; but by 1980 the U.S. share had fallen to 21 percent, that of Germany had risen to 40 percent. And on the other side of the trade equation, American entrepreneurs were losing to foreign competitors a good share of the market at home—in steel, autos, apparel, farm machinery, footwear, electronics, and textile machinery. "The military burden . . . ," observed the Council on Economic Priorities, "has significantly contributed to America's declining competitiveness. While not the only cause of our decreasing efficiency, economic performance has suffered because the United States has devoted a larger share of its output to the military than its competitors."[18] A British economist, Ron Smith, has shown that nations with large military establishments tend to have a lower rate of investment. The reason, according to David Gold, director of the Institute on the Military and the Economy, is that "military spending can push civilian spending aside. Military industry firms outbid civilian companies for engineers, skilled workers, key materials and even loans."[19] This is no small matter because military spending, though only 6 percent of the national product, constitutes almost a third of the durable goods industry, the heartland of the American economy. It is no accident then that a good part of the smokestack industries, for instance steel, are in disarray, and that smokestack companies increasingly resort to artificial methods to shore up profits. Tax gimmicks or buying up other corporations, devices that add nothing to national productivity, are all part of this package. U.S. Steel preferred to purchase Marathon Oil for $5 billion, for instance, rather than revitalize plants such as the one it abandoned in Youngstown, or the one it was in the process of abandoning in Chicago.

One of the leading students of this subject, Seymour Melman of Columbia University, records that by 1968 American industry "operated the world's oldest stock of metal-working machinery." Its railroads were far behind those of Japan, France, and others both in speed and efficiency; its merchant fleet was 23rd in the world, and many industries such as steel and machine tools were beginning to show weakness even in the domestic market.[20] The effects of obsolescence were evident in statistics of growth. Economic growth fell from an average 4.1 percent in the 1960s to 2.9 percent in the 1970s, and even lower in the first two years of the 1980s when we experienced the worst economic downturn since the 1930s. There was a strong revival in 1983–84, but it appears to have been only temporary.

Military spending has imposed other burdens on the economy, some subtle, some not so subtle. Theoretically the Pentagon should provide a great stimulus to the economy. As author Frank Ackerman once wrote, it is the "largest employment agency" in the country, accounting for 3 percent of the labor force directly (2 percent in uniform, 1 percent in civilian jobs), and another 3 percent as a result of procurement of goods and services from private corporations—or a total of 6 percent of the national work force. That 6 percent in turn generates work for another 6 percent of the national work force, since every defense worker and soldier must buy food, clothing, and housing which in turn leads to further employment. Economists call this the "multiplier effect." But the Pentagon's kind of stimulus is the wrong kind: it provides considerably fewer jobs than would be provided by a civilian-oriented economy.[21]

When the rate of unemployment was relatively low it didn't matter too much that militarism was creating fewer jobs than civilian spending would have done. But in the last decade, when unemployment reached as high as 11 percent of the nation's work force, it was something to worry about. The Congressional Budget Office estimates that every $10 billion spent on military products creates 40,000 fewer jobs than if the same $10 billion were spent on civilian endeavors. Others put the number of jobs much higher, twice as much or more. Marion Anderson of the Employment Research Associates in Lansing, Michigan, has calculated that if the proposed $238.6 billion 1984 defense budget were to have been spent on housing, food, and other necessities it would have provided 2,240,000 more jobs.[22]

Strange as it may seem, considering the enormous amount of research and development generated by the Pentagon, military spending inhibits the innovative spirit in the rest of the economy. "Lately," observed *Business Week* on June 30, 1980, "there is frightening evidence that the ability of U.S. industry to innovate—to convert ideas to commercial products and processes—is slipping." While research for the Pentagon is rising, research for the civilian-oriented sector has gone down appreciably. This is reflected in the fact that the number of patents granted American inventors has fallen, while that of foreigners seeking patents here has more than doubled from 1966 to 1975. Moreover, though the military research and development may be of high quality, it is not always applicable to the civilian economy—for instance guidance systems for missile technology. And where an innovation is applicable, it often is not functional for civilian purposes. The two types of production are very different from each other and not always interchangeable. "The nature of the military product is unique," writes Ann R. Markusen in a study for the University of California. "Unlike most other commodities and services, the goal is not to standardize the product, minimize costs of production and saturate markets. Weapons, military equipment and transport vehicles are increasingly few in number and highly sophisticated in nature. They are produced in what are essentially large craft shops rather than assembly lines."[23] In other words the Defense Department seeks a small number of items but of high quality, regardless of cost, whereas a nondefense corporation, working on civilian products, needs to produce large quantities on assembly lines, at low costs. Thus the transfer of technology from military uses to civilian uses has not been automatic, and many items that were developed in the United States are now being produced more cheaply and widely elsewhere. "In the U.S.," reports David Gold, "where transistors, semiconductors, and other innovations in the miniaturization of electronics originated, the emphasis on military-oriented research has reduced the ability of companies to compete with Japanese and European companies."[24] The Japanese, in particular, are making inroads into fields where American military research made the first scientific breakthroughs.

Military spending has another negative economic feature: it has an inherent tendency to expand and perpetuate itself regardless of costs. "Compared to many government expenditures," writes Frank Ackerman in his book *Reaganomics: Rhetoric vs. Reality*, "the Pentagon's budget is more congenial to business interests." Other alternatives would be much less pleasing to private capitalism. Money spent for mass transit, for instance, "would cut into auto sales." Money spent for public housing would compete with private developers. "Social welfare programs that provide cash benefits to individuals weaken the 'work incentives' so popular with employers. The Pentagon does none of this, but instead creates a new high-profit market for certain manufactures."[25] Big business, by and large, prefers that government spend its largesse on weaponry rather than mass transit or housing or other social investments. Thousands of corporations, mayors, city governments, public officials, scientists, and engineers have a stake in those high-profit industries. They and the Pentagon resist fiercely any effort to curb or whittle them down even though these industries pay little heed to costs, cost overruns, and an extravagant use of the taxpayers' money. Everyone has read of toilet seats for which the Pentagon pays $620, or 67 cent transistors for which the military pays $814 each, of $8 wrenches for which the armed services pay out $2,228, of $1.69 screwdrivers which cost the taxpayer $265.50, of 9 cent screws which are billed at $37 each.[26]

The Air Force's Tactical Air squadrons were one of the military growth areas of the late 1970s. Money was largely spent on the latest, most complex and most expensive planes—such as the F-15, at $25 million per plane—whose great cost was due to exotic capabilities which are almost certain never to be used. Planes are designed to fly much faster than they will ever have to fly in battle and vast sums are eaten up to make them that fast. Of the 100,000 flights in planes capable of exceeding Mach 2 during the Vietnam war, only one reached as high as Mach 1.6, for a few seconds, and it ran out of fuel; its pilots were forced to bail out and were captured.

Adding more sophistication than is required is costly and counterproductive. A 1980 Pentagon memo stated that the F-15 was prepared to fly only slightly more than half the time and requires 34 maintenance hours per flight. Another plane, the F111-D is ready to fly only a third of the time and needs almost 100 hours of maintenance to get ready. Yet any attempt to reduce the level of sophistication, cut the number of weapons, or eliminate military bases receives such bitter rebuke from members of Congress—almost all of whom have a stake in continuing the arms race—that cutbacks almost never happen. The military budget is the prime reason for the burgeoning of the national debt from $258 billion in 1945 and 1950 to $1,800 or $1,900 billion, and for the $200 billion a year budget deficits during the Reagan years, three times higher than anything known in the past.

In retrospect it is evident that by 1971 the United States had entered a period of structural crisis from which it is not likely to recover if the permanent war continues. We were buying more from foreign countries than we were selling them—something that has happened rarely since 1893—and we faced a balance of payments deficit of $20 billion dollars (considered an astronomical sum at the time, though in 1984 it was to grow to six times that size). The hoard of gold (then worth $35 an ounce) had fallen from $23.4 billion in 1949 to $10.1 billion, and was likely to fall further unless drastic measures were taken. (The budget too was at a near-record deficit of $23 billion—a sum that today would be considered extremely modest.) To meet the crisis President Nixon introduced a New Economic Program which froze wages and prices for ninety days, then controlled them for a couple of years more. The dollar was devalued and divorced from gold, so that instead of a stable price of $35 an ounce, it fluctuated wildly and reached a peak at one time of $800 an ounce. America was beginning to feel the effects of instability and the soaring debt primarily resulting from militarism. Contrary to NSC-68 the United States could not afford to spend 50 percent of its gross national product on the Pentagon, investments, and foreign assistance. It was having difficulty even with much smaller sums.

The economic debacle of 1971 was followed by a military debacle which also had serious economic consequences. Early in 1973 the Nixon administration, which had pledged "peace with honor" and vowed not to withdraw American troops unless North Vietnam withdrew its forces from South Vietnam first, was compelled to reverse itself. The American military contingent was flown and helicoptered out in what was to be the worst military defeat in American history, causing greater humiliation than the 1950–53 stalemate in Korea or the British occupation of the Executive Mansion during the War of 1812. In the wake of Vietnam the United States became infected by what was to become known as the Vietnam Syndrome, a determination by Americans not to become involved in another engagement of that sort again.

The loss in Vietnam had a serious subsidiary effect; it buoyed the courage of weak nations, who would never have dared to twit the United States in the past, to do so now. In the midst of the 1973 Yom Kippur war in the Mideast, thirteen oil producing countries—none with any serious military force that would have been a challenge to American military might—cut off oil shipments to the United States, then raised prices astronomically. This could not have happened in the past—as is evident by what the CIA did to Mohammed Mossadegh in the 1950s after he nationalized the oil industry of Iran.

In fact there had been gratuitous hints emanating from Washington in the early 1970s that the United States would send in the Marines if ever its Mideast supply of oil was endangered. Secretary of State Henry Kissinger would not have shrunk from such a course—

he later made the threat himself. But with Indochina still in the forefront of national anxiety another invasion would have aroused national angers in ways that the Nixon administration might not have been able to contend with. Kissinger's effort to mobilize the industrial states for a buyers' strike was abortive; the Western powers refused to hang together, each trying to run around the other to make a deal on its own with the oil producing nations. In the face of American weakness, then, the Organization of Petroleum Exporting Countries (OPEC), formed in 1960 and inactive until the early 1970s, exacted tribute on a scale never before witnessed. They increased the posted price by 70 percent in October 1973, another 128 percent on Christmas Eve, and more as the months went by. For a barrel of oil that cost 10 to 20 cents to produce in Saudi Arabia the world was soon paying $12 or $13, and eventually as high as $31.

This was a marked reversal of previous relations between the strong and the weak of the world. In economic terms the essence of imperialism had always been that the prices colonial nations paid to imperial powers for manufactured goods rose more rapidly than the prices the imperial nations paid the colonies and spheres of influence for raw materials. Because of such favorable "terms of trade," the industrial West drained off innumerable billions from the weak nations. Now, in the wake of Vietnam, the process was being reversed insofar as the oil countries were concerned: Saudi Arabia, Iran, Iraq, Nigeria, Venezuela, and the rest drained hundreds of billions from the strong powers to the weak. As the First National Bank of Chicago correctly predicted, the ultimate result of this transfer of wealth would be that the United States would have to cut living standards.

The National Security State found a way to avoid this debacle immediately, but in the process it created other, long-term, problems which, to the naked eye at least, are beyond solution. The oil countries, suffused with dollars from their brigandage, spent some of it for economic development, some for conspicuous consumption, but still had vast sums for which there was no other home but as deposits in American, German, and other Western banks. The West, of course, was happy to have the money—it temporarily reduced balance of payments deficits—but it had to find a use for the additional funds. The problem was solved in part by lending countries such as Brazil and Mexico large amounts to develop their import-substitute industries—their own machine-tool, automobile, and other industrial plants—so that they might cut back on imports, improve their balance of payments position, and perhaps raise living standards.

It was an impressive idea, but it did not work out entirely as expected. Countries such as Brazil, Argentina, and Mexico did indeed build new factories and did strengthen their infrastructure, but to pay for their international loans they had to sell more oil, coffee, and cattle. Unfortunately, the market for such items became increasingly tight as one recession after another hit the industrial world. In the end the debtor countries found they could not pay $800 billion in debts (a figure which will undoubtedly reach a trillion before long) and they had to plead to have the loans refinanced. In turn the Western banks and the International Monetary Fund (IMF) demanded that the debtor states introduce a program of austerity—hold down wages, cut back on social programs. The IMF insistence that living standards be slashed, in turn often led to social upheaval. When the subsidy on bread was reduced in Egypt, as a result of IMF pressure, riots took dozens of lives. The IMF-imposed austerity measures led to a near-revolution in Peru; to strikes in Brazil, with workers demanding their government default on foreign loans rather than accept IMF terms; to a 1983 strike wave in Mexico that was perhaps the largest in that nation's history; and to riots and killings in the Dominican Republic in 1984 when the government raised the price of gasoline and other commodities. Most of the loans have been refinanced and stretched out so that they come due in, say twenty-five years instead of fifteen; but there is a visceral feeling in many places they will never be repaid, or repaid only in part.

Should there be a default, or, more dramatically, a debtors' strike against IMF, the impact on the American and Western banking would be staggering. For example, Citicorp, probably the nation's most prestigious banking institution, had a net worth in 1984, according to *Business Week*, of $10.2 billion and roughly the same amount in loans to five Latin American nations. Brazil alone owed it $5 billion. Since these debts are considerably less than triple A and will certainly not be repaid as scheduled, there is some question as to whether they ought to be at least partly written off. In that case Citicorp's net worth would be considerably less than $10.2 billion and it would have to curtail or call in some of the domestic loans it has outstanding. Multiply this by many big banks and many similar situations and you have the basis of a depression of the 1929-type, or worse.

When Continental Illinois, the eighth largest bank in the nation, tottered on the edge of bankruptcy in 1984, the government had to take extraordinary measures to avoid a debacle like the one of 1873 when Jay Cooke and Company closed its doors, dragging 23,000 other corporations down with it in three years, and triggering one of the worst depressions in history. The Federal Deposit Insurance Corporation (FDIC), which normally insures deposits only up to $100,000, lifted the lid to cover all deposits at Continental Illinois and it mobilized a consortium of sixteen banks to provide a $4 to $5 billion line of credit.[27] The FDIC later purchased most of the bank's bad loans. "In many instances," writes Lester R. Brown in *State of the World—1984*, "outstanding loans by major U.S. banks to debt-burdened Third World countries exceed these banks' capital assets. If a wave of defaults were to engulf the Third World and some of their loans were to go bad, U.S. banks would face collapse unless rescued by Washington."[28]

Perhaps the tenuous banking situation is not enough to bring down the American economy. Perhaps the government will ride out the storms of $200 billion a year annual deficits. Perhaps the farm crisis which in 1985 threatened to drive thousands of farmers out of business will be resolved with less disruption than anticipated. But taking them all together, they bode ill for America's future. The fact is that imperialism is rapidly reaching the point where it no longer pays. Corporate America is still being enriched by it, but the military cost to assure the profits of multinational corporations are considerably higher than the profits the multinationals earn on about $250 billion in foreign investments and about the same or a little more in exports. Assuming a very high return of 30 percent, the profit of U.S. firms on overseas investments and exports is about $150 billion a year. In effect the National Security State is spending $300 billion so that its entrepreneurs might earn a profit half that much. The costs of imperialism clearly outpace the benefits, except that it is the public at large that pays the costs and it is a small number of multinationals that reap the benefits. Even so there must be a point at which the burden becomes unbearable, particularly since a large number of citizens have already had their living standards cut since 1979 to accommodate the burgeoning costs of militarism.

Militarism is no longer the channel to an ever improving standard of living, but rather the opposite. Both President Carter, a Democrat, and President Reagan, a Republican, understood this. They took deliberate steps to lower the standard of living, the first time in American history that any president has taken any such measures by design. Carter reduced the standard of living during the last two years of his term by introducing what was called "voluntary" wage guidelines, but which in effect were mandatory. The guidelines were 4 or 5 percent below the rise in the cost of living. Reagan's technique was more complex. He reduced welfare, Social Security, Medicare, Medicaid, food stamps, and other programs for the disadvantaged, so that there was always a large pool of desperate people willing to take the jobs of strikers, or underbid others seeking work. The "give-back" programs initiated by employers in 1979 to reduce wages and benefits won in previous years, was continued under Reagan, both in the recession years of 1981 and 1982 and the "prosperity" years of 1983 and 1984. Reagan programs, including the appointment of an antiunion National Labor Relations Board, cut deeply into labor's ranks so that the percentage of nonfarm workers in unions fell from 21 to 18 in a couple of years.

The number of poor people in America rose by 6 million from the previous decade, though it fell temporarily, by 1 percent, in 1984. One or two million Americans were homeless and farmers were losing their farms in unprecedented numbers. And the Reagan administration was trying to unravel the reforms of the New Deal and the Great Society as the only means of retaining an exaggerated level of military spending.

Despite the recovery years of 1983–84 there were many indications that the benefits of militarization were turning sour. No leftist could paint a gloomier picture of the future than the recognized organ of big business, *Business Week*. In its October 29, 1984 issue it warned that "Rumblings in the banking system are growing ever louder. Already, bank failures are at a rate unprecedented since the Depression. And the number of problem banks tracked by federal banking regulators has ballooned. . . . More and more banks are concluding that loans to once-rock-solid borrowers in energy, real estate, agriculture, and basic manufacture are uncollectible. . . . " Bank regulators are carefully urging caution, fearing that "the first sign of panic would risk a full-scale crisis that would rock financial markets. . . . "

Even if there is no *panic*, everyone knows there will be a slowdown and that when it comes some of the government's favorite options in dealing with such situations, such as "throwing money" at the crisis, will no longer be available to it. The administration threw vast sums of money at the 1980–82 recession—it gave tax benefits of about $750 billion to the wealthier classes and corporations, and instituted a program of $1.5 trillion for the military. "Because our deficit is already so high in these fat years," writes conservative *New York Times* columnist William Safire, "we no longer have a fiscal weapon [such as higher government expenditures] to rely on in the lean years. We cannot go deeper and deeper into deficit to combat recession because the interest on our mounting debt would get out of hand. . . . " The only alternative would be for the Federal Reserve Bank to pump money into the economy, but that will suffice only "until inflation raises its head again; at that point we would really be in the soup, because we will be out of anti-recession ammunition." The last recession, Safire says, "was needed to stop the greater evil of runaway inflation; the next recession, if its starts with the price level this low and the unemployment this high, will not have the excuse of necessity at all."[29]

In the 1940s and 1950s the United States led the whole capitalist world out of economic crisis; in the 1970s and 1980s it was carrying that same world into the quicksand under the weight of debt caused by militarization. By 1986, the United States will have become a debtor nation, it will owe more dollars to foreign countries than they owe us—just like Brazil, Zaire, or other underdeveloped countries. This is not the way imperialism was supposed to have worked. By 1984 the balance of payments deficit had reached an astronomical $120 billion a year. We owed that to foreigners. We also owed them scores of billions they had placed in our banks or paid for our certificates of deposit, because our interest rates were higher than in Europe. Our misfortune became our momentary fortune—the misfortune that government borrowing (to make up for the big deficit) pushed interest rates far beyond what they were elsewhere, attracting foreigners to deposit money and buy certificates here. In a sense they were financing our deficit. But that is only a temporary phenomenon. Sooner or later they will demand their money and the fat will be in the fire.

The United States, like a compulsive Las Vegas gambler who has lost his stake and keeps borrowing to stay in the game, is sinking into the quagmire of debt. The federal debt is nearing $2 trillion. State, local, corporate, real estate, and consumer debt are two to three times that sum. The stage is set for all kinds of credit crises which will impact unfavorably on the economy. According to the *Monthly Review*, in recent credit "crunches"—such as those caused by Penn Central, Franklin National Bank, Chrysler, and Continental Illinois—"disaster has been avoided each time by emergency injections of money either directly by the Federal Reserve into the banks, or by various forms of government subsidies, loans, or loan guarantees for threatened firms or industries." So far there has been no catastrophic chain reaction, but "no one knows whether the same method will work if the trouble starts not with a single bank or corporation but with a large number simultaneously or in quick succession."[30]

Economic shoals facing the American empire are complemented by political shoals. The Empire is clearly contracting, another testament to the lost momentum of global imperialism. True, the United States has succeeded in drawing China closer to it, but China is not and will never be anymore the colony or sphere of influence of any other nation. It is just too big and too populous. It may help the United States counteract some of the power of the Soviet Union, but it will probably not help suppress revolution. The United States has also picked up one or two additional supporters, such as Egypt. But to counterbalance that, it has lost its base in Indochina and, along with its Khmer allies, it has been unable to regain a viable foothold in Kampuchea. Iran, a subimperial power that was expected to monitor the Persian Gulf area for the American Empire, has fallen to a Shiite enemy of the United States; and if Khomeini is overthrown or dies soon it is unlikely that a pro-American like Shah Pahlevi can be restored to that seat.

The United States has lost other bastions, in Ethiopia, Mozambique, Angola, Nicaragua, and it is on tenuous grounds in El Salvador. Brazil has turned from the military dictatorship imposed on it by the United States in 1964, and it is treading a more normal electoral path. Similar developments have occurred in Argentina, Uruguay, and elsewhere in Latin America. While the Reagan administration contends that these are welcome steps toward democracy, in fact they represent a loosening of Washington's hold. In the Mideast the United States suffered a humiliating defeat when it was forced to take its troops out of Lebanon as a result of Moslem terrorism against its forces, and a second defeat in this vital area was suffered later on when its ally, Israel, was also forced out of the country.

The United States is still a great and imposing power, but it is beginning to carry an increasing aura of impotence and frustration. The promise of imperialism, the promise of what Henry Luce called "The American Century," is not being fulfilled as Roosevelt and Truman had expected. Increasingly it is more burden than boon, and the price that is being paid for it, a permanent war and the installation of a "second government" which uses totalitarian methods to achieve its purposes, seems like a poor bargain indeed.

9

What Next?

One day in the not-too-distant future the American people will have to make a decision of even greater import than those their forebears made in the 1770s, 1860s, and 1930s. They will have to decide whether to continue as at present, toward a totalitarian society, a possible nuclear war, and economic disintegration; or whether they will end the permanent war, dismantle the National Security State, and find a means other than imperialism to achieve economic abundance.

Periodically in history nations and people reach forkroads where they must make basic decisions that will determine events for a long time to come. The years 1776, 1861, and 1932 were forkroads in American history, and if the American people had taken other decisions, the United States would never have become a superpower. It is doubtful if it would have been a *United* States, and it is certain it would not have stretched from the Atlantic to the Pacific. The decisions that Americans must make today are weightier because they involve not only the survival of a nation, but of a world system and perhaps of human life itself.

The decision we must make soon is necessary, indispensable in fact, because the three levers of American power no longer guarantee prosperity, security, or comfort. On the contrary, they assure that all three will be whittled away. When the first atomic device was exploded at Alamogordo, New Mexico, Harry Truman called it "the greatest thing in history," and Bernard Baruch exulted that America now "can get what she wants if she insists on it." But the Bomb, as George F. Kennan and so many others have noted, leads to neither greatness nor victory, but rather, to annihilation. "The nuclear bomb," George F.Kennan, author of the containment policy, now says, "is the most useless weapon ever invented. It can be employed to no rational purpose."[1] The late George Kistiakowsky, science advisor to President Eisenhower, predicted that we will have a nuclear war before the end of the century unless the arms race is stopped. Such sentiments have been echoed by many other former establishment figures. In any case the Soviet Union can no longer be threatened into submission by waving the nuclear stick. It has shown convincingly that it will match one nuclear breakthrough after another—multiple-warhead missiles, the cruise, the Trident, mobile missiles, and when and if the space war begins, space weapons. A nuclear war, for innumerable reasons, is not winnable, or even thinkable; neither is a limited nuclear war or a conventional war between the superpowers, if only because they carry the implicit danger of escalating into nuclear confrontation. And if weapons no longer have the capacity to assure victory, then, not only their military but their political value as well is canceled out.

The Central Intelligence Agency (CIA), like the nuclear and conventional military machine, gives the appearance of a great power but it too lacks the substance of victory. There is no conceivable scenario by which the CIA can achieve the original goals of America's imperial policy: to make the United States predominant and unchallenged in world affairs. At a maximum the CIA may be able to stave off a few successes by leftist forces, say in Latin America, but even that is far from assured. As the economic crisis in the developing world becomes more acute and its people more desperate, the CIA will find it next to impossible to keep pro-American dictators (or even pro-American semidemocrats) in office.

As for America's economic power, there is no gainsaying that a nation which produces $4 trillion of goods and services a year is formidable. But it is no longer formidable in the same way it was in 1945. Four decades ago the United States was able to pull the whole capitalist world out of the quicksand with its economic might. It had surpluses of trade and payments, a vast stockpile of gold, an enormous potential for expansion. Today the surpluses are gone, the stockpile diminished, the potential very much diluted. It is doubtful that the United States can save the world economy as it did after World Wars

I and II; or for that matter save itself from the steady erosion of economic strength, as the level of unemployment grows higher from one recession to another, and insolvencies in business and banking threaten to undermine it.

The goal of imperialism was to assure markets abroad, permanent prosperity, economic stability, and jobs in the United States. "Foreign markets must be regained," proclaimed Franklin Roosevelt. "There is no other way if we would avoid painful economic dislocation, social readjustments and unemployment."[2] But imperialism is no longer viable, and the assumption of Roosevelt, Truman, and their successors that only our present economic system can guarantee our well-being is no longer convincing. The atom bomb, said Secretary of War Henry Stimson in 1945, represents "a revolutionary change in the relations of man and the universe."[3] So is the technological revolution, the military revolution, and the national and social revolution which has been far and away the greatest social upheaval in all history, involving seventy-two nations and more than 2 billion people. To think that the problems accruing from these revolutionary changes can be ministered to without *fundamental* changes in our society is naive. To think that we can leave the so-called free-enterprise system, the nation–state, and the present military system untouched is worse than myopia, it is suicide.

A total program to deal with the present situation is beyond the purview of this work. But a few high points are in order.

To begin with, if we are to jettison the imperialist policy and divorce ourselves from slavish reliance on world markets we must find a substitute economic method. At its fulcrum would be some form of economic planning, perhaps on the model suggested by historian Charles Beard and philosopher John Dewey in the 1930s, or on the order of some of the current planning advocates. There is a tendency by Americans to shy away from such socialist-sounding (or worse still, communist-sounding) terms as *planning*, but if we are terrified by a word in an era that calls for extreme innovation then there is no hope for the United States. The Beard–Dewey prescription called on government to fix a desired national standard of living and plan imports and production so that this standard could be met. The government would make an inventory of what Americans would reasonably be expected to export to other countries, then provide for the import of a similar amount of commodities, and plan national production and the distribution of the national income based on the total of its national and international resources.

Unlike the planning in the Soviet Union, this planning would be decentralized. It would be indicator planning, with the government using its tax policies, material allotment programs, control of banking credit, and import licenses to *prod* various companies and industries in the direction it wants them to take. It would not order them to take these steps, or set quotas and prices by government ukase—it would use indirect means to achieve its goals. Certain facets of the economy, certainly banking, would be under government ownership or control, but exactly how much would depend on developments. The idea of planning, both in the 1930s and today, was embraced not only by communists and socialists, but also by leading capitalists like Gerard Swope, president of General Electric in the 1930s, and leading liberals like Rexford Tugwell, Senator Robert M. La Follette, Jr., and in our own time theorists like Gar Alperovitz and Jeff Faux.

On the political front a coherent program to meet the current adversity would call for:

1. A plan for disarmament, beginning with nuclear disarmament. The tensions of the world cannot be relieved, nor any humanistic substitute programs implemented, unless and until the nations begin to shed themselves of military hardware.
2. An expansion of economic aid to developing countries, providing they are prepared to introduce political and social changes like land reform, and provided also that all military aid cease.
3. The establishment of a worldwide system to resolve international disputes without war. A world court would adjudicate differences between nations, and an international police force—as originally envisioned for the United Nations—would enforce the court's decisions.
4. Creation of four international bodies—with worldwide enforcement powers—to prevent atomic proliferation, control pollution, reduce poverty, rein in population, as proposed by the late Secretary General of the United Nations, U Thant.
5. Liquidation of the National Security State—perhaps by con-

verting the National Security Council into an open and above-board economic planning agency, or conversion into an agency for worldwide economic aid; reducing the military machine to pre-World War II levels or below for the time being, as one step toward total disarmament; returning the FBI to its former role as a law enforcement agency; outright liquidation of such agencies as the CIA and NSA.

Each of these planks has a hundred subplanks and poses dozens of questions: "If we disarm, how can we defend ourselves against Soviet aggression"; "who will be in charge of an international police force"; "will such a force be allowed to use nuclear bombs"; "will economic aid be dispensed by single nations or by a world organization, and who will determine whether it is used appropriately"; "how will an international body stop Pakistan from secretly producing a nuclear bomb"; "what will happen to all the people in the United States who now service the National Security State"; "how will we convert military factories into civilian enterprises?"

The question that will bother Americans most is: What about the Russians? If the United States and the Soviet Union both demilitarize won't the Russians "cheat"; won't they use "secret" weapons to conquer the world? These are the kinds of questions born out of the phobias of a permanent war and they cannot be answered simplistically because they are rooted in emotion rather than reason.

Suffice it to note, however, that the Soviets too have their problems. Their three levers of power—the military, the KGB, and the economy—are no more capable of establishing world rule than are ours. They face the same dilemmas we do about the Bomb and conventional military force, namely that they cannot "win" a war without committing suicide. Nor is their KGB any more likely to dominate the world through covert and paramilitary tactics than is our CIA. As for their economy, it is proceeding ahead but its rate of growth has slowed. It will soon either suffocate or find it necessary to change its mode of planning drastically—along the decentralized lines that Yugoslavia, China, and Hungary are now following—if it is to take the next step forward. And if it decentralizes it must also improve the human rights situation and introduce democratic prerogatives (again as other communist countries are being forced to do). Hundreds of Russian economists understand that their society must make a fundamental change in economic planning; the only justification they give for not having done so before this is that the economy has been forced to allocate far too much of its resources to the arms race. "We are at war, cold war," they say. If the war is relaxed, the Russian hold on its empire and its own people will also loosen.

It is naive to think that Russians are automatons or that the regime feels it can use old Stalinist methods with impunity. An antigovernment emigré from the Soviet Union, using the pseudonym Alex Amersov, told the editor of a socialist publication, *In These Times*, that "in the U.S., for a person to become an active opponent of the system requires a long process of alienation, but in the Soviet Union, to place yourself in a position in opposition to the system very often is just a matter of strengthening the ties with other people." There are, he said, "hundreds of thousands of small, independent networks or groups where people get together and express their opinions about all of political and social life—that is normal in the Soviet Union. . . . The KGB can't clamp down on the small groups, because they are based on family and friends and are very extensive. . . . "[4]

A turnabout for the United States would probably result in a confrontation between segments of the population. It is not likely that a campaign to end the permanent war and dissolve the National Security State can proceed without a clash between those who want to cling to the past and those who want to effect basic change. The permanent war has lasted too long and the institutions and people who endorse it have become too entrenched for a change to be effected without bitterness.

To the extent that Americans educate themselves to the futility of the permanent war, they will mitigate the pending confrontation. We do not, under any circumstances, have the luxury of choice. History has already made it for us. Our only useful option is to understand what it dictates, and act accordingly.

Notes

1. The Permanent War.

1. Catton, Bruce. *War Lords of Washington*, 40–41. New York: Harcourt, Brace, 1948.

2. Barnet, Richard J. *Roots of War*, 24. New York: Atheneum, 1972.

3. Baldwin, Hanson, Quoted in de Riencourt, Amaury. *The American Empire*, 100. New York: Dial, 1968.

4. See Cathy Perkus, ed., *Cointelpro*. New York: Monad Press, 1975.

5. Two interviews with Regino Boti, Cuban Minister of Economics, December 1960 and August 1961.

6. Hinckle, Warren, and William Turner. *The Fish is Red*, 17. New York: Harper & Row, 1981.

7. Wise, David, and Thomas B. Ross. *Invisible Government*, 26–31. New York: Freedom House, 1964.

8. Hersh, Seymour, *New York Times*, quoted in *New Yorker* (May 10, 1978): 44–49.

9. *New York Times* and *The Washington Post* quoted in ibid., 60–61.

10. Williams, William Appleman, Quoted in Houghton, N.D., ed. *Struggle Against History*, 2. New York: Simon and Schuster, 1968.

11. Ekirch, Arthur A., Jr. *The Civilian and the Military*, 19. Oxford University Press, 1956.

12. Continental Congress quoted in, Dupuy, R. Ernest. *A Compact History of the United States Army*, 38. New York: Hawthorne, 1961.

13. Washington, George, quoted in Dupuy, R. Ernest, and Trevor N. Dupuy. *The Military Heritage of America*, 19. New York: McGraw-Hill. 1956.

14. Madison, James, Quoted in Ambrose, Stephen E. and James Alden Barber, Jr. *The Military and American Society*, 1. New York: Free Press, 1972.

15. Pusey, Merlo J. *The U.S.A. Astride the Globe*, 15–18. Boston: Houghton Mifflin, 1971.

16. Ambrose and Barber, *The Military*, 4., 10–11.

17. Eisenhower, Dwight D., Quoted in Commager, Henry Steele, ed.

Documents of American History, 9th ed., Vol. 2, 653. Englewood Cliffs, NJ: Prentice-Hall, 1973.

18. *Nation* (October 28, 1968): 284–85.
19. *New York Times* (May 9, 1951).
20. *Conscription News*, (February 2, 1956); also quoted in *Progressive* (January 1959):5.
21. Wilson, Woodrow, quoted in "The Militarization of America." National Council Against Conscription (January 1948):13.
22. Ambrose and Barber, *The Military*, 4.
23. Weinberg, Albert K. *Manifest Destiny*, 22. New York: Quadrangle, 1963.
24. Smith, Howard K. *The State of Europe*, 71. New York: Alfred A. Knopf, 1949.
25. Eakins, David W. "Business Planners and American Postwar Expansion." In *Corporations and the Cold War*, edited by David Horowitz, 152. New York: Monthly Review Press, 1969.
26. Hofstadter, Richard. *American Political Tradition*, 349. New York: Vintage, 1984.
27. Chomsky, Noam. *Towards a New Cold War*, 97. New York: Pantheon, 1982.
28. Interview by author with Richard J. Barnet.
29. Goodpaster, Andrew J., and Samuel P. Huntington. *Civil-Military Relations*, 7. Washington, DC: American Enterprise Institute for Public Policy Research, 1977.
30. Madison, James, quoted in *Progressive* (September 1978): 9.

2. The Second Government.

1. Sherwood, Robert E. *Roosevelt and Hopkins, An Intimate History*, Vol. 2, 516. New York: Bantam, 1948.
2. Fleming, D.F. *The Cold War and Its Origins, 1950–1960*, Vol. 2, 1060. Garden City, NY: Doubleday, 1961; Deutscher, Isaac. *Russia: What Next*, 99–101. New York: Oxford University Press, 1953.
3. Seton-Watson, Hugh. *From Lenin to Malenkov*, 223. New York: Praeger, 1954.
4. Williams, William Appleman. *The Tragedy of American Diplomacy*, 166. New York: World, 1959.
5. Ambrose and Barber. *The Military*, 8.
6. Magdoff, Harry. *The Age of Imperialism*, 117. New York: Monthly Review Press, 1969.
7. Stone, I.F. *The Truman Era*, 75. New York: Monthly Review Press, 1953.
8. Gardner, Lloyd C. *Architects of Illusion*, 120. New York: Quadrangle, 1970.

9. Baruch, Bernard, Quoted in Horowitz, David. *The Free World Colossus*, 264. New York: Hill and Wang, 1965.
10. Alperovitz, Gar. *Atomic Diplomacy: Hiroshima and Potsdam*, 188. London: Secker & Warburg, 1965.
11. Stimson, Henry L., Quoted in Alperovitz, *Atomic Diplomacy*, 227.
12. Byrnes, James F. *Speaking Frankly*, 203. New York: Harper, 1947.
13. Fleming, D.F. *The Cold War and Its Origins 1917–1950*, Vol. 1, 323. Garden City, NY: Doubleday, 1961.
14. Fleming, *The Cold War*, ibid.
15. Sixty-two page document in Clark Clifford's possession. Shown to author by Clifford.
16. Goshal, Kumar. *People in Colonies*, 268. Dobbs Ferry, NY: Sheridan House, 1968.
17. U.S. Congress. Senate. Committee on Foreign Relations. *Hearings on Nonproliferation Treaty*. 90th Cong., 2nd sess. February 18, 20, 1969, 509.
18. Pomeroy, William J. *Guerrilla and Counter-Guerrilla Warfare*, 63, 70–71. New York: International Publishers, 1964.
19. Drummond, Roscoe, and Gaston Coblentz. *Duel at the Brink*. Garden City, NY: Doubleday, 1960.
20. Stillwell, Joseph W. *The Stillwell Papers*, 320. AMS Press, 948.
21. Hailey, Foster. *Half of One World*, 44. New York: Macmillan, 1950.
22. Truman, Harry S. *Memoirs*, Vol. 1, 421. Garden City, NY: Doubleday, 1955.
23. *Time* (January 21, 1980).
24. Kennan, George F., Quoted in *Chicago Sun-Times* (May 20, 1981).
25. Truman, *Memoirs*, Vol. 2, 3–6.
26. Rodberg, Leonard S., and Derek Shearer. *The Pentagon Watchers*, 35. Garden City, NY: Doubleday/Anchor, 1970.
27. Wise, David. *The Politics of Lying*, 109. New York: Random House, 1973.
28. Goldberg, Arthur, Quoted in *Harvard Law Review*, 85, no. 6 (April 1972): 1201.
29. Paine, Thomas, Quoted in *Hastings Constitutional Law Quarterly*, 9, no. 4 (Summer 1982): 749 note.
30. U.S. Congress. House. Leneice N. Wu, Library of Congress. *Report to House Committee on Foreign Affairs*. Report prepared by 92nd Cong., 2nd sess., 1972.
31. Bernstein, Barton J., and Allen J. Matusow. *The Truman Administration: A Documentary History*, 221–24. New York: Harper, 1966.
32. Truman, Harry S., Quoted in Commager, *Documents of American History*, 527.
33. George F. Kennan. "The Sources of Soviet Conduct." *Foreign Affairs* (July 1947): 566–82. Under pseudonym "x".

34. Lippmann, Walter, Quoted in LaFeber, Walter. *America, Russia, and the Cold War, 1945–71*, 17. New York: John Wiley & Sons, 1972.

35. MacArthur, Douglas. speech, Lansing, Michigan (May 15 1952). Reported in national press.

36. Fleming, D.F. *The Cold War and Its Origins 1917–1950*, Vol. 1, 443–445. Garden City, NY: Doubleday, 1961.

37. One-page leaflet. Union of Concerned Scientists and United Campuses to Prevent Nuclear War.

38. Reagan, Ronald, Quoted in *Wall Street Journal* and *Defense Monitor* (June 1980): 1

39. U.S. Congress. House and Senate. *Annual Report to Congress, Fiscal 1983*. 98th Cong., 1st sess. p. II-3. Report prepared by Caspar Weinberger.

40. *Washington Spectator* (June 1, 1982). p. 3.

41. Hughes was consistent. He defended the socialists from attacks by Attorney General A. Mitchell Palmer eight years later.

42. Acheson, Dean. *Present At the Creation*, 736. New York: W.W. Norton, 1969.

43. Rodberg, Leonard S., and Derek Shearer, eds. *Pentagon Watchers: Students Report on the National Security State*. Garden City, NY: Doubleday/Anchor, 1970.

44. *Law and Contemporary Problems*. Durham, NC: School of Law, Duke University. *Presidential Power*. Part 2, 40, no. 3 (Summer 1976): 175.

45. U.S. Congress. Senate. *Final Report of the Select Committee to Study Governmental Operations With Respect to Intelligence Activities* (hereinafter called Church Committee Report), Vol. 1, 132. 1976.

46. Halperin, Morton H. and Jerry J. Berman, Robert L. Borosage, and Christine M. Marwick. *The Lawless State*, 136. Baltimore, MD: Penguin Books, 1976.

47. *New York Times* (January 4, 1975).

48. *Chicago Sun-Times* (March 8, 1983).

49. *Law and Contemporary Problems*, 168; *New York Times* (May 1, 1972).

3. The President's Wars.

1. Schlesinger, Arthur, M. Jr. *The Imperial Presidency*, 50–51. Boston: Houghton Mifflin, 1973.

2. Schlesinger, *Imperial* 21.

3. ibid. 5.

4. ibid. 42.

5. Commager, *Documents*, 2:1–4.

6. ibid. 2:128–30.

7. ibid. 2:451–52.

8. Schlesinger, *Imperial* 17.

9. *Law and Contemporary Problems*, 87–88.

10. Schlesinger, *Imperial* 173, 174, 176.

11. *Law and Contemporary Problems* 94.
12. Sorenson, Theodore C. *Kennedy*, 764. New York: Harper, 1965.
13. Keating, Kenneth, Quoted in Schlesinger, Arthur M. Jr. *A Thousand Days*, 800, 801, 834, 836. Boston: Houghton Mifflin, 1965.
14. Sorenson, *Kennedy* 770.
15. Stimson, Henry L., quoted in Bernstein, Barton J., and Allen J. Matusow, eds. *The Truman Administration. A Documentary History*, 221. New York: Harper Torchbooks, 1968.
16. Groueff, Stephane, quoted in *Bulletin of Atomic Scientists* (November 1975): 22.
17. ibid.
18. Sherwin, Martin J. *A World Destroyed*, 204–205. New York: Alfred A. Knopf, 1975.
19. Berstein and Matusow, *Truman Administration* 43, 46.
20. Aron, Raymond. *The Great Debate*, 14. Garden City, NY: Doubleday/Anchor, 1965.
21. Published in *National War College Review* (May–June 1975): 51, 65, 81.
22. Barnet, Richard J. *The Giants: Russia and America*. 18–20. New York: Simon and Schuster, 1977; *Chicago Sun-Times* (March 15, 1977).
23. *Monthly Review* (September 1981): 20–26, footnote.
24. Wyden, Peter. *Day One*, 18. New York: Simon and Schuster, 1984.
25. Norman Solomon. *Progressive* (July 1979): 21, 22, 26.
26. Pauling, Linus, Quoted in Wasserman, Harvey, and Norman Solomon. *Killing Our Own*, 96, 97. New York: Delacorte, 1982.
27. *Washington Spectator* (November 1, 1984): 2.
28. Rodberg and Shearer, *Pentagon Watchers* 50.
29. U.S. Congress. Report to Congress. James Schlesinger. 94th Cong., 1st Sess. May 30, 1975.
30. *New York Times* (September 6, 1983).
31. Stone, Jeremy J., and Cox, Chapman B., Quoted in *Chicago Tribune* (September 9, 1984).
32. Lippmann, Walter, quoted in *America, Russia* 55; Rodman and Shearer, *Pentagon Watchers* 50.
33. Ibid.
34. Wise, David. *The Politics of Lying*, 43ff. New York: Random House. 1973.
35. Kahin, George McTurman, and John W. Lewis. *The United States in Vietnam*, 163. New York: Delta, 1967.
36. Schlesinger, *Imperial* 179.
37. Shawcross, William. *Sideshow: The Secret War in Cambodia*, 26–28, 277. New York: Simon and Schuster, 1979.
38. ibid. 332–33.
39. *Law and Contemporary Problems* 96 ff.
40. Rodberg and Shearer, *Pentagon Watchers* 54.

4. *The Secret Wars.*

1. Moynihan, Daniel Patrick, Quoted in the *New York Times* (November 28, 1984).

2. Church Committee Report, Book 1 9.

3. Horowitz, David, ed. *Corporations and the Cold War*, 164. New York: Monthly Review Press, 1969.

4. Barnet, Richard J. *Intervention and Revolution*, 4, 9. New York: World, 1968.

5. Marchetti, Victor, and John D. Marks. *The CIA and the Cult of Intelligence*, 113. New York: Alfred A. Knopf. 1974.

6. Kennan, George, Quoted in Barnet, *The Alliance* 139.

7. ibid. 39 ff.

8. Marchetti and Marks, *CIA and the Cult* 36.

9. Church Committee Report, Book 1 12.

10. ibid. 132.

11. Kennan, George, Quoted in Halperin et al., *Lawless State* 37.

12. Truman, Harry S., quoted in Borosage, Robert L., and John Marks, eds. *The CIA File*, 10. New York: Grossman, 1976.

13. Rowe, Harry Howe, Quoted by Senator Frank Church. Speech. "Covert Action: Swampland of American Foreign Policy," Delivered in Washington, DC, December 4, 1975.

14. *Law and Contemporary Problems*, 196–97.

15. Borosage and Marks, *CIA File* 9.

16. Rodberg and Shearer, *Pentagon Watchers* 21.

17. Marchetti and Marks, *CIA and the Cult* 23

18. Tully, Andrew. *CIA: The Inside Story*, 88. New York: William Morrow, 1962.

19. Barnet, Richard J. *Intervention and Revolution*, 228. New York: World.

20. ibid. 232.

21. *New York Times* (January 28, 1982).

22. *Chicago Sun-Times* (May 12, 1983).

23. Church Committee Report, Book 1 46.

24. Horowitz, David, ed. *Containment and Revolution*, 71. New York: Beacon, 1967.

25. *New Republic* (September 12, 1960).

26. Agee, Philip. *Inside the Company: CIA Diary*, 218 ff. Middlesex, England: Penguin Books, 1975.

27. Church, Senator Frank, "Covert Action: Swampland of American Foreign Policy." Speech delivered in Washington, DC, December 4, 1975, 4.

28. ibid.

29. Halperin, et al., *Lawless State* 44, 45.

30. Hinckle, *Fish is Red.* 34 ff, 76, 104–105, 203.
31. Halperin, et al., *Lawless State* 46.
32. *Chicago Tribune* (October 23, 1984); *New York Times* (November 13, 1984).
33. Tully, *CIA: Inside Story* 198.
34. *Progressive* (May 1984).
35. Borosage and Marks, *CIA File* 46–48.
36. ibid. 67.
37. ibid. 48.
38. Marchetti and Marks, *CIA and the Cult* 253–54.
39. ibid. 80.
40. Center for National Security Studies. Press release (July 18, 1983).

5. *The Authoritarian Syndrome.*

1. Stokes, Rose Pastor. Letter to the editor. *Kansas City Star*, cited in Shannon, David A. *The Socialist Party of America: A History*, 113. New York: Macmillan, 1955.
2. Ibid. 114
3. Church Committee Report, Book 2 25, 27–28.
4. ibid. Book 4 35.
5. Zinn, Howard. *A People's History of the United States*, 407. New York: Harper & Row, 1980.
6. Rodberg and Shearer, *Pentagon Watchers* 45.
7. "The Militarization of America." National Council Against Conscription. (January 1948): 13.
8. U.S. Congress. Senate. *Foreign Relations Committee.* Report prepared by Library of Congress. Cong. Sess. 1971.
9. Wise, *Politics of Lying* 67.
10. U.S. Congress. Subcommittee Foreign Relations Committee. 91st Cong., 2nd Sess. December 1970; see Heberling, Peter D. W., and Etzioni, Amitai. Position paper prepared for the Center for Policy Research. Mimeograph. Comment by Senator J. William Fulbright: 3.
11. ibid.
12. Quoted in Wise, *Politics of Lying* 111.
13. Schlesinger, *Imperial* 341.
14. ibid. 356.
15. ibid. 342.
16. ibid. 344.
17. *New York Times* (June 14, 1984).
18. *New York Times* (December 22, 1984).
19. Morris, Christopher. *The Day They Lost the H-Bomb.* 10, 32, 46, 47, 89. New York: Coward-McCann, 1966.
20. Reuters Report, Quoted in *Chicago Tribune* (March 1, 1983).

21. *Chicago Sun–Times Book Week Review*. (December 19, 1982).
22. Houghton, N.D., ed. *The Struggle Against History*, 96–97. New York: Simon and Schuster, 1968.
23. Eisenhower, Dwight D. *The White House Years*, Vol. 1, 613–14. Garden City, NY: Doubleday, 1965.
24. Wise, *Politics of Lying* 42.
25. Heberling, Etzioni. *Offense Against the Constitution*, 4. Mimeographed. Washington, DC: Center for Policy Research, no date.
26. *New York Times* (November 3, 1984).
27. *Chicago Tribune* (November 15, 1984).
28. Peterzell, Jay. *Reagan's Secret Wars*, rev. ed., 16–17. Washington, DC: Center for National Security Studies, 1983.
29. Wise, *Politics of Lying* 43–44.
30. *The Pentagon Papers* 234–35. New York: Quadrangle, 1971.
31. ibid. 516–17.
32. MacArthur, Douglas, quoted in *Parade* magazine (October 10, 1971).
33. *The Threat of Nuclear War.* 1 page leaflet. Union of Concerned Scientists and United Campuses to Prevent Nuclear War, no date.
34. Church Committee Report, Book 2 2–3.
35. ibid. Book 2 15.
36. ibid. Book 3 3.
37. ibid. Book 3 37.
38. ibid. Book 3 12.
39. Halperin et al., *Lawless State* 95.
40. Church Committee Report, Book 3 439–45.
41. ibid. 449.
42. ibid. 235–38.
43. Wise, *American Police State* 146–47.
44. Church Committee Report, Book 3 26.
45. ibid. 31–32, 45.
46. *COINTELPRO. The FBI's Secret War on Political Freedom*, 8–10. New York: Random House Vintage, 1975.
47. ibid. 12.
48. Wise, *American Police State* 319.
49. Church Committee Report, Book 3 158–59.
50. ibid. 117.
51. Halperin et al., *Lawless State* 138 ff.
52. ibid. 140–41.
53. ibid. 151.
54. Wise, *American Police State* 398.
55. Church Committee Report, Book 3 936ff, 955–56.
56. Cooper, Marc. "Civil Liberties: The Untranquil State of the Union." *Los Angeles Weekly* (October 19–25, 1984).
57. American Civil Liberties Union. *Free Speech, 1984. The Rise of Govern-*

ment Controls on Information, Debate and Association, 3. Washington, DC: American Civil Liberties Union, 1984.

58. Glasser, Ira. Symposium on the Civil Liberties Implications of Nuclear Power Development. *New York University Review of Law and Social Change*, 10, no. 2 (1980–1981): 354–55.

59. Church Committee Report, Book 3 222.

6. The Rearrangement of Power.

1. *Law and Contemporary Problems*, 196–97.
2. ibid. 10.
3. ibid. 10.
4. Church Committee Report. Book 4 157.
5. Madison, James. *The Federalist*. no. 47. Quoted in *Law and Contemporary Problems* 2.
6. ibid. 37.
7. *Chicago Sun-Times* (July 12, 1969).
8. *Law and Contemporary Problems* 184.
9. ibid.
10. Goodpaster, Andrew J., and Samuel P. Huntington. *Civil-Military Relations*. 8–9. Brochure. Washington, DC: American Enterprise Institute for Public Policy Research.
11. *Chicago Daily News* (April 15, 1969).
12. Interview with author.
13. Wood, David. *Los Angeles Times* (July 10, 1983).
14. ibid.
15. Tempest, Rone. *Los Angeles Times* (October 7, 1983).
16. *Washington Post* (June 24, 1981).
17. *Washington Spectator* (December 1, 1984): 1.
18. Johnson, Haynes. *Washington Post* quoted in *Washington Spectator*, ibid.
19. quoted ibid.
20. quoted ibid.
21. *St. Louis Post-Dispatch* (April 17, 1983).
22. *St. Louis Post-Dispatch* (April 27, 1983).
23. *Common Cause* (March 4, 1984): 12; (April 21, 1983): 9.
24. *St. Louis Post-Dispatch* (April 22, 1983).
25. *New York Times* (July 8, 1969).
26. Swomley, John M. Jr. *Our Military Government*, 13. National Council Against Conscription. Pamphlet.
27. U.S. Congress. *Report of the Congressional Conference on the Military Budget and National Priorities*. 91st Cong., 1st sess. 1969. 30ff.
28. MacDonald, Ralph. Quoted in *The Militarization of America*. National Council Against Conscription. January 1968.

7. *The Co-optation of Dissenters.*

1. Ambrose and Barber. *The Military and American Society* 63.
2. Nossiter, Bernard. *Washington Post* (April 28, 1969).
3. Radosh, Ronald. *American Labor and United States Foreign Policy.* 307. New York: Random House, 1969; Lens, Sidney. "Lovestone Diplomacy." *Nation* (July 5, 1965).
4. Radosh, *American Labor* 323.
5. Reuther, Victor G. *The Brothers Reuther.* 413–14. Boston: Houghton Mifflin, 1976.
6. Radosh, *American Labor* 393–405.
7. Hirsch, Fred. *An Analysis of our AFL-CIO Role in Latin America; Or Under the Covers with the CIA*, 7. Pamphlet. April 1974.
8. ibid. 4.
9. Interview with author.
10. Hirsch, *Analysis of our AFL-CIO Role* 25.
11. Radosh, *American Labor*, 426.
12. Hirsch, *Analysis of our AFL-CIO Role* 36–37.
13. *New York Times* (August 2, 1969).
14. Interview with author.
15. Kerr, Clark, Quoted in Greer, Edward. *Viet-Report.* (January 1968): 5.
16. *Philadelphia Inquirer* (May 16, 1969).
17. Hersh, Seymour M. *Chemical and Biological Warfare, America's Hidden Arsenal*, 139. Garden City, NY: Doubleday/Anchor, 1969.
18. Klare, Michael. "Universities in Vietnam." *Viet-Report* (Jan. 1968):14, 37.
19. Scheer, Robert. *How the United States Got Involved in Vietnam*, 34–37. Center for the Study of Democratic Institutions, 1965.
20. *Chicago Daily News* (April 11, 1969).
21. Eynon, Bret. *Military Research on Campus: U of M Re-Enlists.* Mimeograph. University of Michigan, (April 15, 1982).
22. NARMIC, American Friends Service Committee. *Uncle Sam Goes to School*, 1.
23. *Dollars and Sense* (September 1982): 13.
24. Burkholder, Steve. *Progressive* (June 1981): 25–31.
25. *"Going for Broke." The University and the Military-Industrial Complex*, 19–20. Ann Arbor, Michigan: Committee for Non-Violent Research, 1982.
26. "The University and the Military." Committee on the University and the Military, State University of New York at Stony Brook, 1981. Mimeographed flyer.
27. Glasser, Ira. "The Bill of Rights: Should It Apply to the Military," 20. Paper delivered to ACLU Biennial Conference at Ann Arbor June 20–25, 1968. Mimeograph.

28. "Militarism and Education. Racism, Sexism and Militarism: The Links." *Interracial Books for Children. Bulletin.* 13, nos. 6 & 7 (1982): 15ff.
29. ibid. 22, 46.
30. *Reader's Digest* Ad. October 1982; *Chicago Tribune* (April 8, 1982).
31. *Nation* (April 5, 1975); *New York Times* (June 3, 1979).
32. Church Committee Report. Book 1 184.
33. ibid. footnote 184.
34. ibid. 185.
35. ibid. 189–90; Halperin et al. *Lawless State* 48–49.
36. *National Catholic Reporter* (May 7, 1976).
37. *National Catholic Reporter* (December 26, 1975)

8. *The Other Costs of Militarism.*

1. Alperovitz, *Atomic Diplomacy: Hiroshima and Potsdam* 151.
2. Horowitz, *Free World Colossus* 263
3. *New Republic* (August 8, 1982).
4. Wasserman, Harvey, and Norman Solomon. *Killing Our Own*, 4. New York: Delacorte, 1982.
5. ibid. 17.
6. ibid. 275.
7. Beardslee, William, and John Mack. "Impact on Children," 67–68. Mimeograph reprint.
8. Lifton, Robert J., and Richard Falk. *Indefensible Weapons*, 51. New York: Basic Books, 1982.
9. ibid.
10. Jezer, Marty. *The Dark Ages. Life in the United States 1945–1960*, 237 Boston:South End Press, 1982.
11. ibid. 240.
12. Interview with author.
13. Shadows of the Nuclear Age. "Nuclear Anxiety—Coping with the Eve of Destruction." #viii. SANE Education Fund interviews. Interview with Robert J. Lifton.
14. *Naval War College Review* (May–June 1975): 102.
15. McMillan, James, and Bernard Harris. *The American Takeover of Britain*. Hart Publishing Company, 1968.
16. Quoted in DeGrasse, Robert Jr. *The Cost and Consequences of Reagan's Military Buildup*, 1. Prepared by the Council on Economic Priorities.
17. "Going for Broke," 26.
18. DeGrasse, *Cost and Consequences* 13.
19. Interview with author.
20. Melman, Seymour. *Pentagon Capitalism*, 3. New York: McGraw-Hill, 1970.
21. *Dollars & Sense*. (July 1981): 30.

22. *Chicago Sun-Times* (February 7, 1983).
23. Markusen, Ann R. "Defense Spending: A Successful Industrial Policy?" 5–6. Unpublished paper.
24. Gold, David. "Fewer Jobs, Slower Growth. Military Spending Drains the Economy." *Dollars & Sense:* (no date): 8
25. Ackerman, Frank, Quoted in *Dollars & Sense*, 30.
26 Comeau, Lori. *Nuts and Bolts at the Pentagon: A Spare Parts Catalogue.* Center on Budget & Policy Priorities, August 1984.
27. Lens, Sidney. "Averting Economic Catastrophe." *Christian Century* (July 18–25, 1984): 707.
28. Brown, Lester. *State of the World*, 17. New York: W.W. Norton, 1984.
29. *Monthly Review* (January 1985): 11.
30. ibid. 10, 11.

9. What Next?

1. *Chicago Sun-Times* (May 20, 1981).
2. Williams, William Appleman. *The Contours of American History*, 454–55. New York: World, 1961.
3. Sherwin, Martin. *A World Destroyed.* 204–205. New York: Alfred A. Knopf, 1975.
4. *In These Times* (February 20, 1985).

Index